STAR WARS™
BOUNTY HUNTERS

TARGET VALANCE

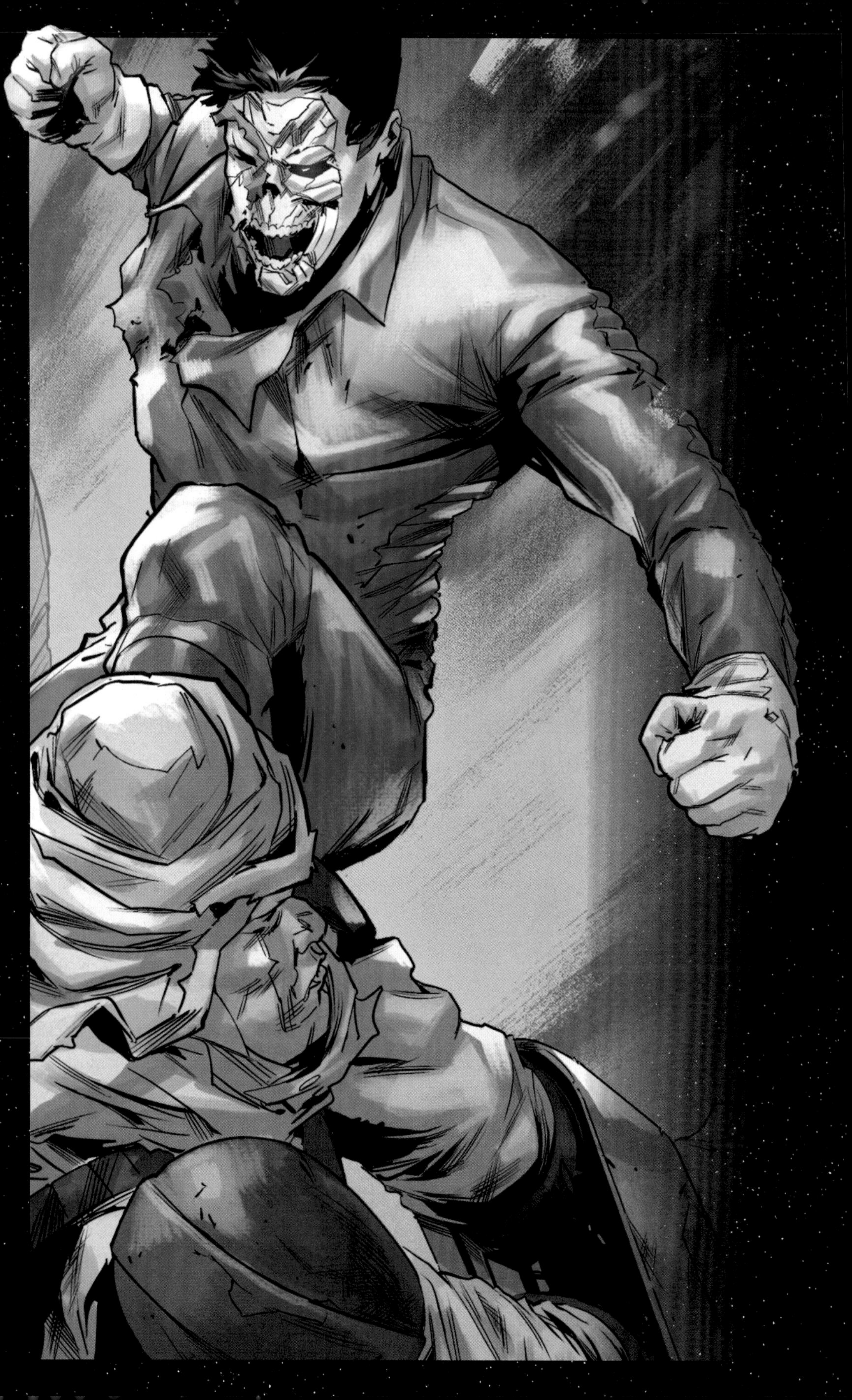

STAR WARS

BOUNTY HUNTERS

TARGET VALANCE

Writer
ETHAN SACKS

Artist
PAOLO VILLANELLI

Color Artist
ARIF PRIANTO

Letterer
VC's TRAVIS LANHAM

Cover Art
LEE BERMEJO (#6-7), **PAOLO VILLANELLI** & **ARIF PRIANTO** (#8) and **MATTIA DE IULIS** (#9-11)

Assistant Editor
TOM GRONEMAN

Editor
MARK PANICCIA

Collection Editor	**JENNIFER GRÜNWALD**		
Assistant Editor	**DANIEL KIRCHHOFFER**		
Assistant Managing Editor	**MAIA LOY**		
Assistant Editor	**LISA MONTALBANO**		
VP Production & Special Projects	**JEFF YOUNGQUIST**		
Book Designer	**ADAM DEL RE**		
SVP Print, Sales & Marketing	**DAVID GABRIEL**		
Editor in Chief	**C.B. CEBULSKI**		

For Lucasfilm:

Senior Editor	**ROBERT SIMPSON**
Creative Director	**MICHAEL SIGLAIN**
Art Director	**TROY ALDERS**
Lucasfilm Story Group	**MATT MARTIN**
	PABLO HIDALGO
	EMILY SHKOUKANI
Lucasfilm Art Department	**PHIL SZOSTAK**

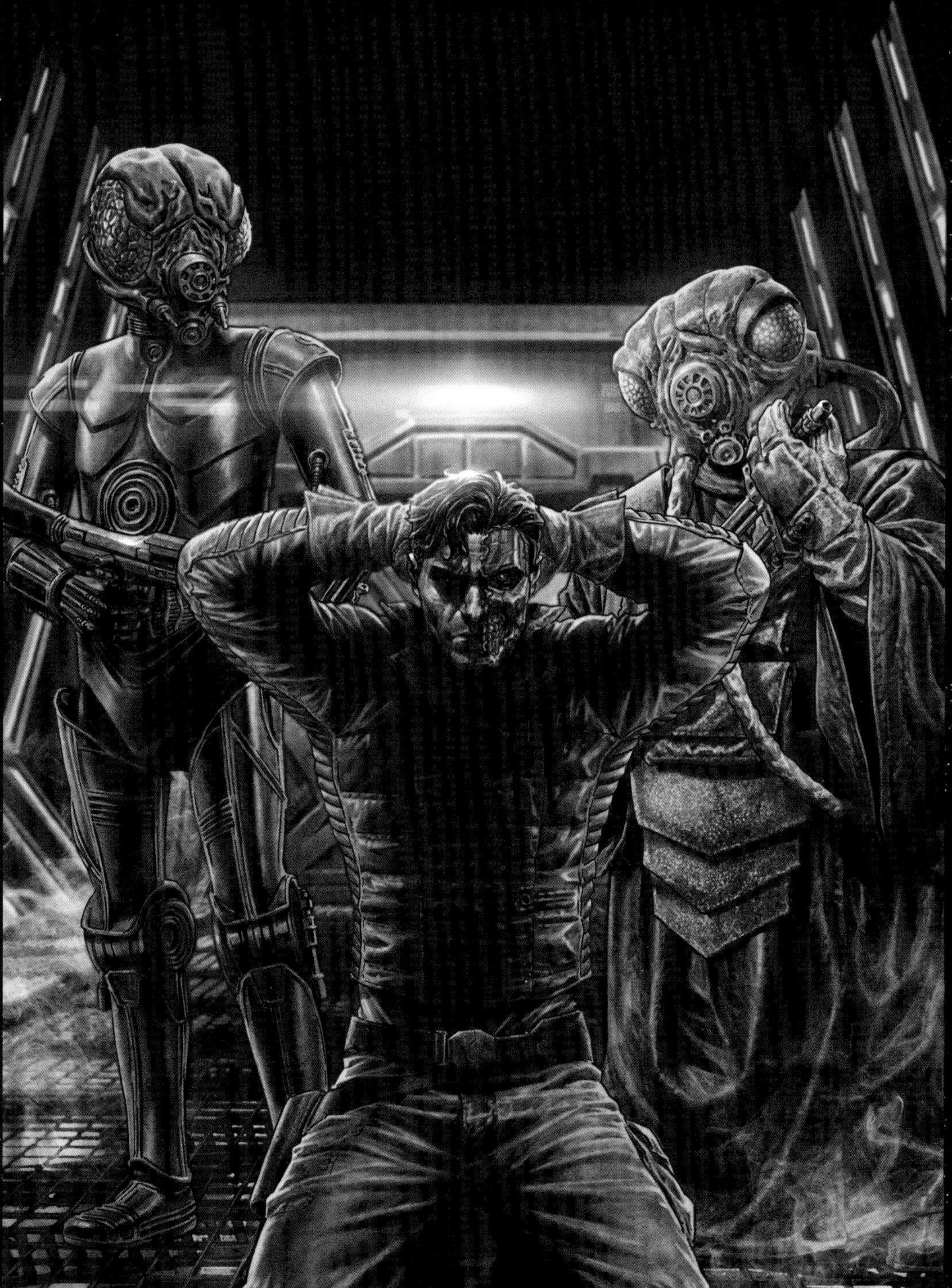

6

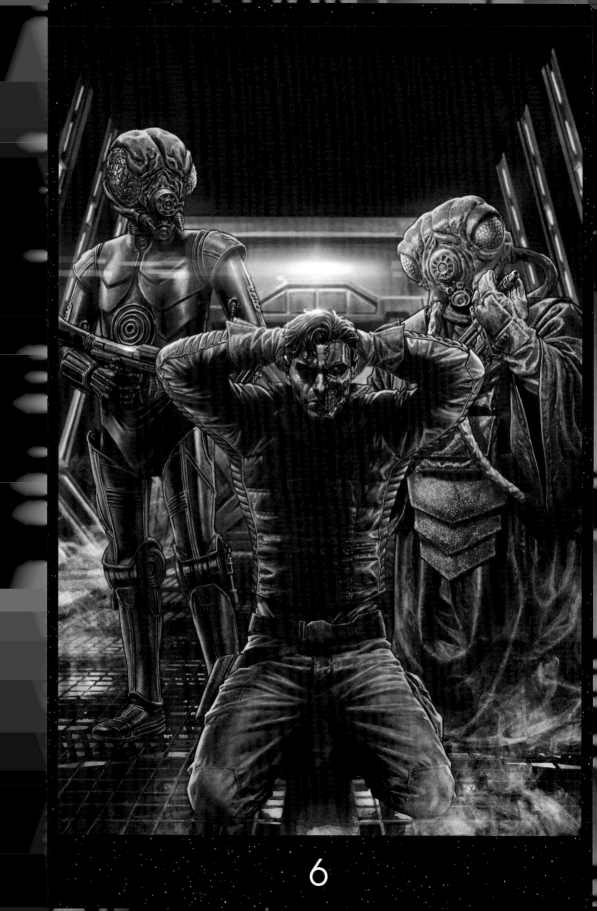

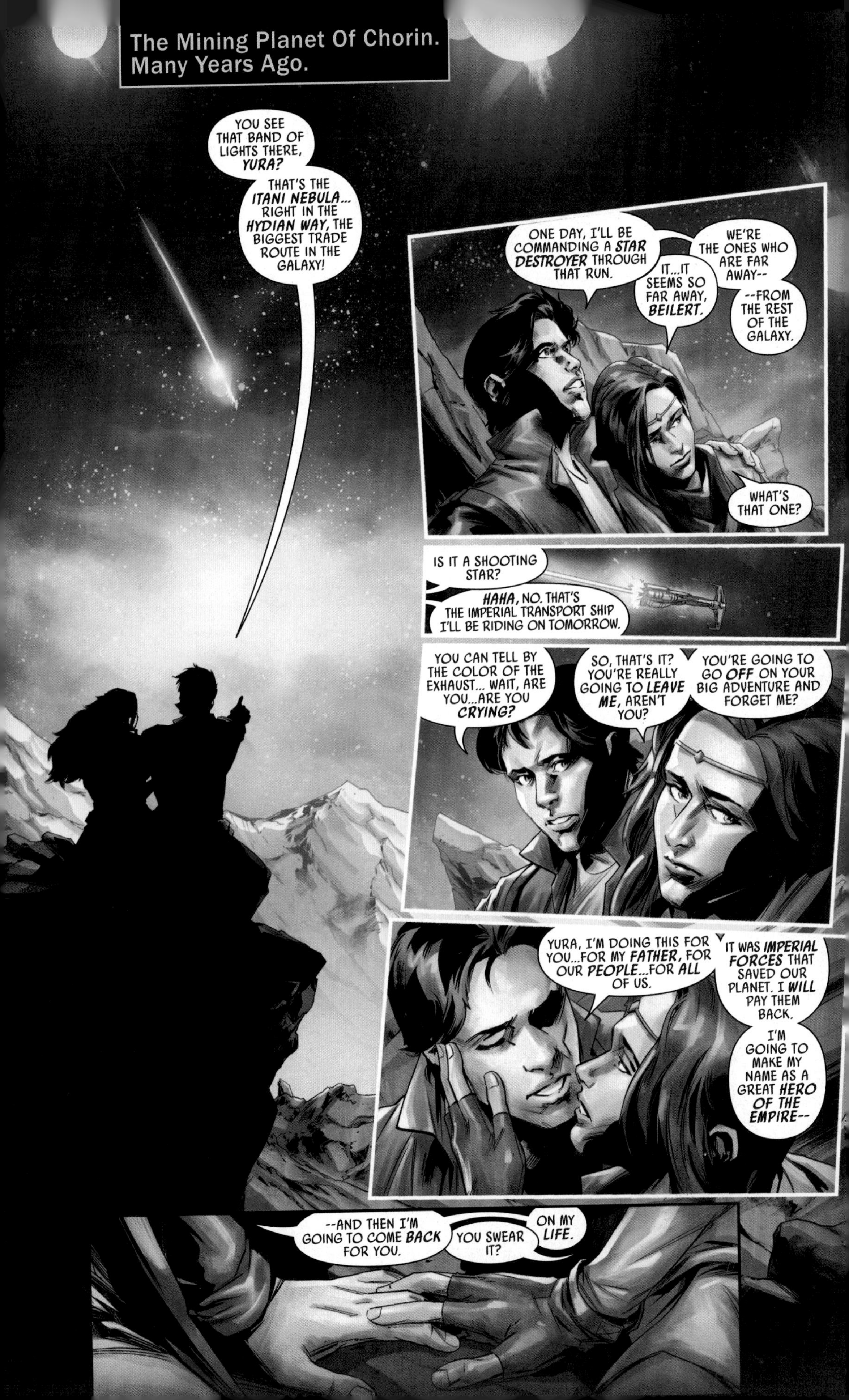
The Mining Planet Of Chorin. Many Years Ago.
YOU SEE THAT BAND OF LIGHTS THERE, YURA?
THAT'S THE ITANI NEBULA... RIGHT IN THE HYDIAN WAY, THE BIGGEST TRADE ROUTE IN THE GALAXY!
ONE DAY, I'LL BE COMMANDING A STAR DESTROYER THROUGH THAT RUN.
IT...IT SEEMS SO FAR AWAY, BEILERT.
WE'RE THE ONES WHO ARE FAR AWAY--
--FROM THE REST OF THE GALAXY.
WHAT'S THAT ONE?
IS IT A SHOOTING STAR?
HAHA, NO. THAT'S THE IMPERIAL TRANSPORT SHIP I'LL BE RIDING ON TOMORROW.
YOU CAN TELL BY THE COLOR OF THE EXHAUST... WAIT, ARE YOU...ARE YOU CRYING?
SO, THAT'S IT? YOU'RE REALLY GOING TO LEAVE ME, AREN'T YOU?
YOU'RE GOING TO GO OFF ON YOUR BIG ADVENTURE AND FORGET ME?
YURA, I'M DOING THIS FOR YOU...FOR MY FATHER, FOR OUR PEOPLE...FOR ALL OF US.
IT WAS IMPERIAL FORCES THAT SAVED OUR PLANET. I WILL PAY THEM BACK.
I'M GOING TO MAKE MY NAME AS A GREAT HERO OF THE EMPIRE--
--AND THEN I'M GOING TO COME BACK FOR YOU.
YOU SWEAR IT?
ON MY LIFE.

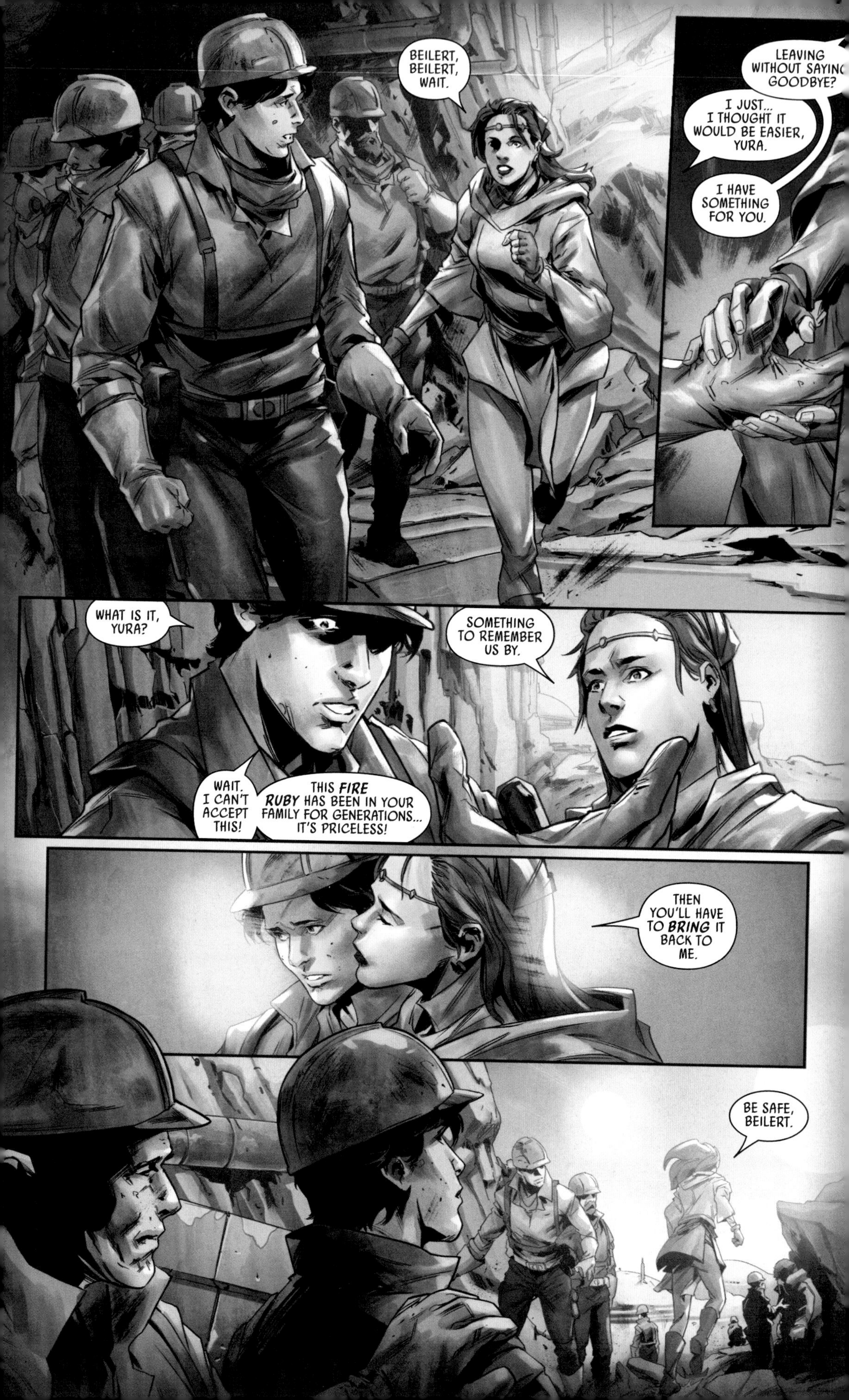
BEILERT, BEILERT, WAIT.
LEAVING WITHOUT SAYING GOODBYE?
I JUST... I THOUGHT IT WOULD BE EASIER, YURA.
I HAVE SOMETHING FOR YOU.
WHAT IS IT, YURA?
SOMETHING TO REMEMBER US BY.
WAIT. I CAN'T ACCEPT THIS!
THIS FIRE RUBY HAS BEEN IN YOUR FAMILY FOR GENERATIONS... IT'S PRICELESS!
THEN YOU'LL HAVE TO BRING IT BACK TO ME.
BE SAFE, BEILERT.

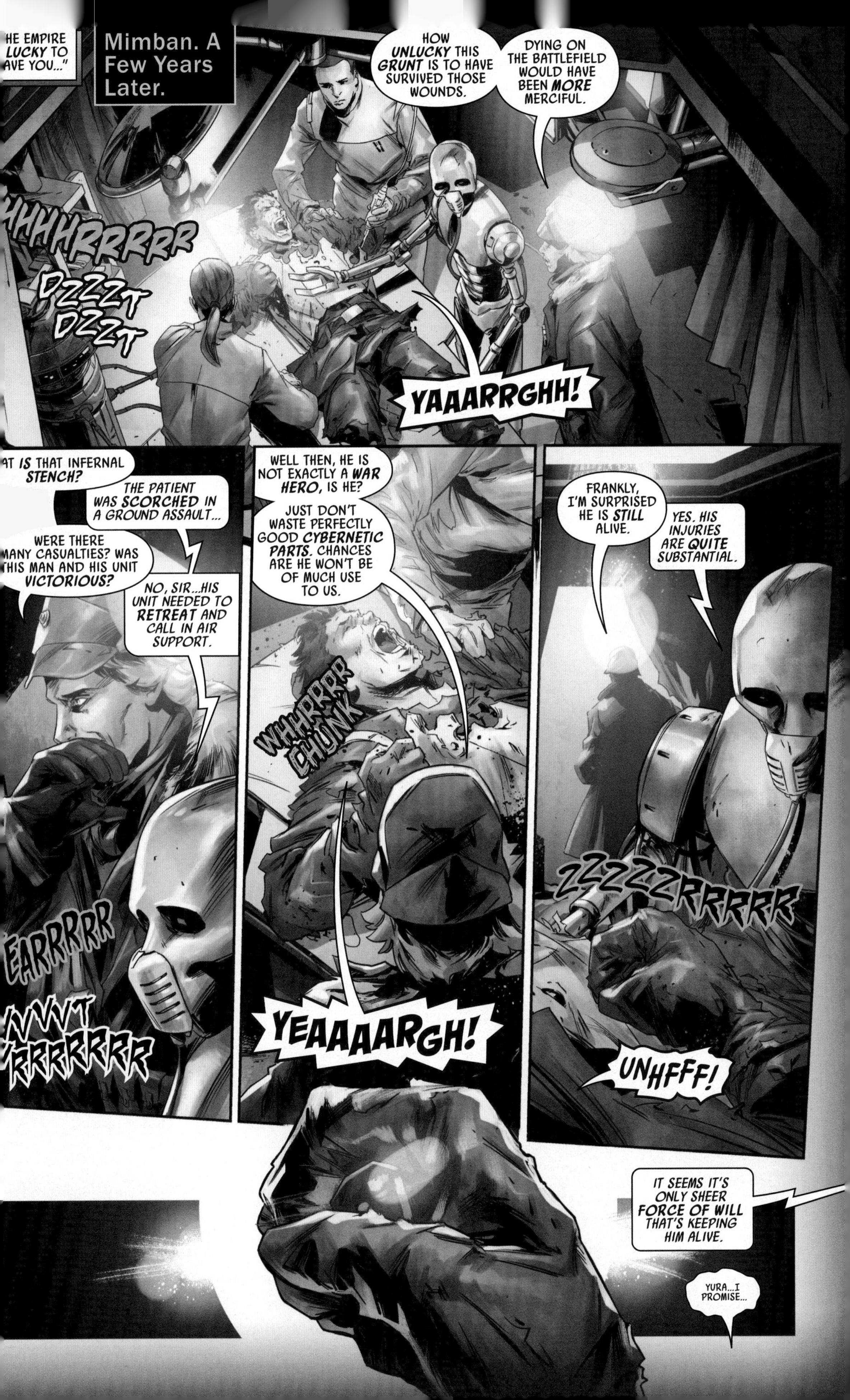
HE EMPIRE LUCKY TO AVE YOU..."
Mimban. A Few Years Later.
HOW UNLUCKY THIS GRUNT IS TO HAVE SURVIVED THOSE WOUNDS.
DYING ON THE BATTLEFIELD WOULD HAVE BEEN MORE MERCIFUL.
HHHHRRRRRR
DZZZT DZZT
YAAARRGHH!
AT IS THAT INFERNAL STENCH?
THE PATIENT WAS SCORCHED IN A GROUND ASSAULT...
WERE THERE MANY CASUALTIES? WAS THIS MAN AND HIS UNIT VICTORIOUS?
NO, SIR...HIS UNIT NEEDED TO RETREAT AND CALL IN AIR SUPPORT.
EARRRRR
VVVT RRRRRRR
WELL THEN, HE IS NOT EXACTLY A WAR HERO, IS HE?
JUST DON'T WASTE PERFECTLY GOOD CYBERNETIC PARTS. CHANCES ARE HE WON'T BE OF MUCH USE TO US.
WHHRRRR CHUNK
YEAAAARGH!
FRANKLY, I'M SURPRISED HE IS STILL ALIVE.
YES. HIS INJURIES ARE QUITE SUBSTANTIAL.
ZZZZZRRRRR
UNHFFF!
IT SEEMS IT'S ONLY SHEER FORCE OF WILL THAT'S KEEPING HIM ALIVE.
YURA...I PROMISE...

VALANCE   CADELIAH   ZUCKUSS   4-LOM

STAR WARS
BOUNTY HUNTERS

TARGET VALANCE

The cyborg bounty hunter Valance is on the run after narrowly escaping the Unbroken Clan syndicate.

With her dying breath, Valance's mentor asked him to protect the young Cadeliah, the only hope to end years of conflict between the syndicates.

Now Valance and Cadeliah are currently the galaxy's most wanted....

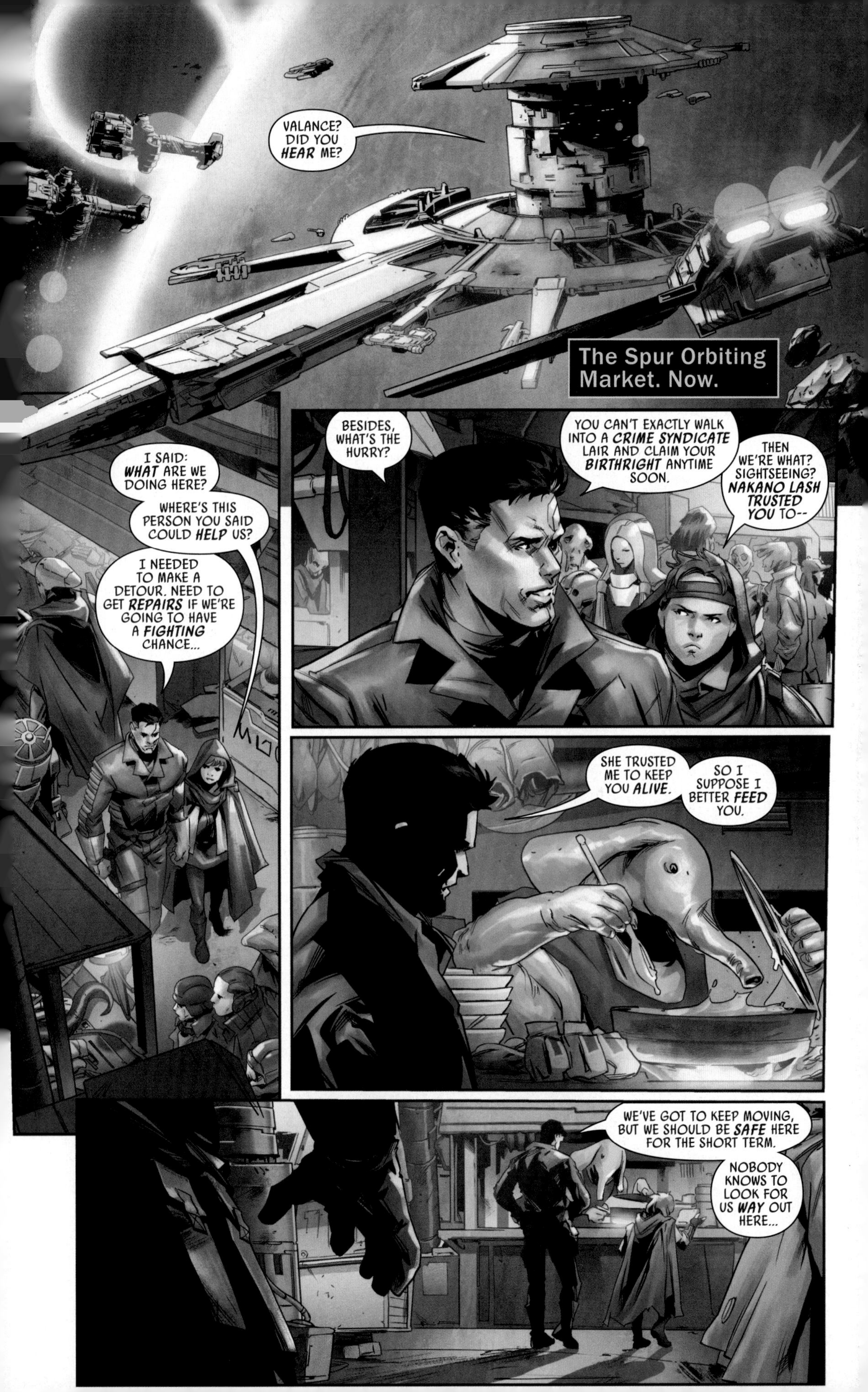
VALANCE? DID YOU HEAR ME?
The Spur Orbiting Market. Now.
I SAID: WHAT ARE WE DOING HERE?
WHERE'S THIS PERSON YOU SAID COULD HELP US?
I NEEDED TO MAKE A DETOUR. NEED TO GET REPAIRS IF WE'RE GOING TO HAVE A FIGHTING CHANCE...
BESIDES, WHAT'S THE HURRY?
YOU CAN'T EXACTLY WALK INTO A CRIME SYNDICATE LAIR AND CLAIM YOUR BIRTHRIGHT ANYTIME SOON.
THEN WE'RE WHAT? SIGHTSEEING? NAKANO LASH TRUSTED YOU TO--
SHE TRUSTED ME TO KEEP YOU ALIVE.
SO I SUPPOSE I BETTER FEED YOU.
WE'VE GOT TO KEEP MOVING, BUT WE SHOULD BE SAFE HERE FOR THE SHORT TERM.
NOBODY KNOWS TO LOOK FOR US WAY OUT HERE...

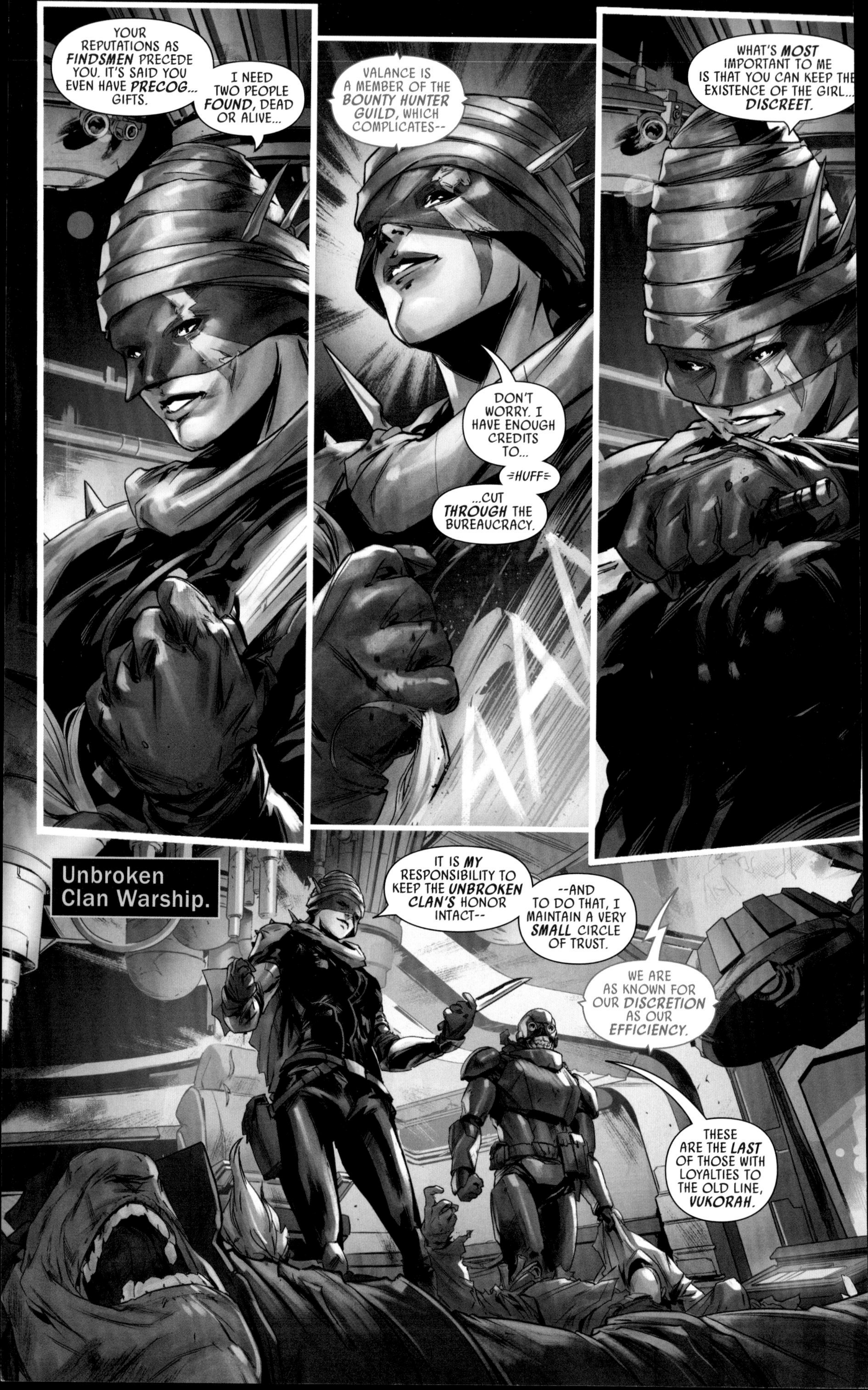
YOUR REPUTATIONS AS FINDSMEN PRECEDE YOU. IT'S SAID YOU EVEN HAVE PRECOG... GIFTS.
I NEED TWO PEOPLE FOUND, DEAD OR ALIVE...
VALANCE IS A MEMBER OF THE BOUNTY HUNTER GUILD, WHICH COMPLICATES--
DON'T WORRY. I HAVE ENOUGH CREDITS TO...
HUFF
...CUT THROUGH THE BUREAUCRACY.
WHAT'S MOST IMPORTANT TO ME IS THAT YOU CAN KEEP THE EXISTENCE OF THE GIRL... DISCREET.
Unbroken Clan Warship.
IT IS MY RESPONSIBILITY TO KEEP THE UNBROKEN CLAN'S HONOR INTACT--
--AND TO DO THAT, I MAINTAIN A VERY SMALL CIRCLE OF TRUST.
WE ARE AS KNOWN FOR OUR DISCRETION AS OUR EFFICIENCY.
THESE ARE THE LAST OF THOSE WITH LOYALTIES TO THE OLD LINE, VUKORAH.

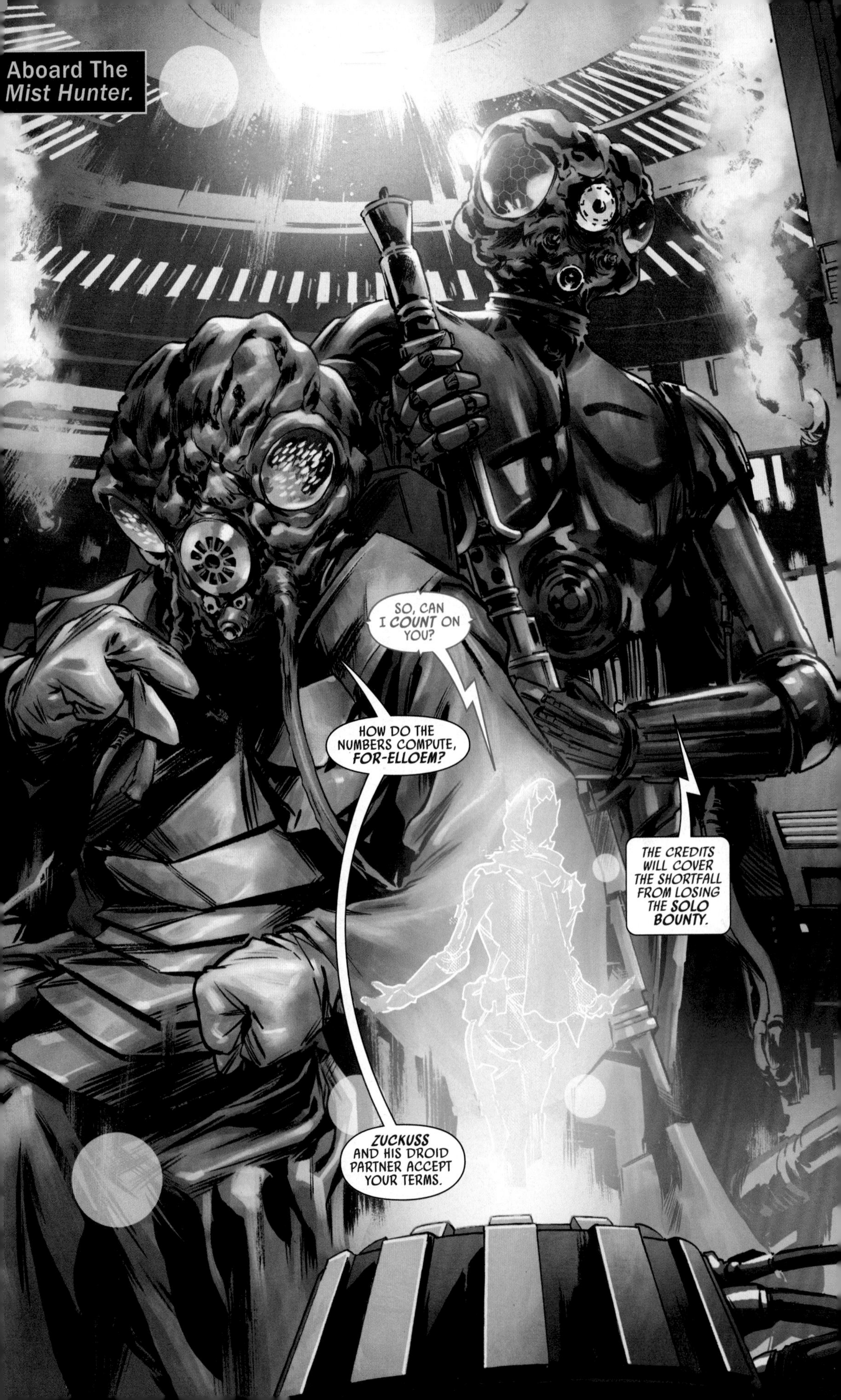
Aboard The *Mist Hunter.*
SO, CAN I COUNT ON YOU?
HOW DO THE NUMBERS COMPUTE, FOR-ELLOEM?
THE CREDITS WILL COVER THE SHORTFALL FROM LOSING THE SOLO BOUNTY.
ZUCKUSS AND HIS DROID PARTNER ACCEPT YOUR TERMS.

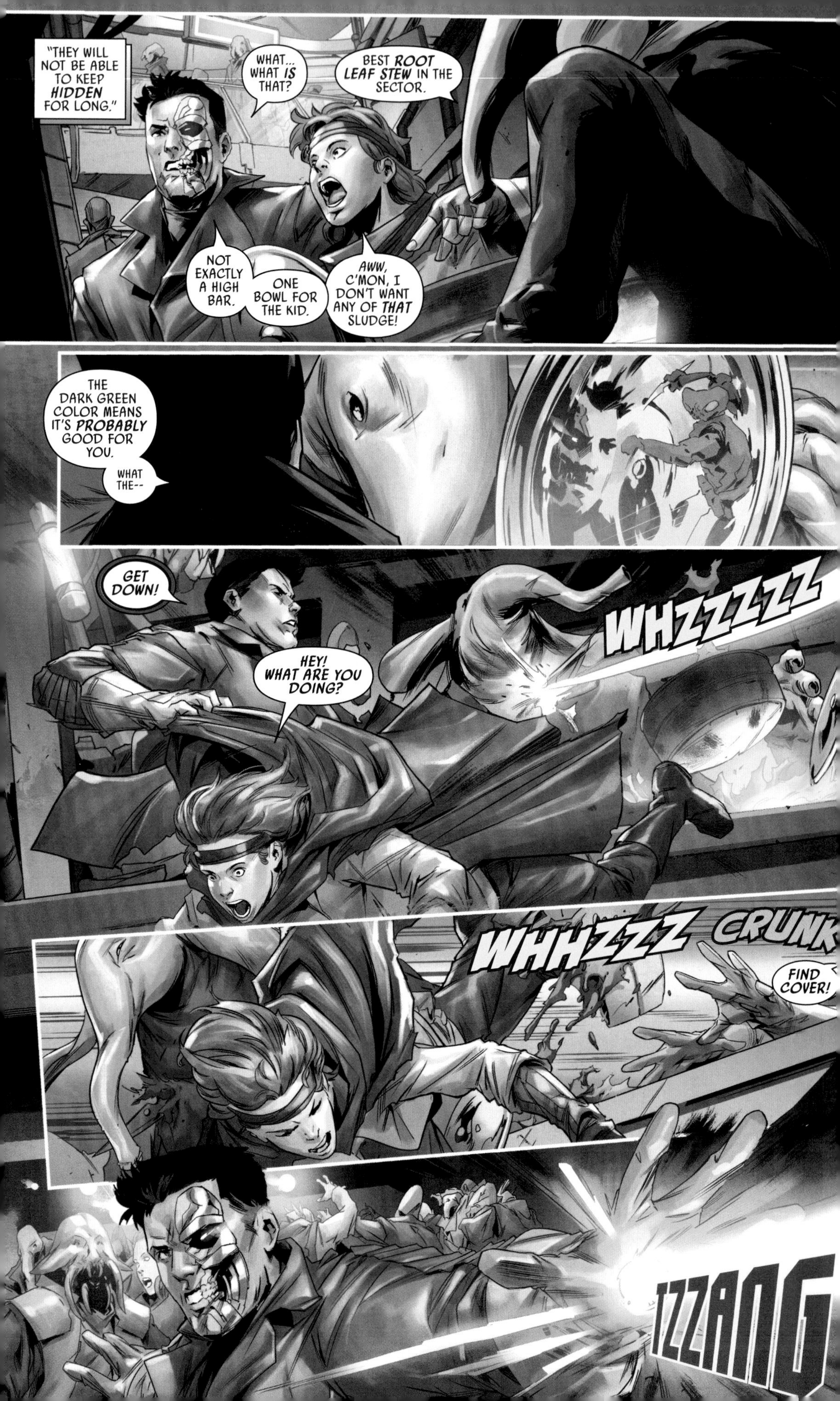

"THEY WILL NOT BE ABLE TO KEEP HIDDEN FOR LONG."
WHAT... WHAT IS THAT?
BEST ROOT LEAF STEW IN THE SECTOR.
NOT EXACTLY A HIGH BAR.
ONE BOWL FOR THE KID.
AWW, C'MON, I DON'T WANT ANY OF THAT SLUDGE!
THE DARK GREEN COLOR MEANS IT'S PROBABLY GOOD FOR YOU.
WHAT THE--
GET DOWN!
HEY! WHAT ARE YOU DOING?
WHZZZZZ
WHHZZZ
CRUNK
FIND COVER!
TZZANG

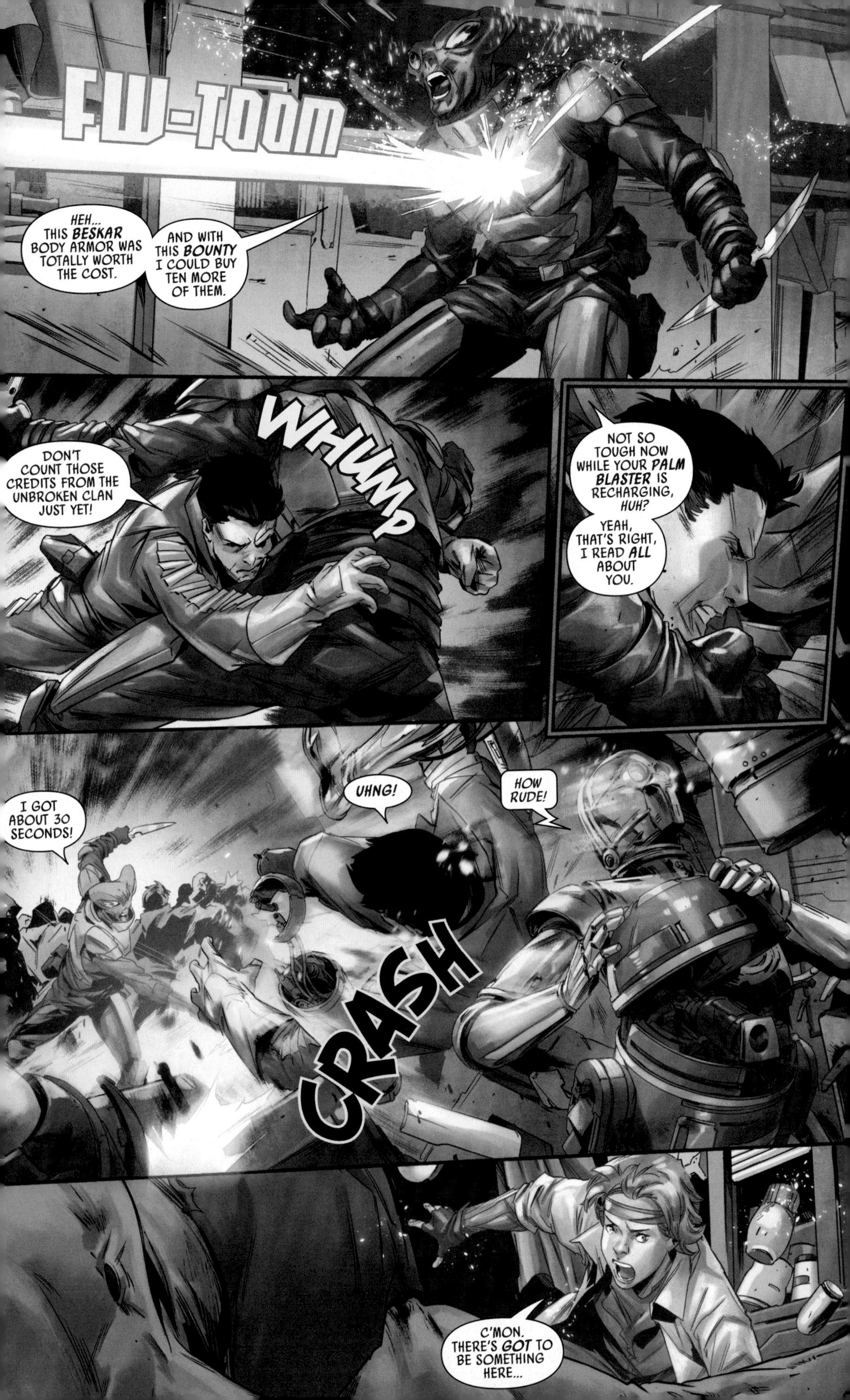
FW-TOOM
HEH... THIS BESKAR BODY ARMOR WAS TOTALLY WORTH THE COST.
AND WITH THIS BOUNTY I COULD BUY TEN MORE OF THEM.
WHUMP
DON'T COUNT THOSE CREDITS FROM THE UNBROKEN CLAN JUST YET!
NOT SO TOUGH NOW WHILE YOUR PALM BLASTER IS RECHARGING, HUH?
YEAH, THAT'S RIGHT, I READ ALL ABOUT YOU.
I GOT ABOUT 30 SECONDS!
UHNG!
HOW RUDE!
CRASH
C'MON. THERE'S GOT TO BE SOMETHING HERE...

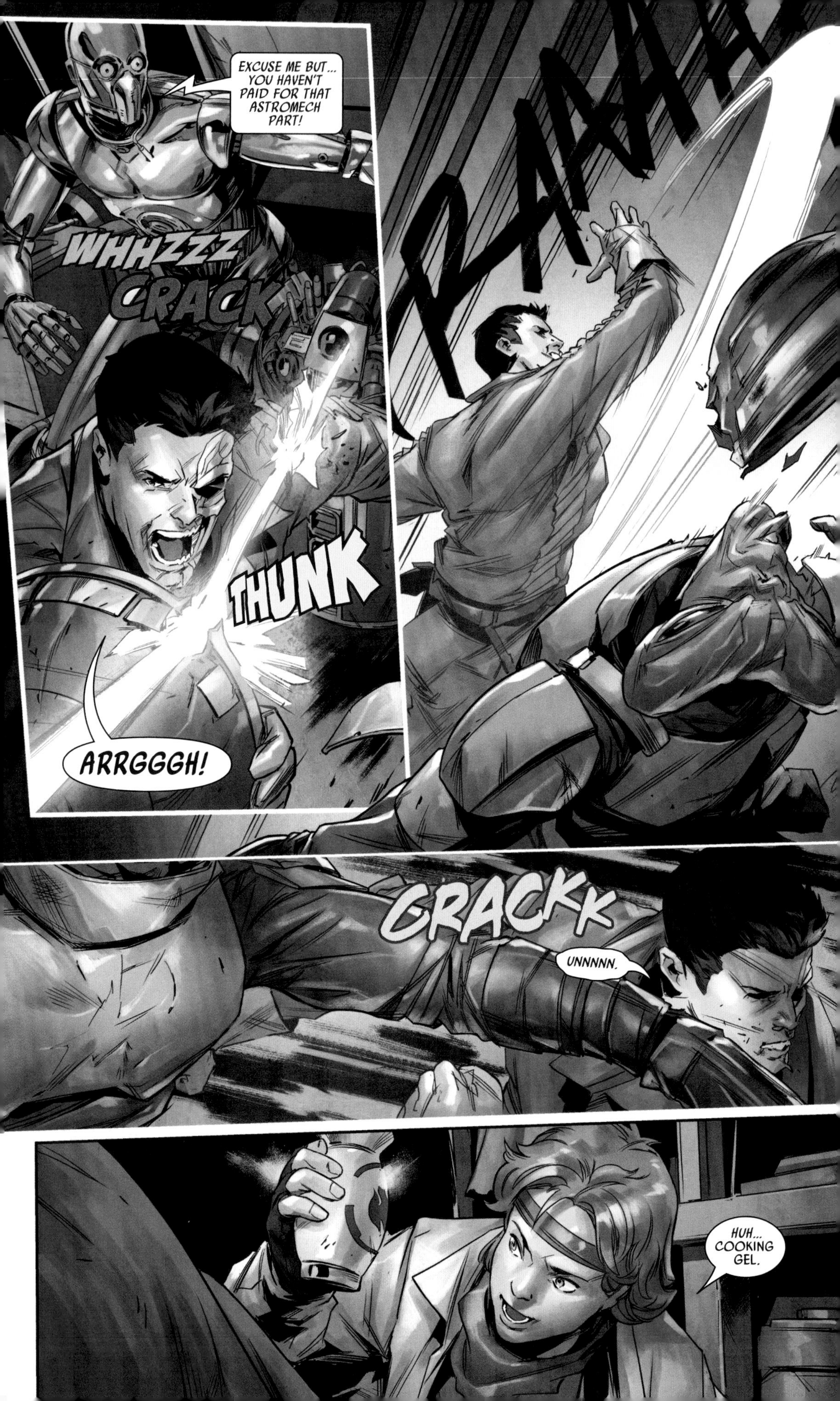

EXCUSE ME BUT... YOU HAVEN'T PAID FOR THAT ASTROMECH PART!
WHHZZZ
CRACK
THUNK
ARRGGGH!
RAAAAH
CRACKK
UNNNNN.
HUH... COOKING GEL.

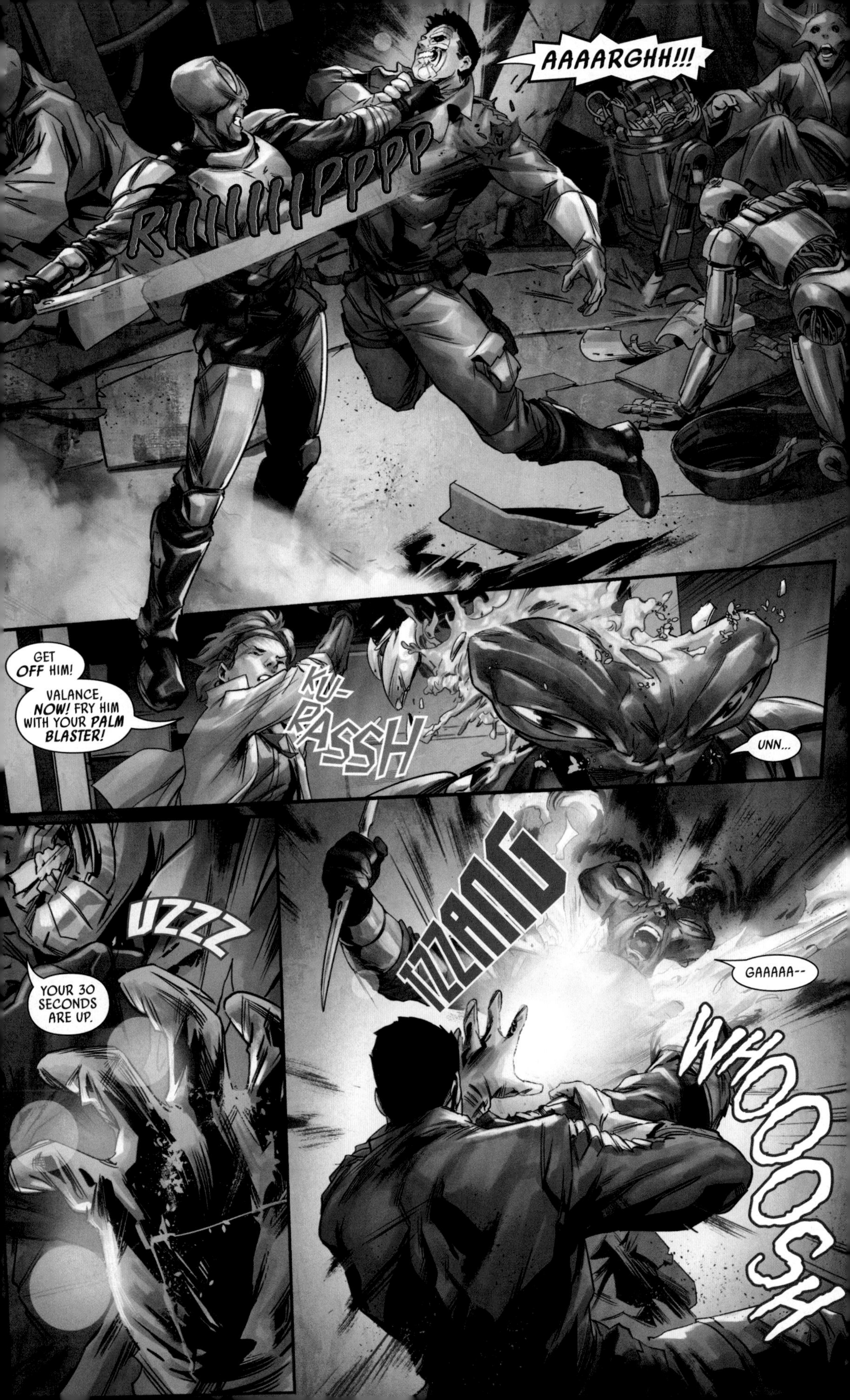
AAAARGHH!!!
RIIIIIIIPPPPP
GET OFF HIM!
VALANCE, NOW! FRY HIM WITH YOUR PALM BLASTER!
KU-RASSH
UNN...
VZZZ
YOUR 30 SECONDS ARE UP.
TZZANG
GAAAAA--
WHOOOSH

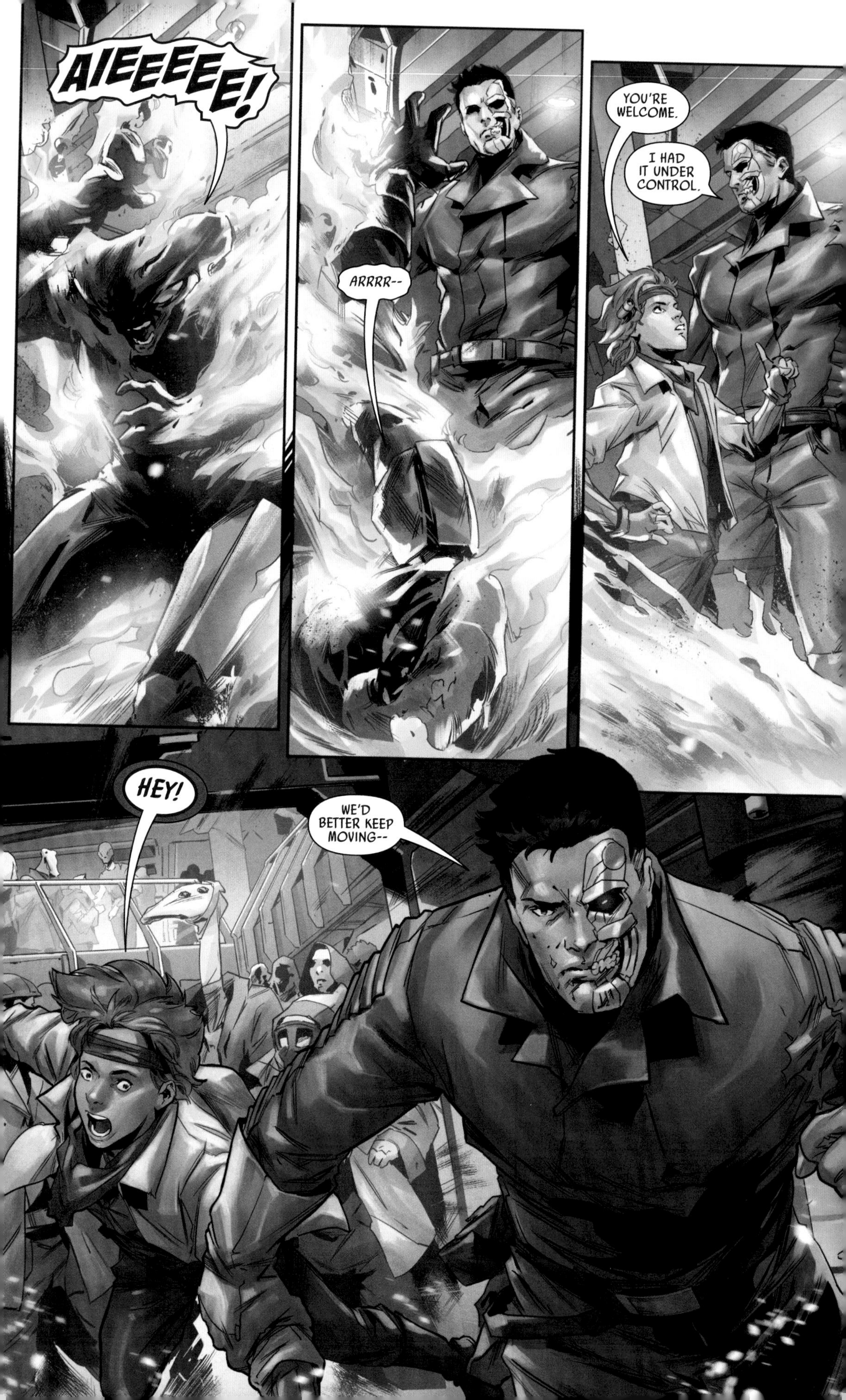
AIEEEEEE!
ARRRR--
YOU'RE WELCOME.
I HAD IT UNDER CONTROL.
HEY!
WE'D BETTER KEEP MOVING--

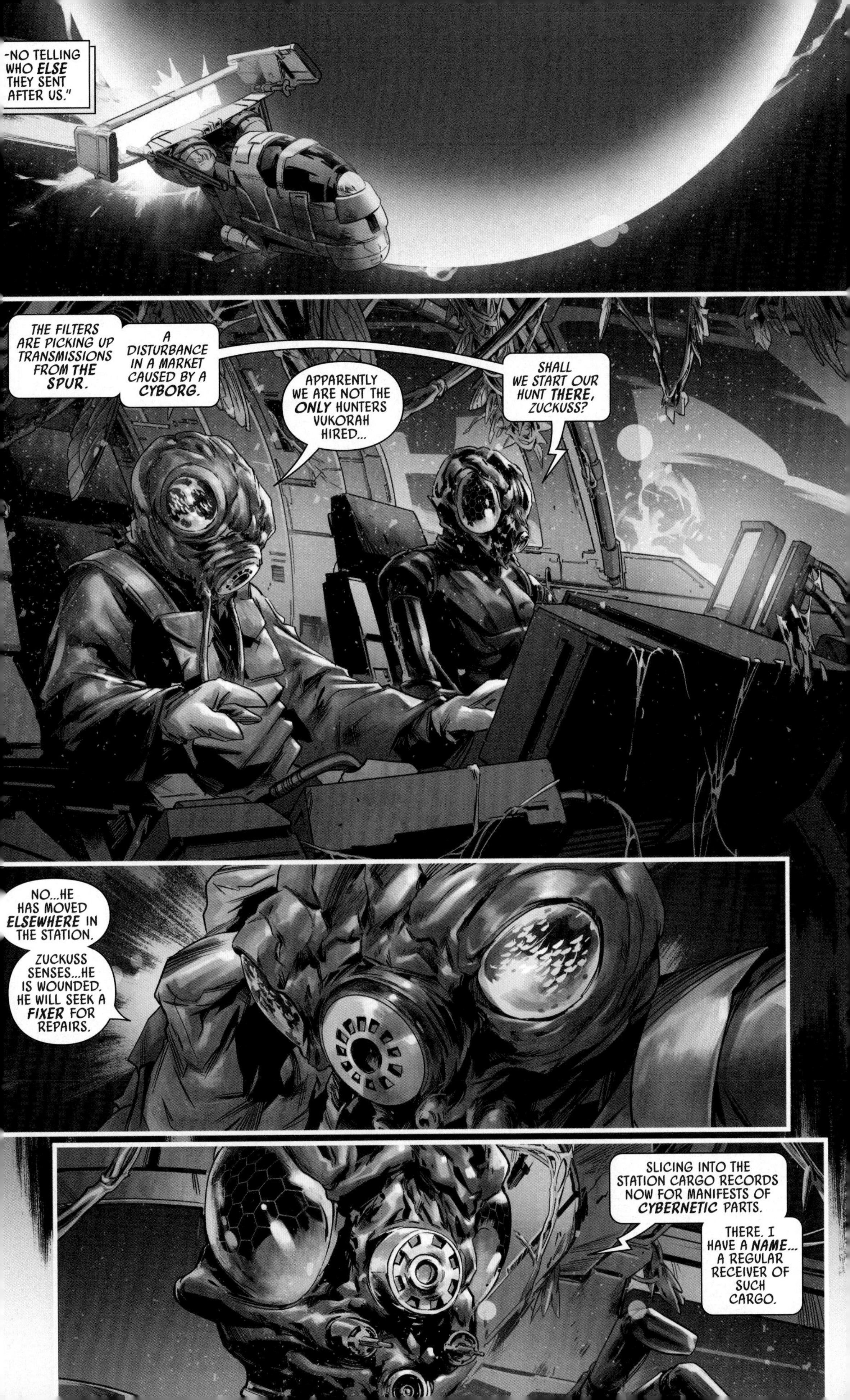
-NO TELLING WHO ELSE THEY SENT AFTER US."
THE FILTERS ARE PICKING UP TRANSMISSIONS FROM THE SPUR.
A DISTURBANCE IN A MARKET CAUSED BY A CYBORG.
APPARENTLY WE ARE NOT THE ONLY HUNTERS VUKORAH HIRED...
SHALL WE START OUR HUNT THERE, ZUCKUSS?
NO...HE HAS MOVED ELSEWHERE IN THE STATION.
ZUCKUSS SENSES...HE IS WOUNDED. HE WILL SEEK A FIXER FOR REPAIRS.
SLICING INTO THE STATION CARGO RECORDS NOW FOR MANIFESTS OF CYBERNETIC PARTS.
THERE. I HAVE A NAME... A REGULAR RECEIVER OF SUCH CARGO.

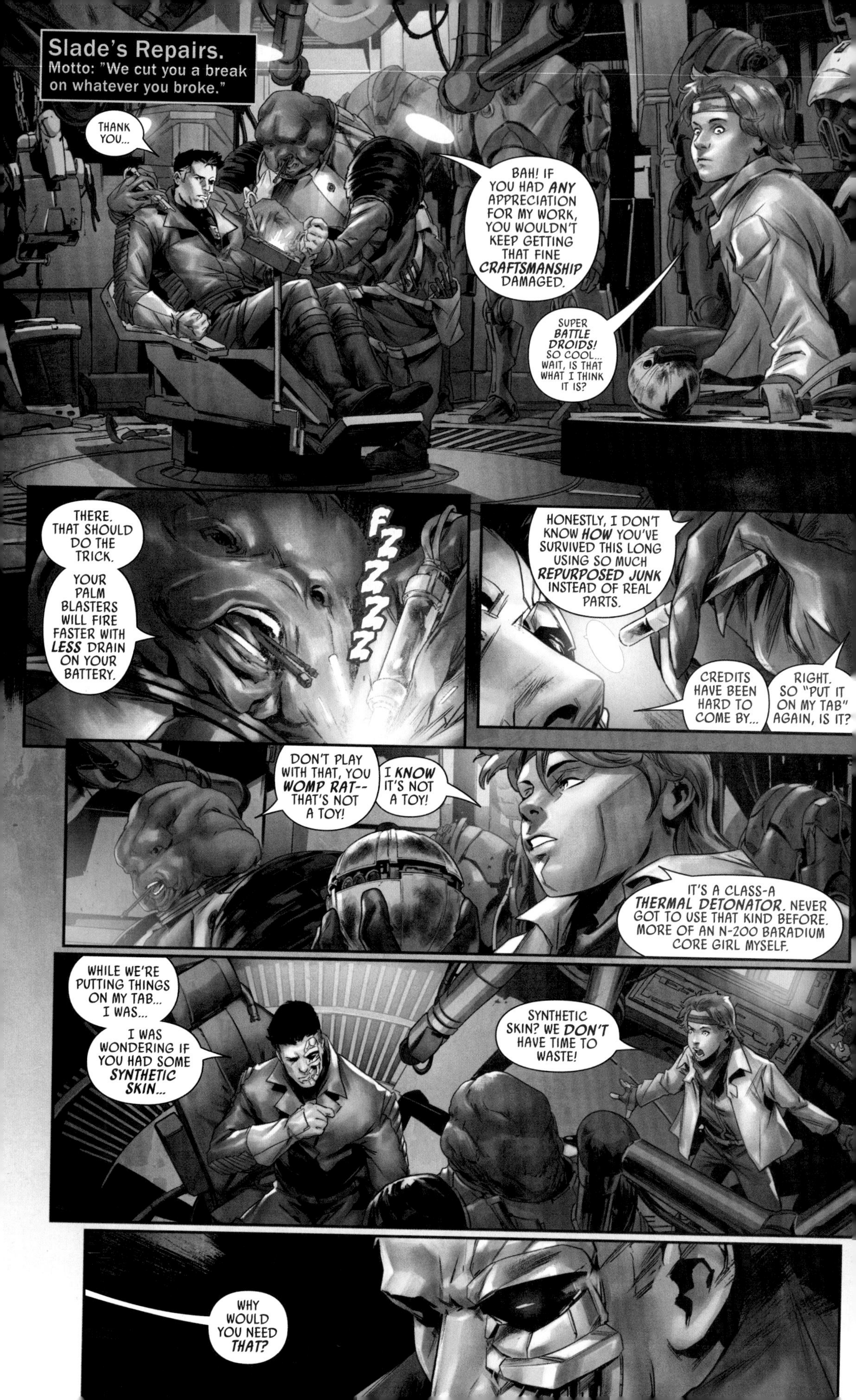
Slade's Repairs.
Motto: "We cut you a break on whatever you broke."
THANK YOU...
BAH! IF YOU HAD ANY APPRECIATION FOR MY WORK, YOU WOULDN'T KEEP GETTING THAT FINE CRAFTSMANSHIP DAMAGED.
SUPER BATTLE DROIDS! SO COOL... WAIT, IS THAT WHAT I THINK IT IS?
THERE. THAT SHOULD DO THE TRICK.
YOUR PALM BLASTERS WILL FIRE FASTER WITH LESS DRAIN ON YOUR BATTERY.
FZZZZZ
HONESTLY, I DON'T KNOW HOW YOU'VE SURVIVED THIS LONG USING SO MUCH REPURPOSED JUNK INSTEAD OF REAL PARTS.
CREDITS HAVE BEEN HARD TO COME BY...
RIGHT. SO "PUT IT ON MY TAB" AGAIN, IS IT?
DON'T PLAY WITH THAT, YOU WOMP RAT-- THAT'S NOT A TOY!
I KNOW IT'S NOT A TOY!
IT'S A CLASS-A THERMAL DETONATOR. NEVER GOT TO USE THAT KIND BEFORE. MORE OF AN N-200 BARADIUM CORE GIRL MYSELF.
WHILE WE'RE PUTTING THINGS ON MY TAB... I WAS...
I WAS WONDERING IF YOU HAD SOME SYNTHETIC SKIN...
SYNTHETIC SKIN? WE DON'T HAVE TIME TO WASTE!
WHY WOULD YOU NEED THAT?

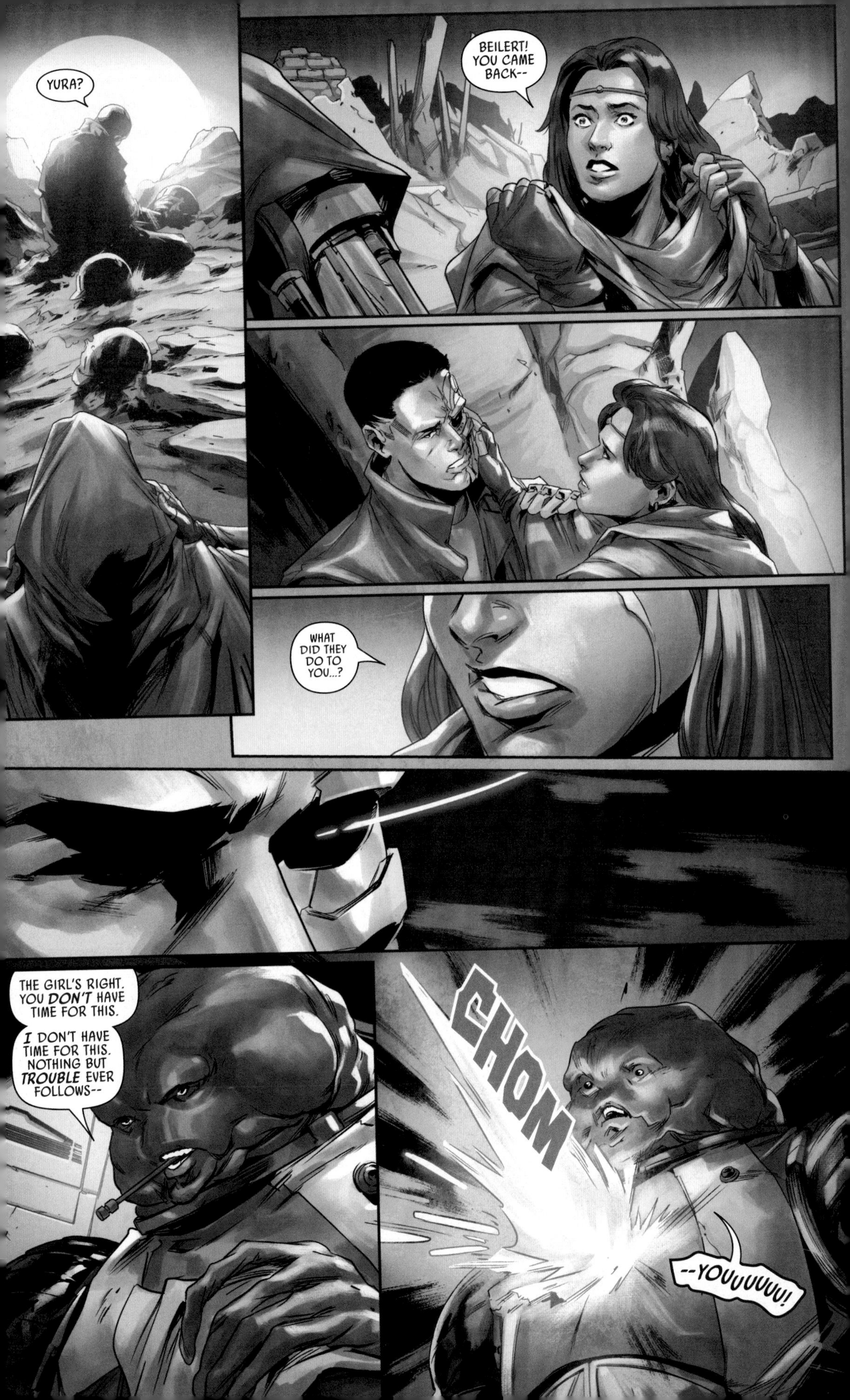
YURA?
BEILERT! YOU CAME BACK--
WHAT DID THEY DO TO YOU...?
THE GIRL'S RIGHT. YOU ***DON'T*** HAVE TIME FOR THIS.
I DON'T HAVE TIME FOR THIS. NOTHING BUT ***TROUBLE*** EVER FOLLOWS--
CHOM
--YOUUUUUU!

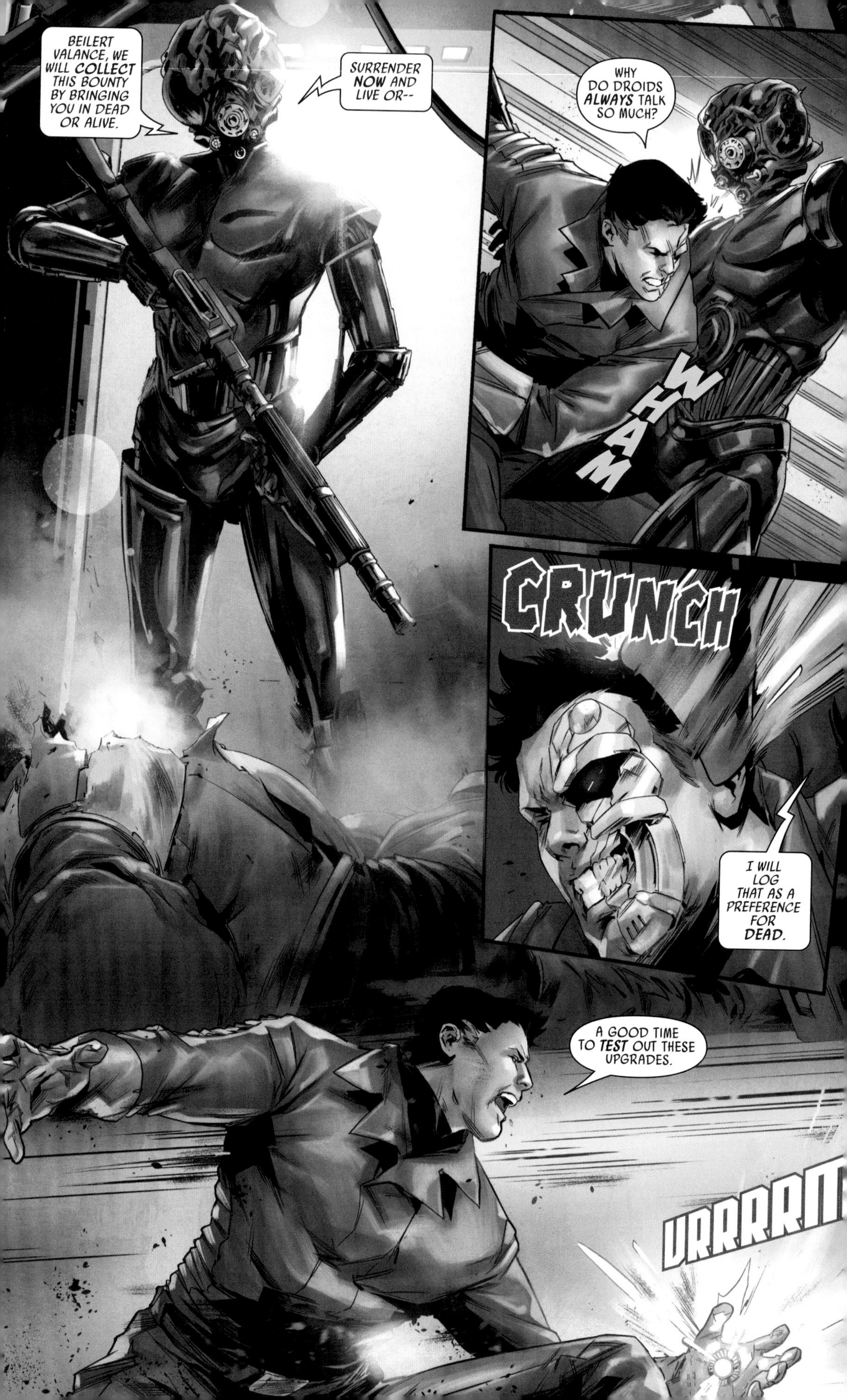
BEILERT VALANCE, WE WILL COLLECT THIS BOUNTY BY BRINGING YOU IN DEAD OR ALIVE.
SURRENDER NOW AND LIVE OR--
WHY DO DROIDS ALWAYS TALK SO MUCH?
WHAM
CRUNCH
I WILL LOG THAT AS A PREFERENCE FOR DEAD.
A GOOD TIME TO TEST OUT THESE UPGRADES.
URRRRM

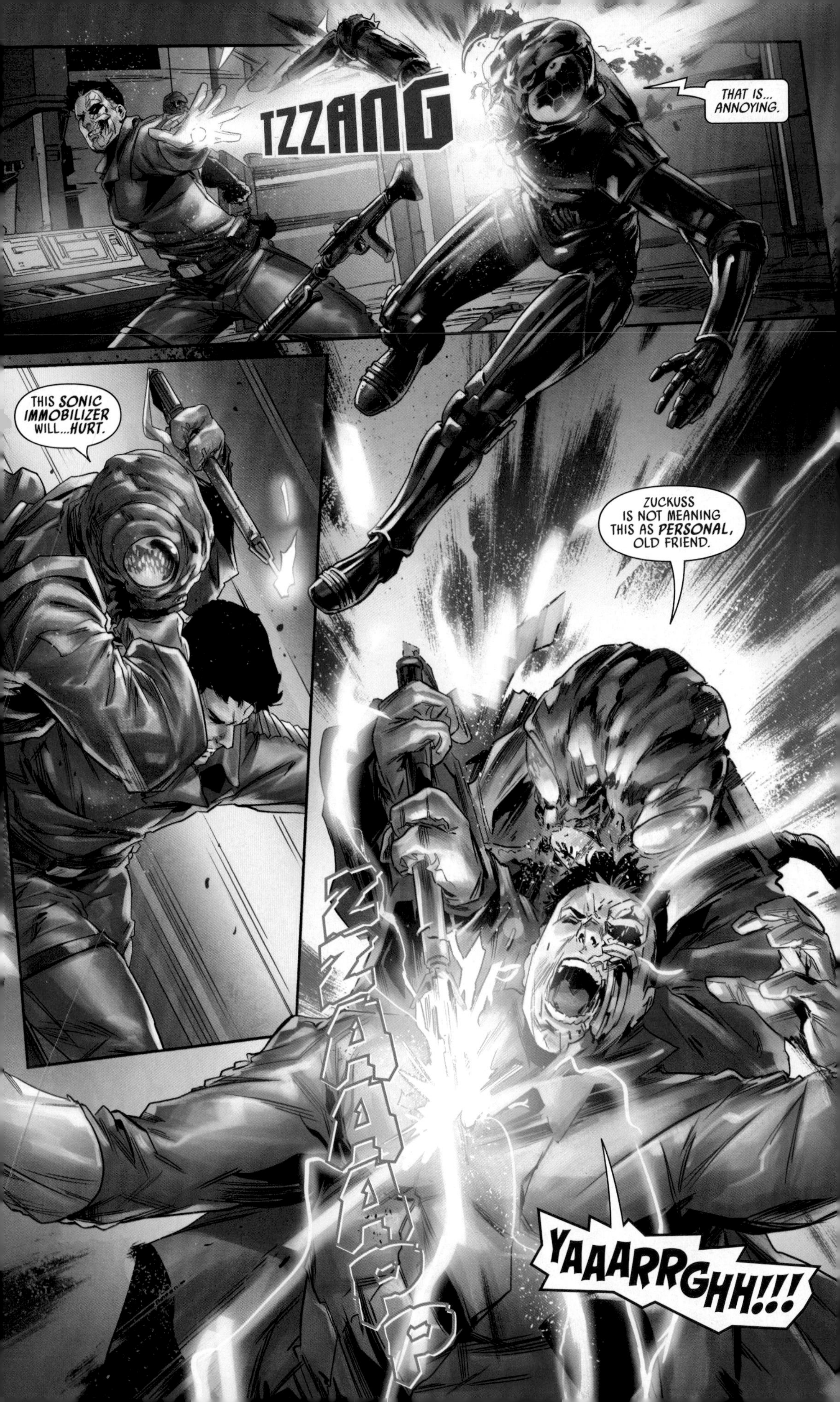

TZZANG
THAT IS... ANNOYING.
THIS SONIC IMMOBILIZER WILL...HURT.
ZUCKUSS IS NOT MEANING THIS AS PERSONAL, OLD FRIEND.
YAAARRGHH!!!

JUST GOT CHARGED... GOOD CREDITS...TO GET FIXED UP...YOU SON OF A RATHTAR!
GAAAAHHH!
YANNNK
I'M... TAKING IT...VERY PERSONAL...
WHOOSH
A WASTED EFFORT.
A GAND FINDSMAN CAN SENSE YOUR ATTACK EVEN BEFORE YOU STRIKE!
IS THAT SO?
WHRRRR CLK

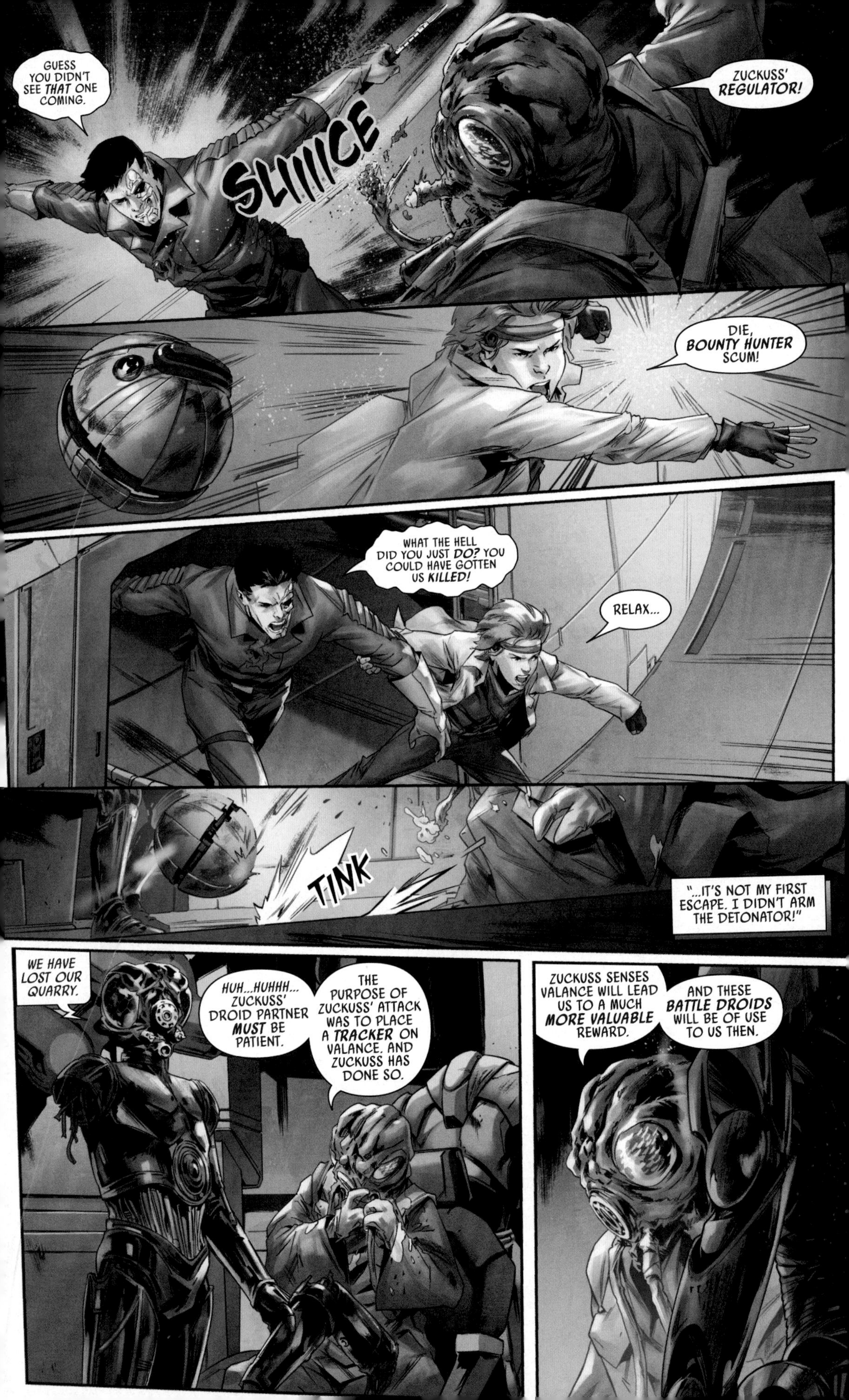
GUESS YOU DIDN'T SEE THAT ONE COMING.
SLIIICE
ZUCKUSS' REGULATOR!
DIE, BOUNTY HUNTER SCUM!
WHAT THE HELL DID YOU JUST DO? YOU COULD HAVE GOTTEN US KILLED!
RELAX...
TINK
"...IT'S NOT MY FIRST ESCAPE. I DIDN'T ARM THE DETONATOR!"
WE HAVE LOST OUR QUARRY.
HUH...HUHHH... ZUCKUSS' DROID PARTNER MUST BE PATIENT.
THE PURPOSE OF ZUCKUSS' ATTACK WAS TO PLACE A TRACKER ON VALANCE. AND ZUCKUSS HAS DONE SO.
ZUCKUSS SENSES VALANCE WILL LEAD US TO A MUCH MORE VALUABLE REWARD.
AND THESE BATTLE DROIDS WILL BE OF USE TO US THEN.

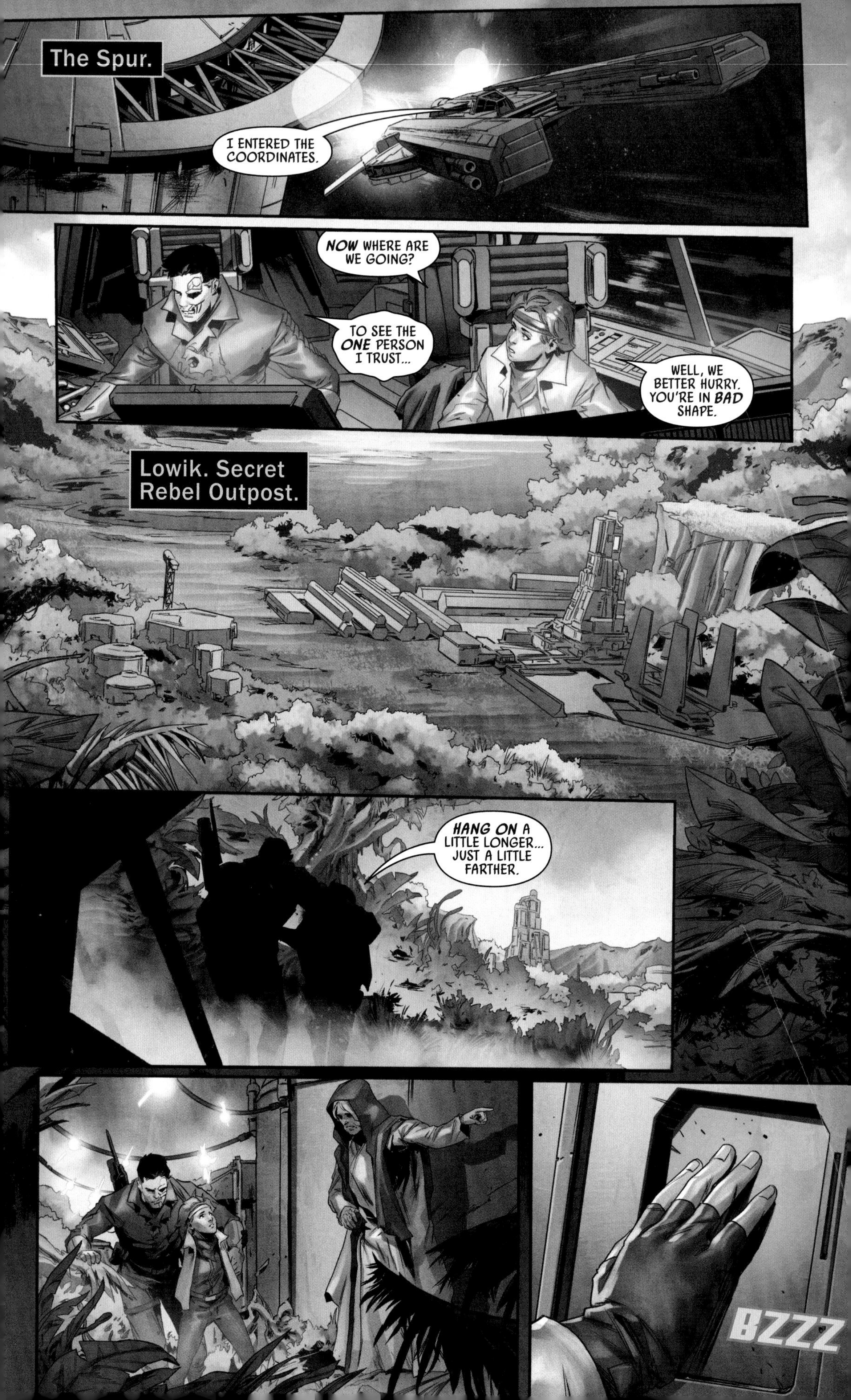
The Spur.
I ENTERED THE COORDINATES.
NOW WHERE ARE WE GOING?
TO SEE THE ONE PERSON I TRUST...
WELL, WE BETTER HURRY. YOU'RE IN BAD SHAPE.
Lowik. Secret Rebel Outpost.
HANG ON A LITTLE LONGER... JUST A LITTLE FARTHER.
BZZZ

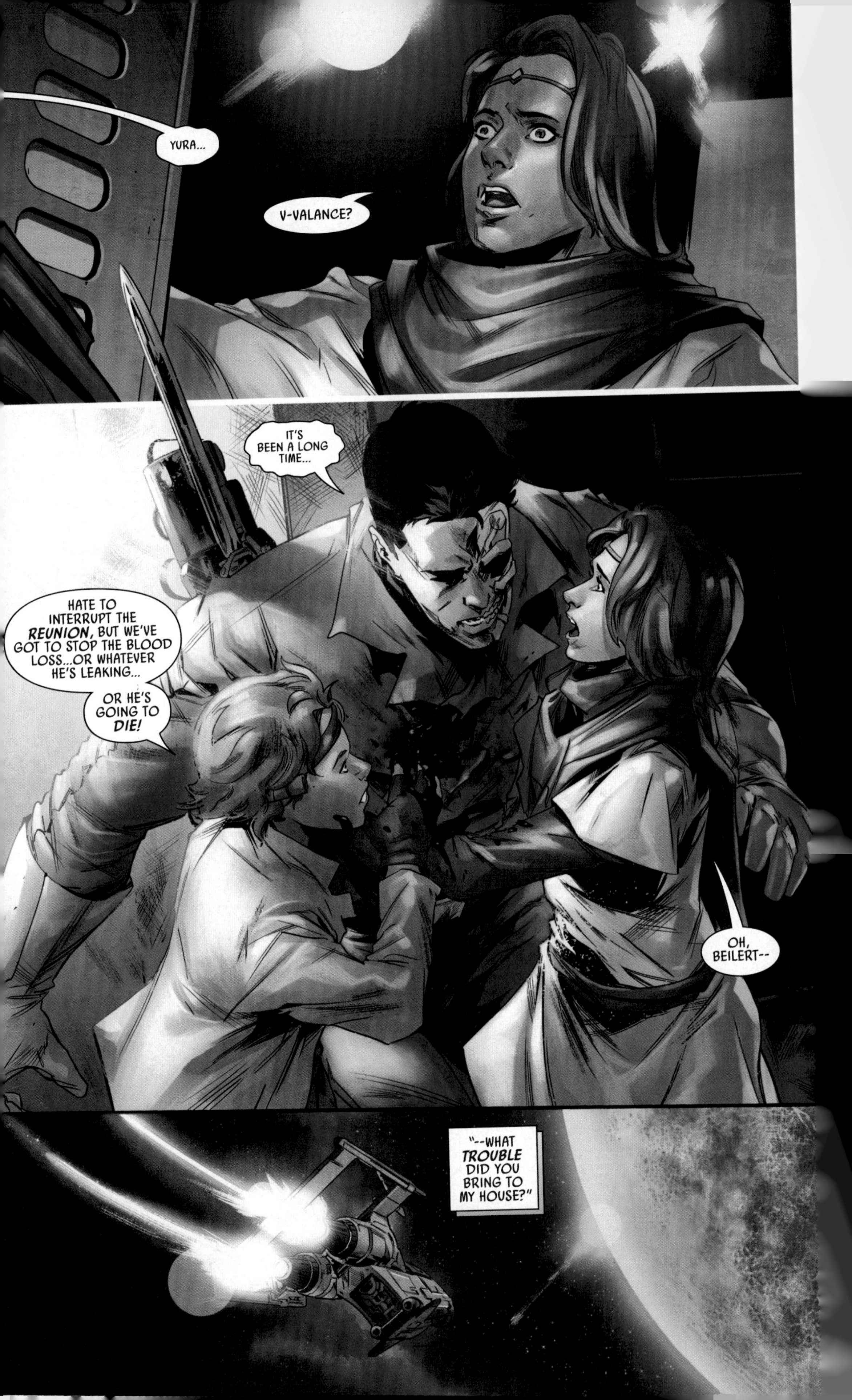
YURA...
V-VALANCE?
IT'S BEEN A LONG TIME...
HATE TO INTERRUPT THE REUNION, BUT WE'VE GOT TO STOP THE BLOOD LOSS...OR WHATEVER HE'S LEAKING...
OR HE'S GOING TO DIE!
OH, BEILERT--
"--WHAT TROUBLE DID YOU BRING TO MY HOUSE?"

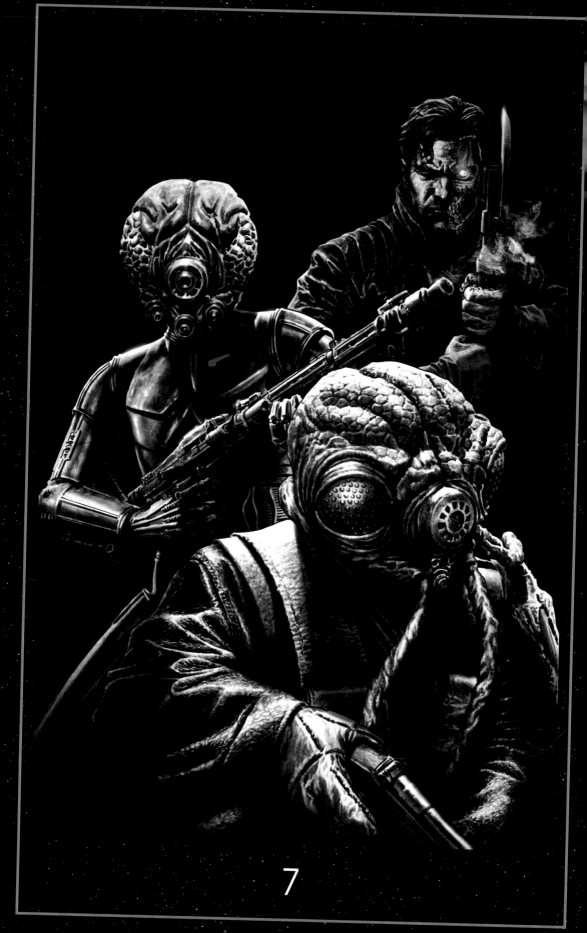

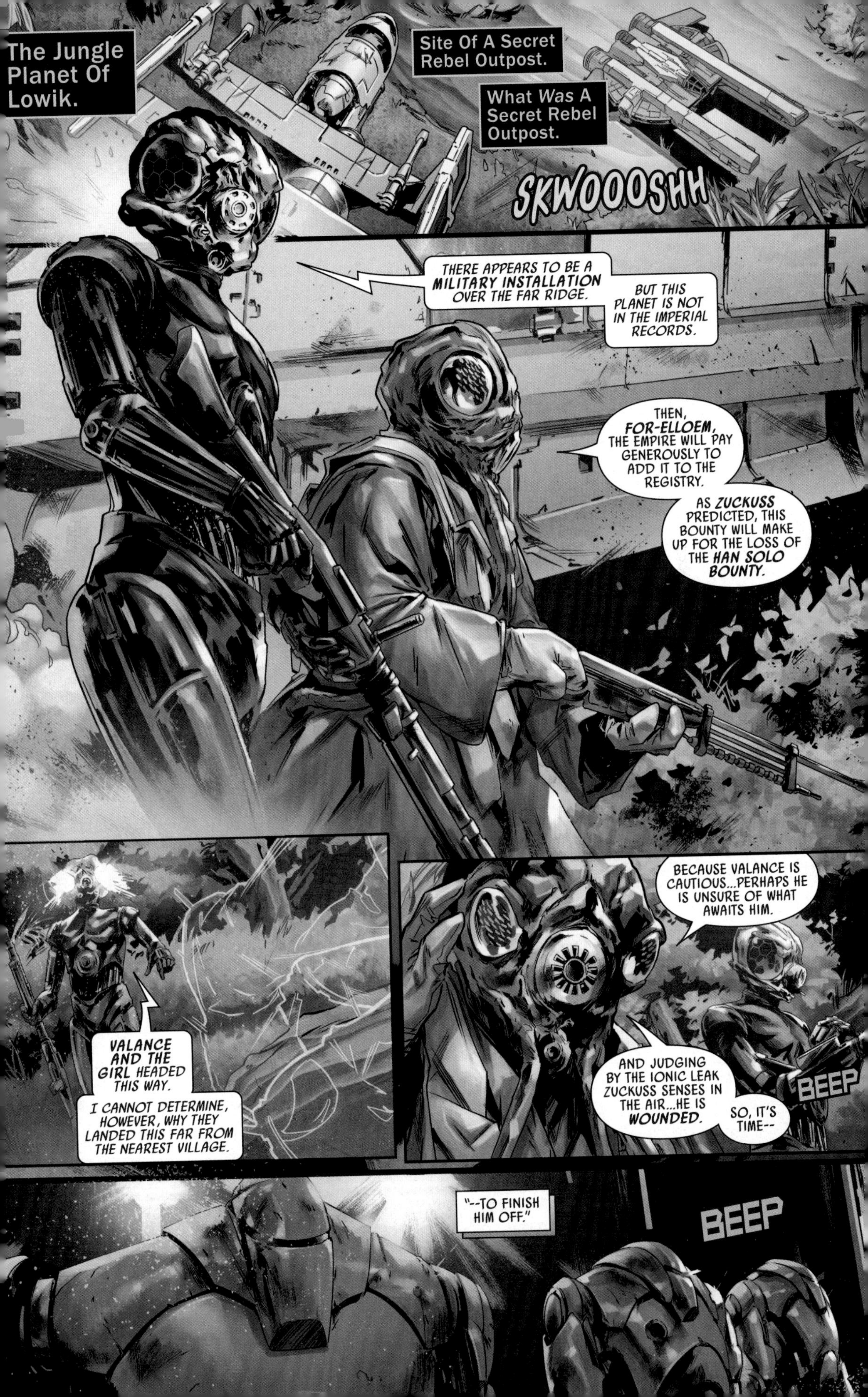
The Jungle Planet Of Lowik.
Site Of A Secret Rebel Outpost.
What *Was* A Secret Rebel Outpost.
SKWOOOSHH
THERE APPEARS TO BE A **MILITARY INSTALLATION** OVER THE FAR RIDGE.
BUT THIS PLANET IS NOT IN THE IMPERIAL RECORDS.
THEN, **FOR-ELLOEM,** THE EMPIRE WILL PAY GENEROUSLY TO ADD IT TO THE REGISTRY.
AS **ZUCKUSS** PREDICTED, THIS BOUNTY WILL MAKE UP FOR THE LOSS OF THE **HAN SOLO BOUNTY.**
VALANCE AND THE GIRL HEADED THIS WAY.
I CANNOT DETERMINE, HOWEVER, WHY THEY LANDED THIS FAR FROM THE NEAREST VILLAGE.
BECAUSE VALANCE IS CAUTIOUS...PERHAPS HE IS UNSURE OF WHAT AWAITS HIM.
AND JUDGING BY THE IONIC LEAK ZUCKUSS SENSES IN THE AIR...HE IS **WOUNDED.**
SO, IT'S TIME--
BEEP
"--TO FINISH HIM OFF."
BEEP

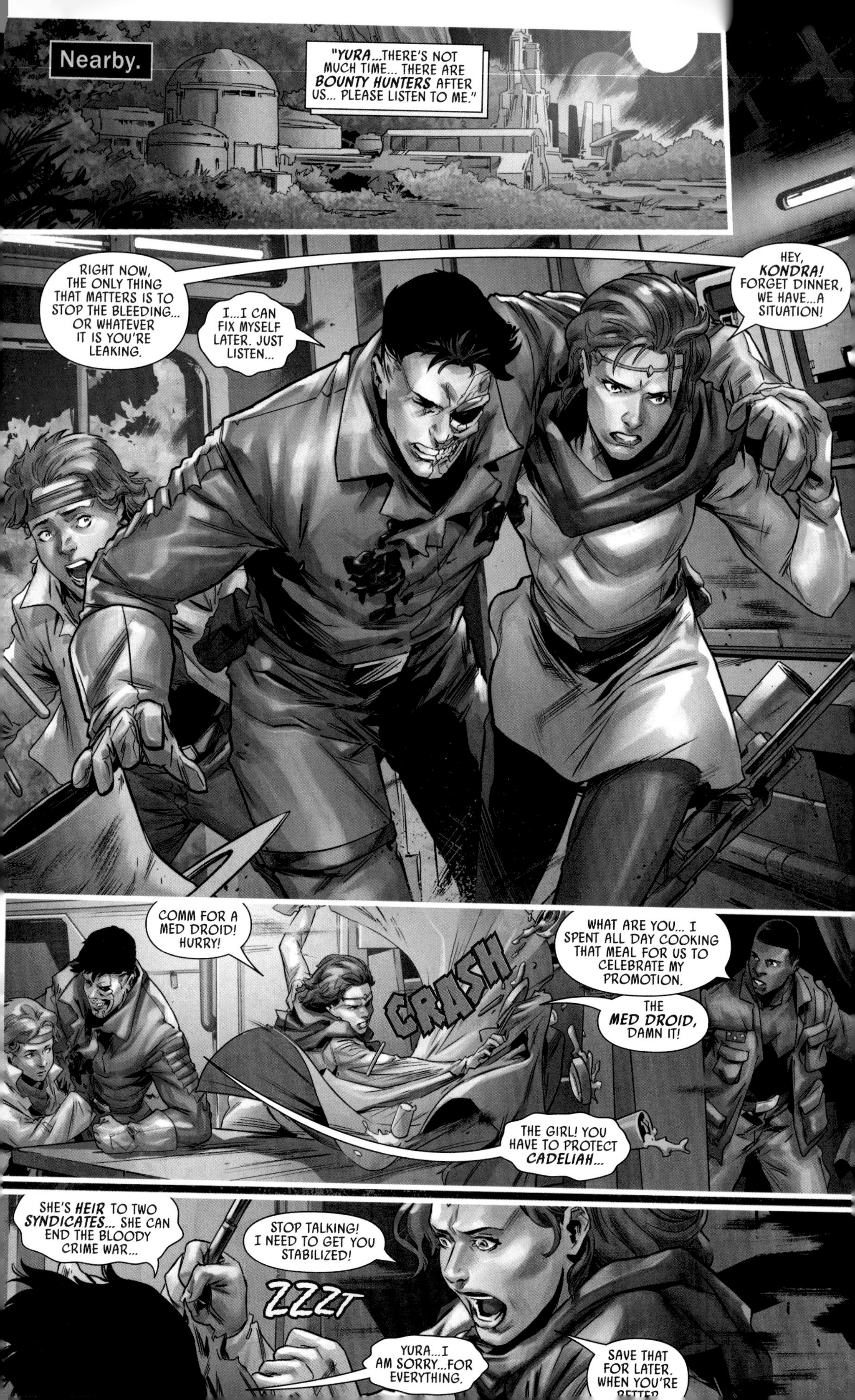
Nearby.
"YURA...THERE'S NOT MUCH TIME... THERE ARE BOUNTY HUNTERS AFTER US... PLEASE LISTEN TO ME."
HEY, KONDRA! FORGET DINNER, WE HAVE...A SITUATION!
RIGHT NOW, THE ONLY THING THAT MATTERS IS TO STOP THE BLEEDING... OR WHATEVER IT IS YOU'RE LEAKING.
I...I CAN FIX MYSELF LATER. JUST LISTEN...
COMM FOR A MED DROID! HURRY!
CRASH
WHAT ARE YOU... I SPENT ALL DAY COOKING THAT MEAL FOR US TO CELEBRATE MY PROMOTION.
THE MED DROID, DAMN IT!
THE GIRL! YOU HAVE TO PROTECT CADELIAH...
SHE'S HEIR TO TWO SYNDICATES... SHE CAN END THE BLOODY CRIME WAR...
STOP TALKING! I NEED TO GET YOU STABILIZED!
ZZZT
YURA...I AM SORRY...FOR EVERYTHING.
SAVE THAT FOR LATER. WHEN YOU'RE

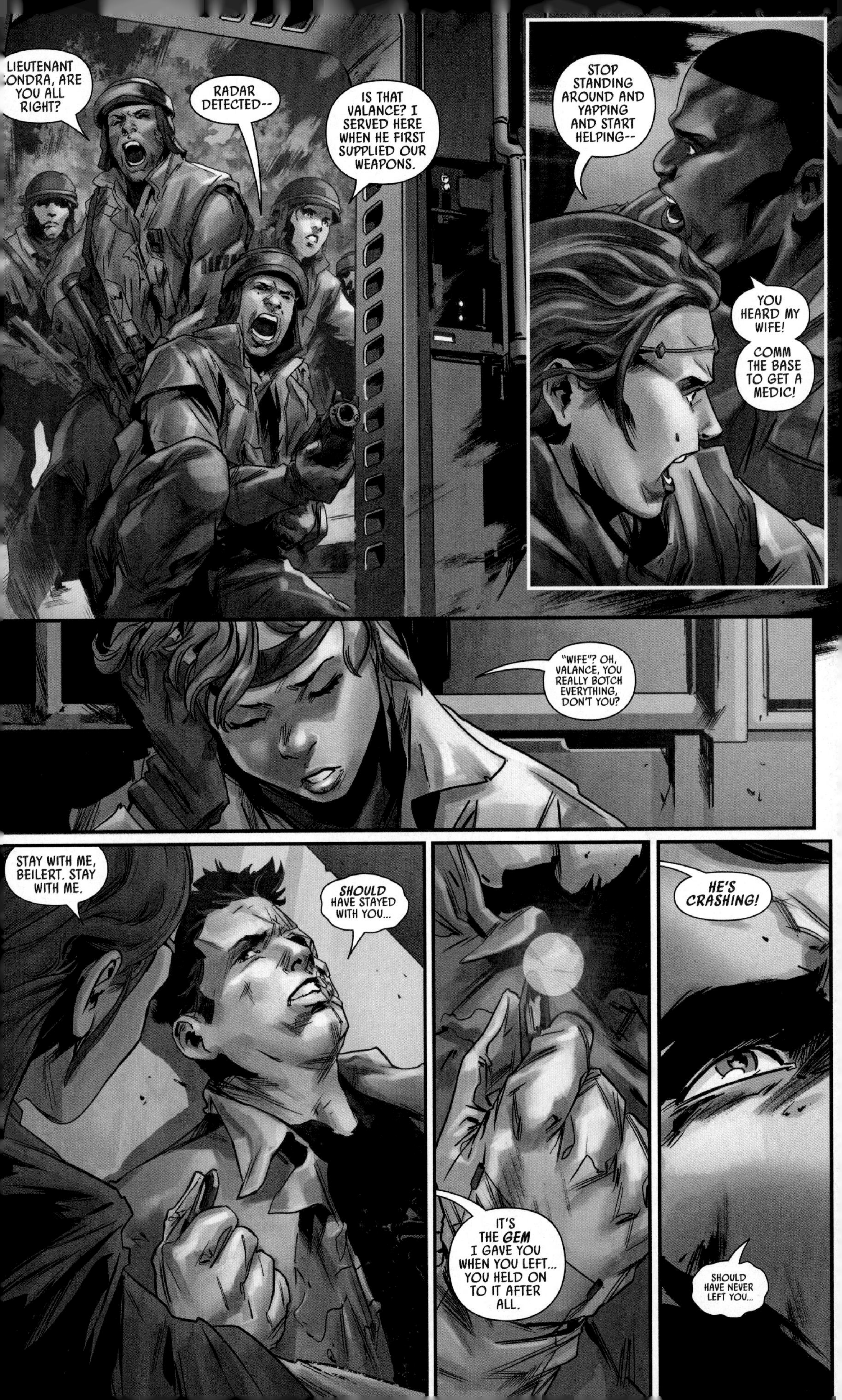

LIEUTENANT KONDRA, ARE YOU ALL RIGHT?
RADAR DETECTED--
IS THAT VALANCE? I SERVED HERE WHEN HE FIRST SUPPLIED OUR WEAPONS.
STOP STANDING AROUND AND YAPPING AND START HELPING--
YOU HEARD MY WIFE!
COMM THE BASE TO GET A MEDIC!
"WIFE"? OH, VALANCE, YOU REALLY BOTCH EVERYTHING, DON'T YOU?
STAY WITH ME, BEILERT. STAY WITH ME.
SHOULD HAVE STAYED WITH YOU...
IT'S THE GEM I GAVE YOU WHEN YOU LEFT... YOU HELD ON TO IT AFTER ALL.
HE'S CRASHING!
SHOULD HAVE NEVER LEFT YOU...

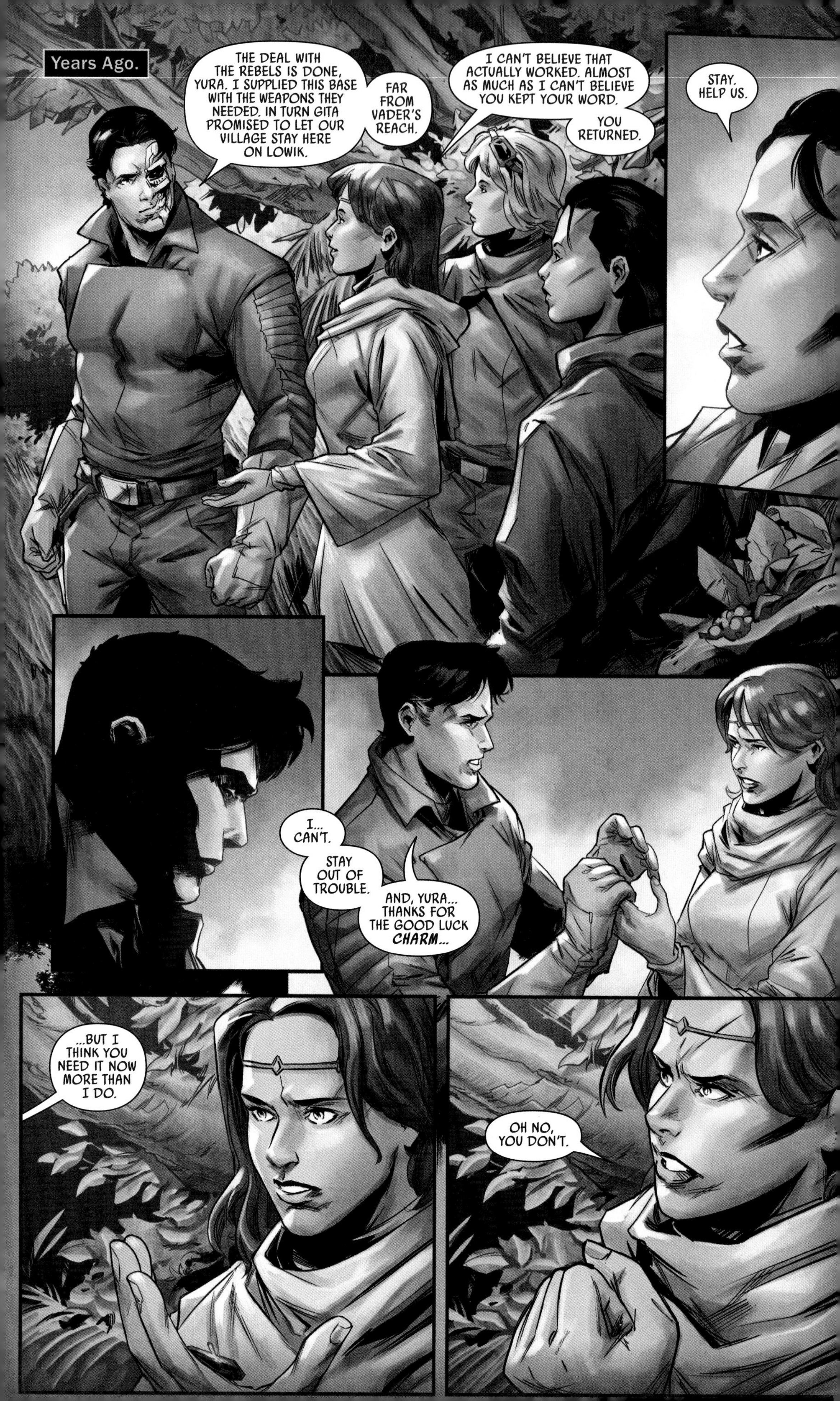
Years Ago.
THE DEAL WITH THE REBELS IS DONE, YURA. I SUPPLIED THIS BASE WITH THE WEAPONS THEY NEEDED. IN TURN GITA PROMISED TO LET OUR VILLAGE STAY HERE ON LOWIK.
FAR FROM VADER'S REACH.
I CAN'T BELIEVE THAT ACTUALLY WORKED. ALMOST AS MUCH AS I CAN'T BELIEVE YOU KEPT YOUR WORD.
YOU RETURNED.
STAY. HELP US.
I... CAN'T.
STAY OUT OF TROUBLE.
AND, YURA... THANKS FOR THE GOOD LUCK CHARM...
...BUT I THINK YOU NEED IT NOW MORE THAN I DO.
OH NO, YOU DON'T.

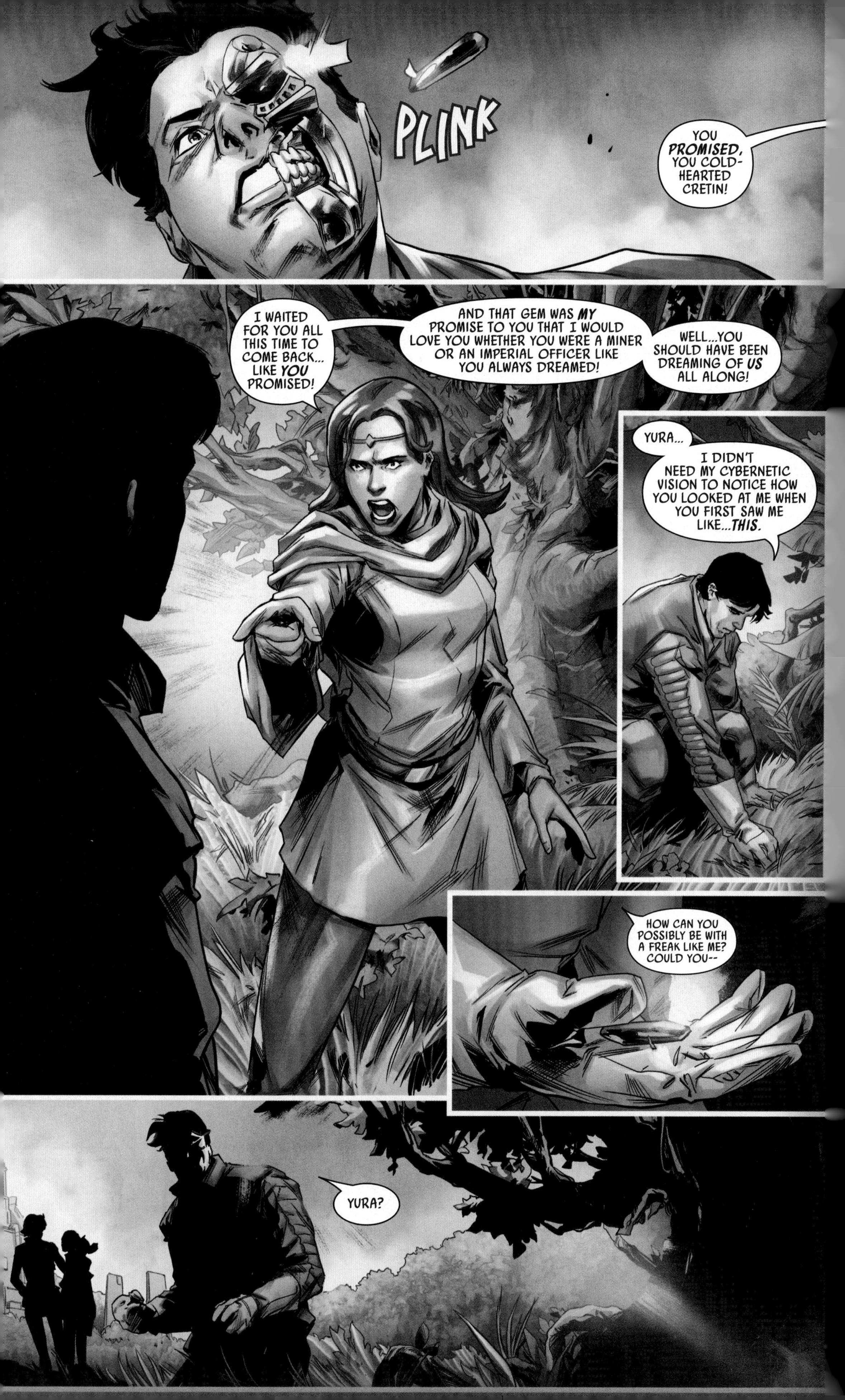
PLINK
YOU PROMISED, YOU COLD-HEARTED CRETIN!
I WAITED FOR YOU ALL THIS TIME TO COME BACK... LIKE YOU PROMISED!
AND THAT GEM WAS MY PROMISE TO YOU THAT I WOULD LOVE YOU WHETHER YOU WERE A MINER OR AN IMPERIAL OFFICER LIKE YOU ALWAYS DREAMED!
WELL...YOU SHOULD HAVE BEEN DREAMING OF US ALL ALONG!
YURA...
I DIDN'T NEED MY CYBERNETIC VISION TO NOTICE HOW YOU LOOKED AT ME WHEN YOU FIRST SAW ME LIKE...THIS.
HOW CAN YOU POSSIBLY BE WITH A FREAK LIKE ME? COULD YOU--
YURA?

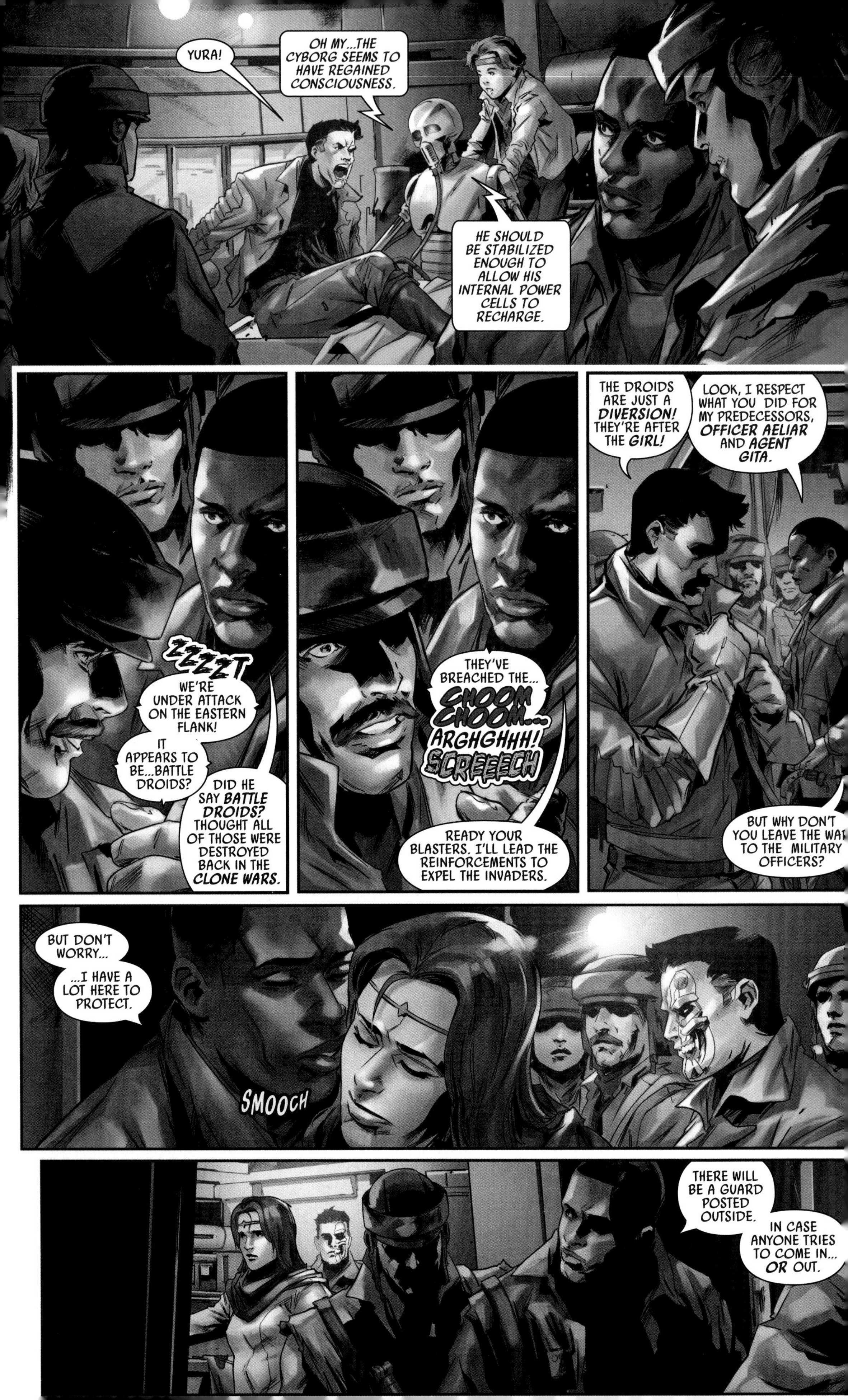
YURA!
OH MY...THE CYBORG SEEMS TO HAVE REGAINED CONSCIOUSNESS.
HE SHOULD BE STABILIZED ENOUGH TO ALLOW HIS INTERNAL POWER CELLS TO RECHARGE.
ZZZZT
WE'RE UNDER ATTACK ON THE EASTERN FLANK!
IT APPEARS TO BE...BATTLE DROIDS?
DID HE SAY BATTLE DROIDS? THOUGHT ALL OF THOSE WERE DESTROYED BACK IN THE CLONE WARS.
THEY'VE BREACHED THE...
CHOOM CHOOM...
ARGHGHHH!
SCREEEECH
READY YOUR BLASTERS. I'LL LEAD THE REINFORCEMENTS TO EXPEL THE INVADERS.
THE DROIDS ARE JUST A DIVERSION! THEY'RE AFTER THE GIRL!
LOOK, I RESPECT WHAT YOU DID FOR MY PREDECESSORS, OFFICER AELIAR AND AGENT GITA.
BUT WHY DON'T YOU LEAVE THE WA TO THE MILITARY OFFICERS?
BUT DON'T WORRY...
...I HAVE A LOT HERE TO PROTECT.
SMOOCH
THERE WILL BE A GUARD POSTED OUTSIDE.
IN CASE ANYONE TRIES TO COME IN... OR OUT.

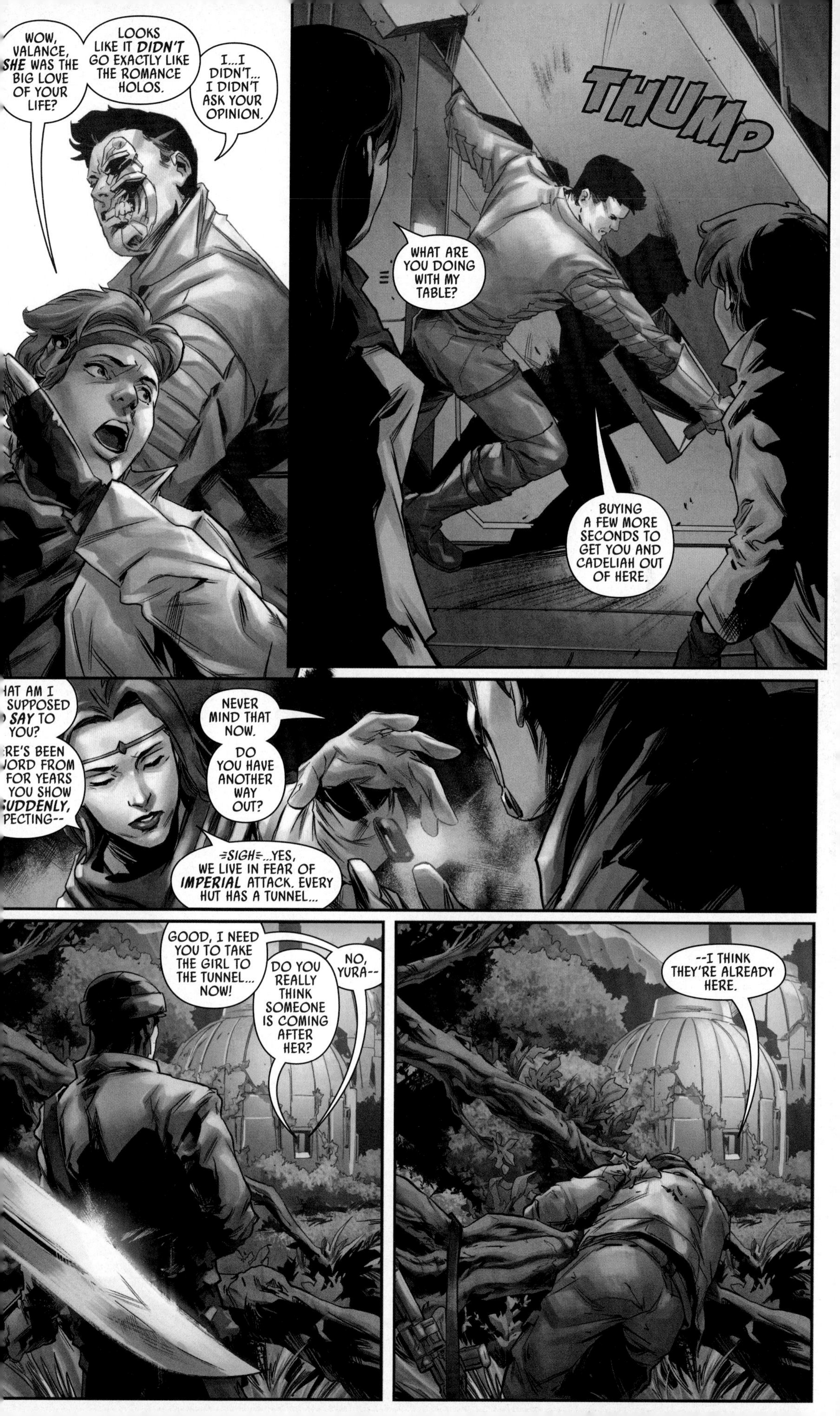
WOW, VALANCE, SHE WAS THE BIG LOVE OF YOUR LIFE?
LOOKS LIKE IT DIDN'T GO EXACTLY LIKE THE ROMANCE HOLOS.
I...I DIDN'T... I DIDN'T ASK YOUR OPINION.
THUMP
WHAT ARE YOU DOING WITH MY TABLE?
BUYING A FEW MORE SECONDS TO GET YOU AND CADELIAH OUT OF HERE.
HAT AM I SUPPOSED SAY TO YOU? RE'S BEEN ORD FROM FOR YEARS YOU SHOW SUDDENLY, PECTING--
NEVER MIND THAT NOW.
DO YOU HAVE ANOTHER WAY OUT?
SIGH...YES, WE LIVE IN FEAR OF IMPERIAL ATTACK. EVERY HUT HAS A TUNNEL...
GOOD, I NEED YOU TO TAKE THE GIRL TO THE TUNNEL... NOW!
DO YOU REALLY THINK SOMEONE IS COMING AFTER HER?
NO, YURA--
--I THINK THEY'RE ALREADY HERE.

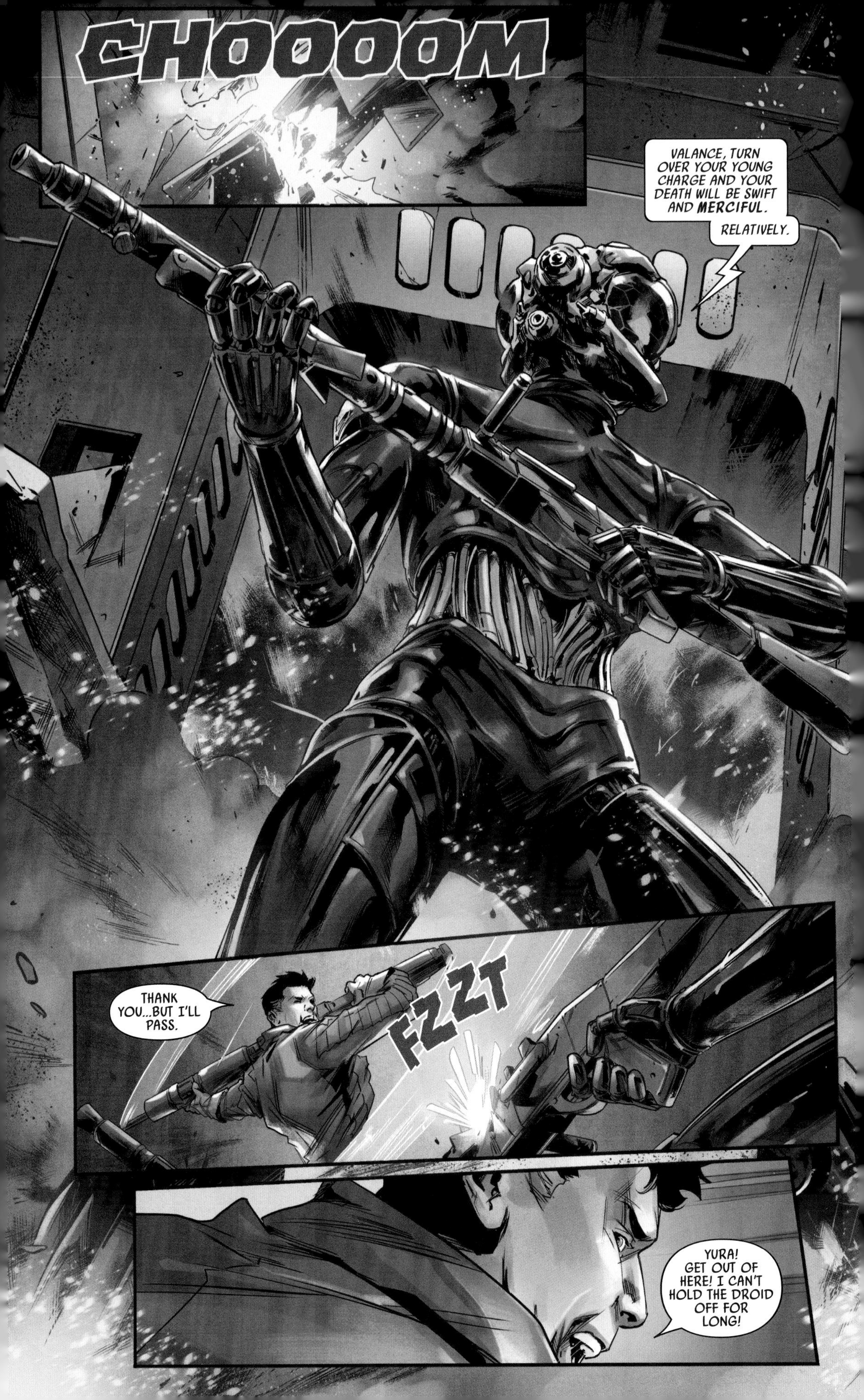
CHOOOOM
VALANCE, TURN OVER YOUR YOUNG CHARGE AND YOUR DEATH WILL BE SWIFT AND MERCIFUL.
RELATIVELY.
THANK YOU...BUT I'LL PASS.
FZZT
YURA! GET OUT OF HERE! I CAN'T HOLD THE DROID OFF FOR LONG!

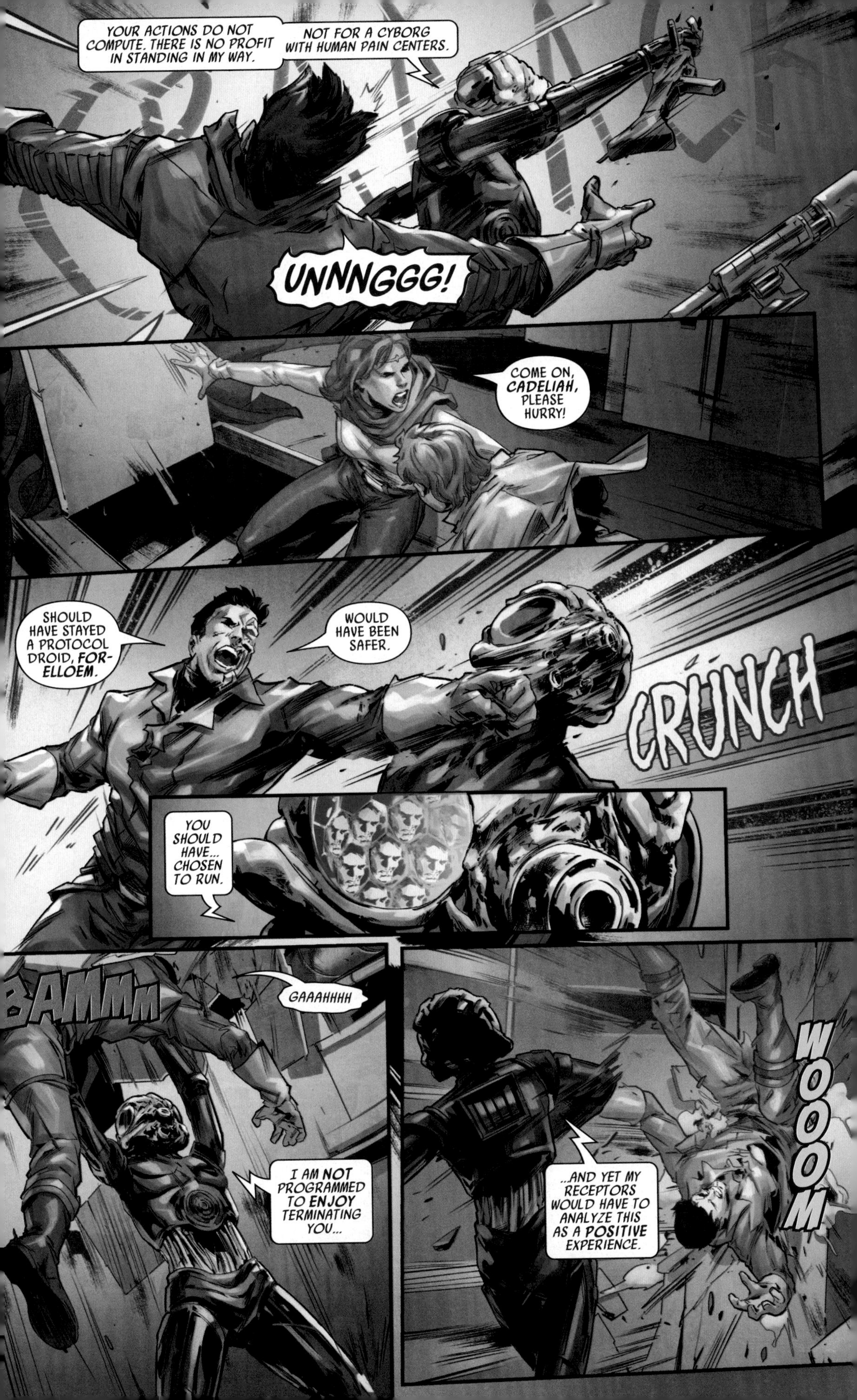
YOUR ACTIONS DO NOT COMPUTE. THERE IS NO PROFIT IN STANDING IN MY WAY.
NOT FOR A CYBORG WITH HUMAN PAIN CENTERS.
UNNNGGG!
COME ON, CADELIAH, PLEASE HURRY!
SHOULD HAVE STAYED A PROTOCOL DROID, FOR-ELLOEM.
WOULD HAVE BEEN SAFER.
CRUNCH
YOU SHOULD HAVE... CHOSEN TO RUN.
BAMMM
GAAAHHHH
I AM NOT PROGRAMMED TO ENJOY TERMINATING YOU...
...AND YET MY RECEPTORS WOULD HAVE TO ANALYZE THIS AS A POSITIVE EXPERIENCE.
WOOOM

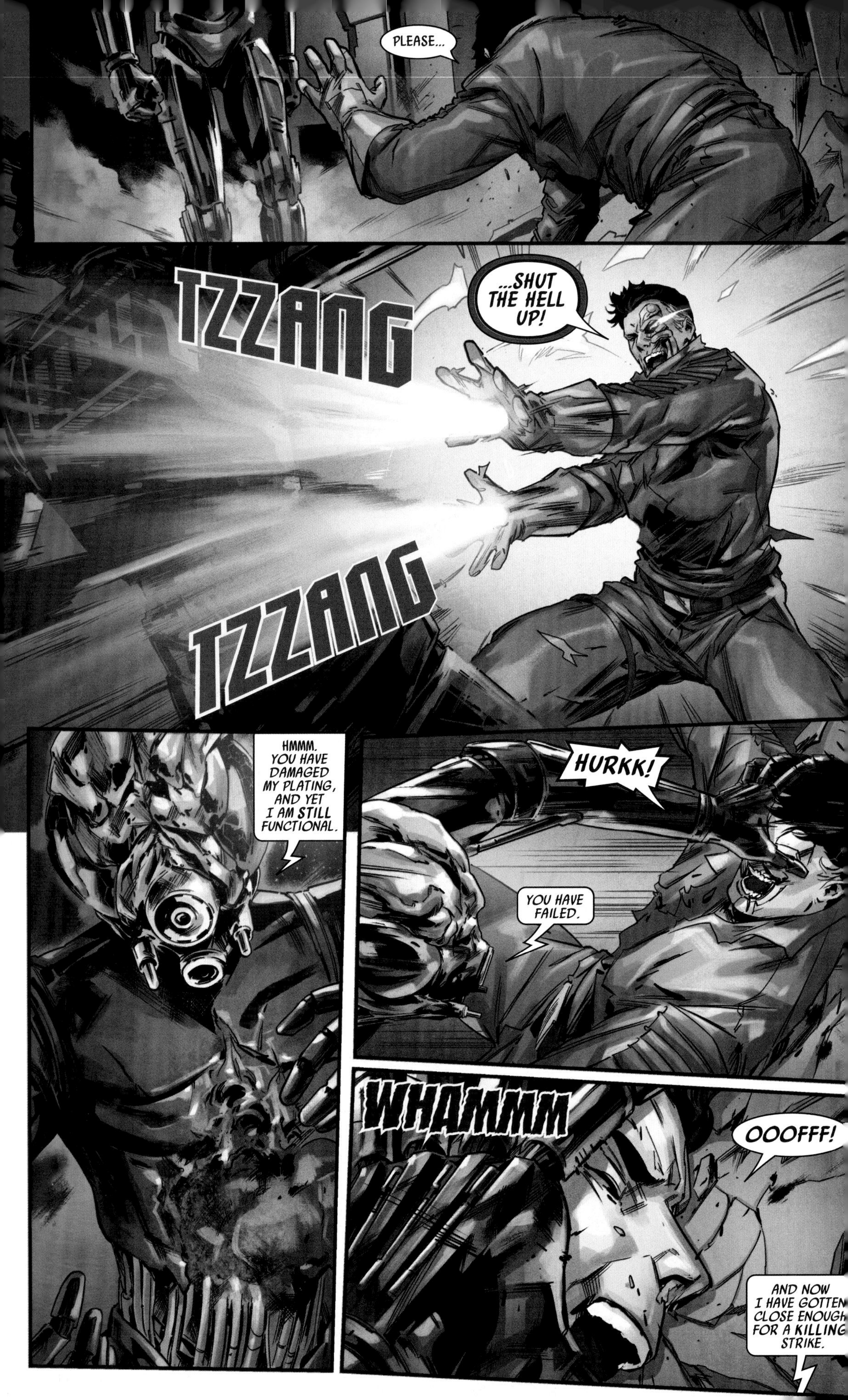
PLEASE...
TZZANG
...SHUT THE HELL UP!
TZZANG
HMMM. YOU HAVE DAMAGED MY PLATING, AND YET I AM STILL FUNCTIONAL.
HURKK!
YOU HAVE FAILED.
WHAMMM
OOOFFF!
AND NOW I HAVE GOTTEN CLOSE ENOUGH FOR A KILLING STRIKE.

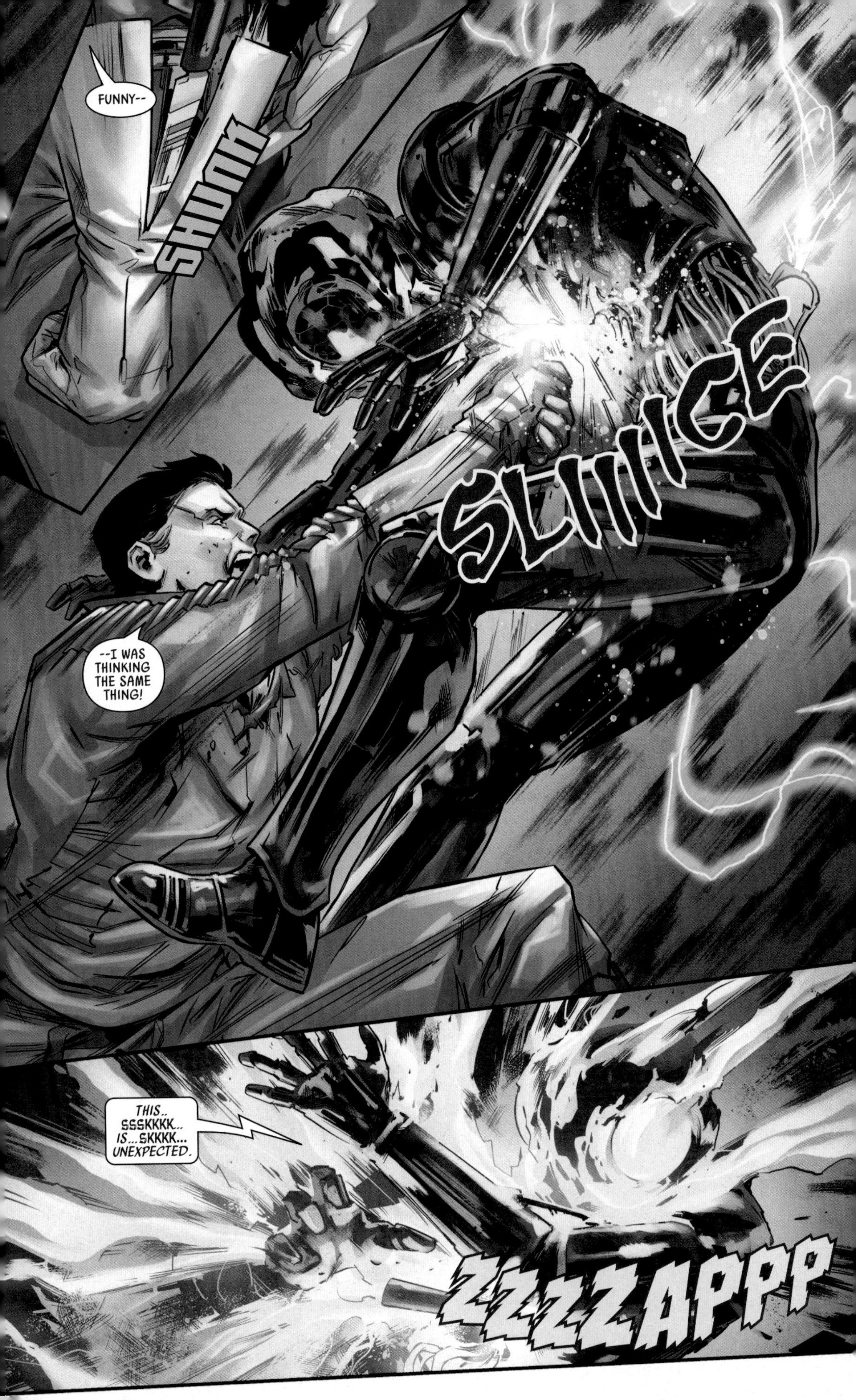
FUNNY--
SHUNK
SLIIIICE
--I WAS THINKING THE SAME THING!
THIS.. SSSKKKK... IS...SKKKK... UNEXPECTED.
ZZZZAPPP

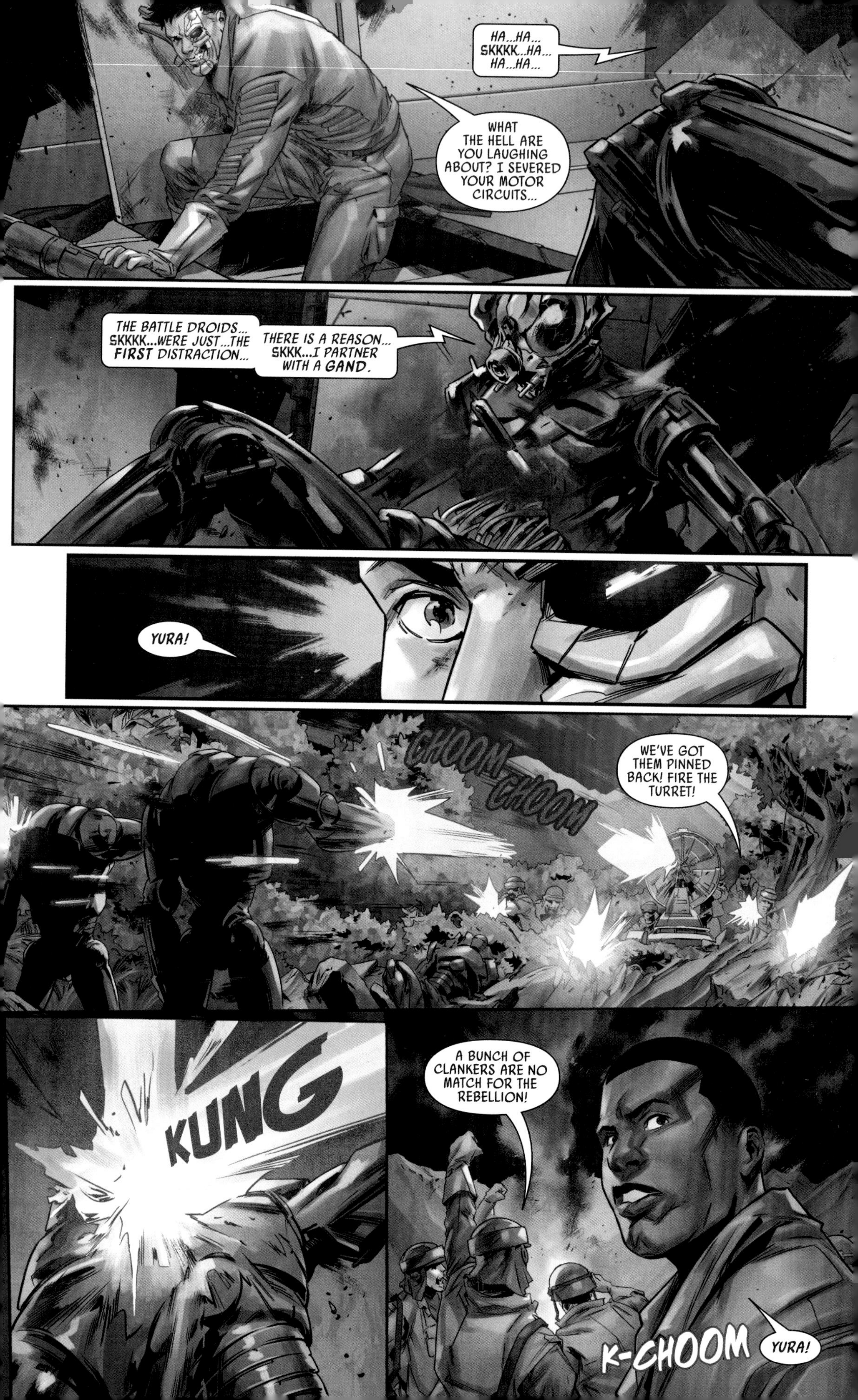
HA...HA... SKKKK...HA... HA...HA...
WHAT THE HELL ARE YOU LAUGHING ABOUT? I SEVERED YOUR MOTOR CIRCUITS...
THE BATTLE DROIDS... SKKKK...WERE JUST...THE FIRST DISTRACTION...
THERE IS A REASON... SKKK...I PARTNER WITH A GAND.
YURA!
CHOOM CHOOM
WE'VE GOT THEM PINNED BACK! FIRE THE TURRET!
KUNG
A BUNCH OF CLANKERS ARE NO MATCH FOR THE REBELLION!
K-CHOOM
YURA!

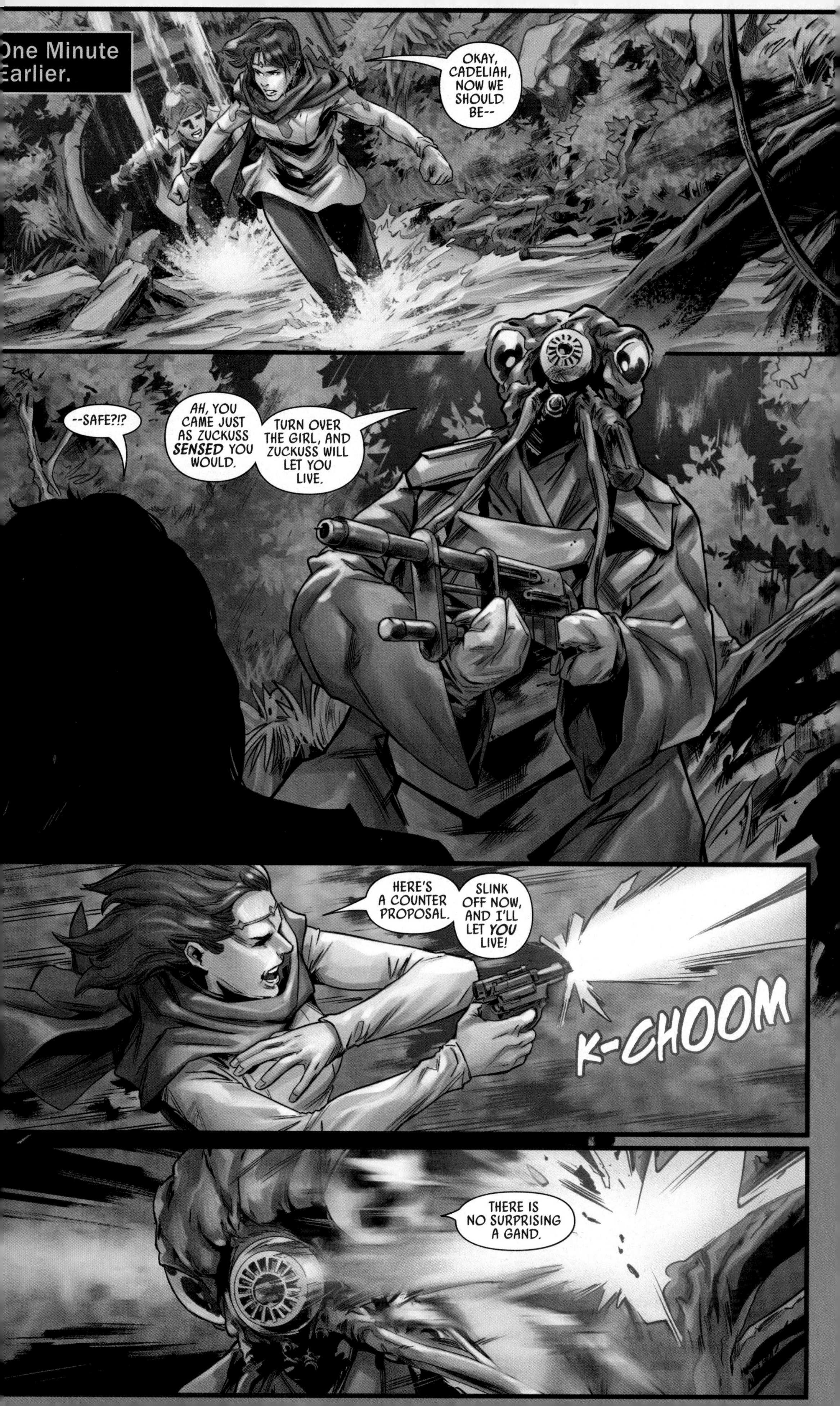

One Minute Earlier.
OKAY, CADELIAH, NOW WE SHOULD BE--
--SAFE?!?
AH, YOU CAME JUST AS ZUCKUSS SENSED YOU WOULD.
TURN OVER THE GIRL, AND ZUCKUSS WILL LET YOU LIVE.
HERE'S A COUNTER PROPOSAL.
SLINK OFF NOW, AND I'LL LET YOU LIVE!
K-CHOOM
THERE IS NO SURPRISING A GAND.

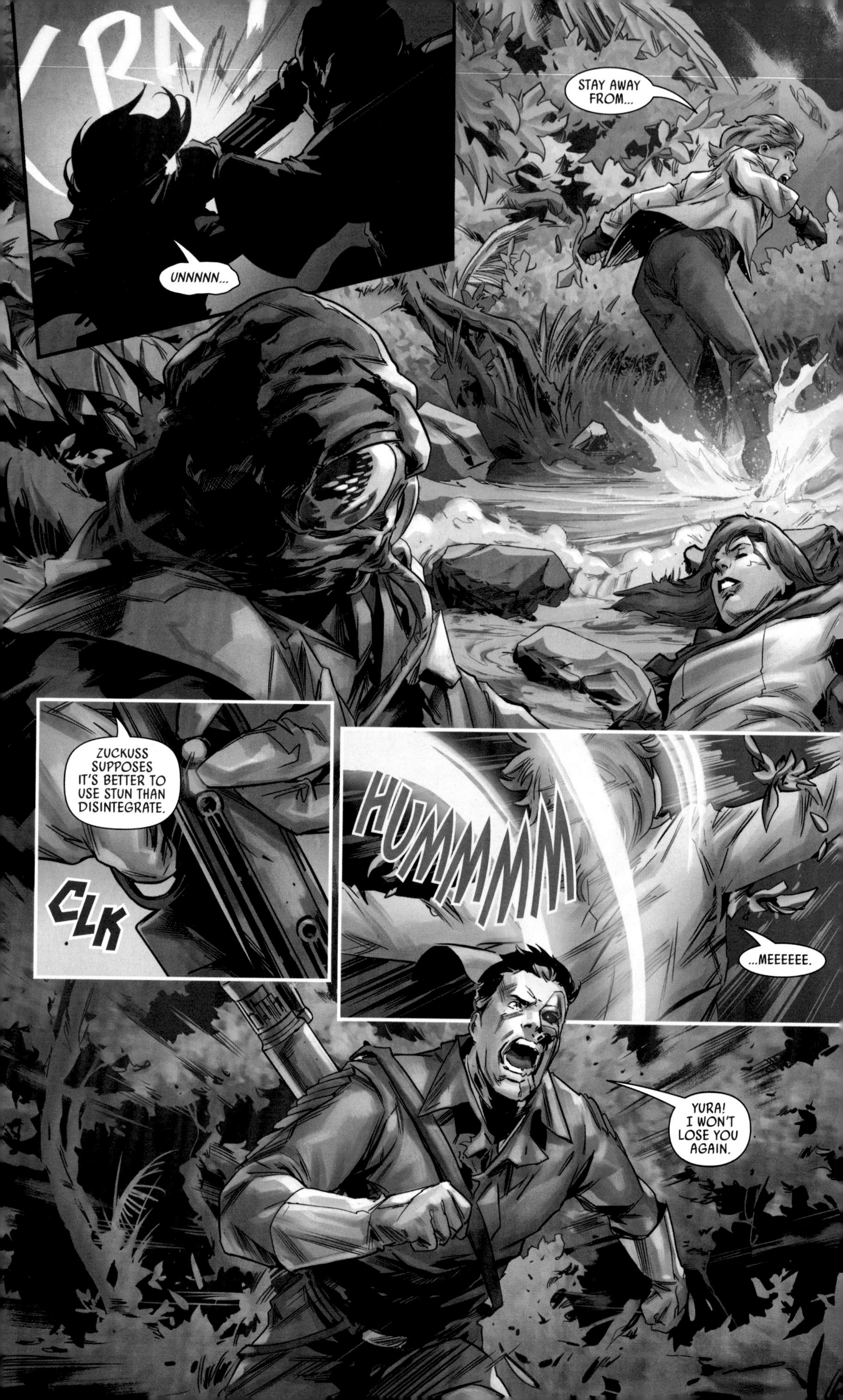
UNNNNN...
STAY AWAY FROM...
ZUCKUSS SUPPOSES IT'S BETTER TO USE STUN THAN DISINTEGRATE.
CLK
HUMMMMM
...MEEEEEE.
YURA! I WON'T LOSE YOU AGAIN.

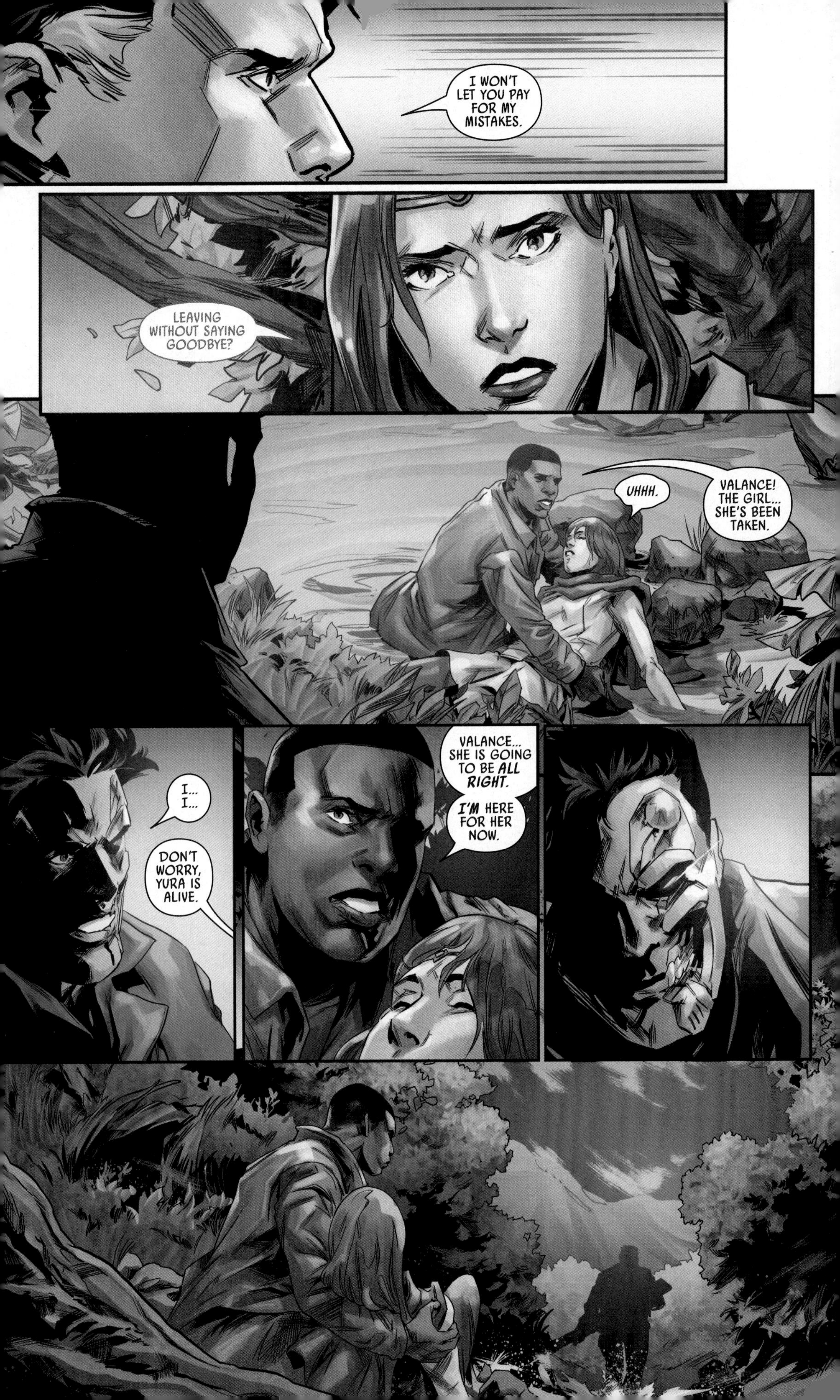

I WON'T LET YOU PAY FOR MY MISTAKES.
LEAVING WITHOUT SAYING GOODBYE?
VALANCE! THE GIRL... SHE'S BEEN TAKEN.
UHHH.
I... I...
DON'T WORRY, YURA IS ALIVE.
VALANCE... SHE IS GOING TO BE ALL RIGHT.
I'M HERE FOR HER NOW.

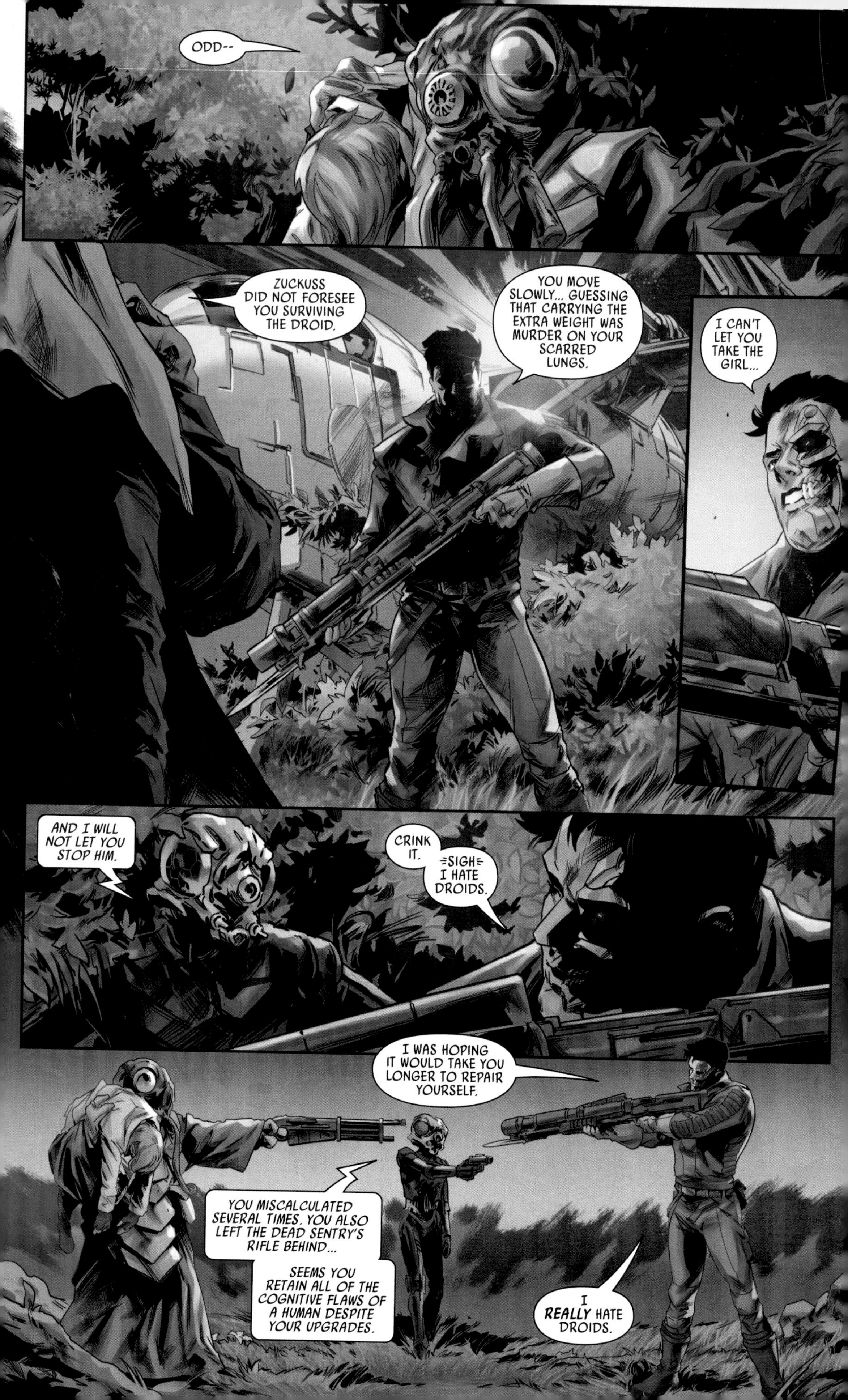
ODD--
ZUCKUSS DID NOT FORESEE YOU SURVIVING THE DROID.
YOU MOVE SLOWLY... GUESSING THAT CARRYING THE EXTRA WEIGHT WAS MURDER ON YOUR SCARRED LUNGS.
I CAN'T LET YOU TAKE THE GIRL...
AND I WILL NOT LET YOU STOP HIM.
CRINK IT.
=SIGH= I HATE DROIDS.
I WAS HOPING IT WOULD TAKE YOU LONGER TO REPAIR YOURSELF.
YOU MISCALCULATED SEVERAL TIMES. YOU ALSO LEFT THE DEAD SENTRY'S RIFLE BEHIND...
SEEMS YOU RETAIN ALL OF THE COGNITIVE FLAWS OF A HUMAN DESPITE YOUR UPGRADES.
I **REALLY** HATE DROIDS.

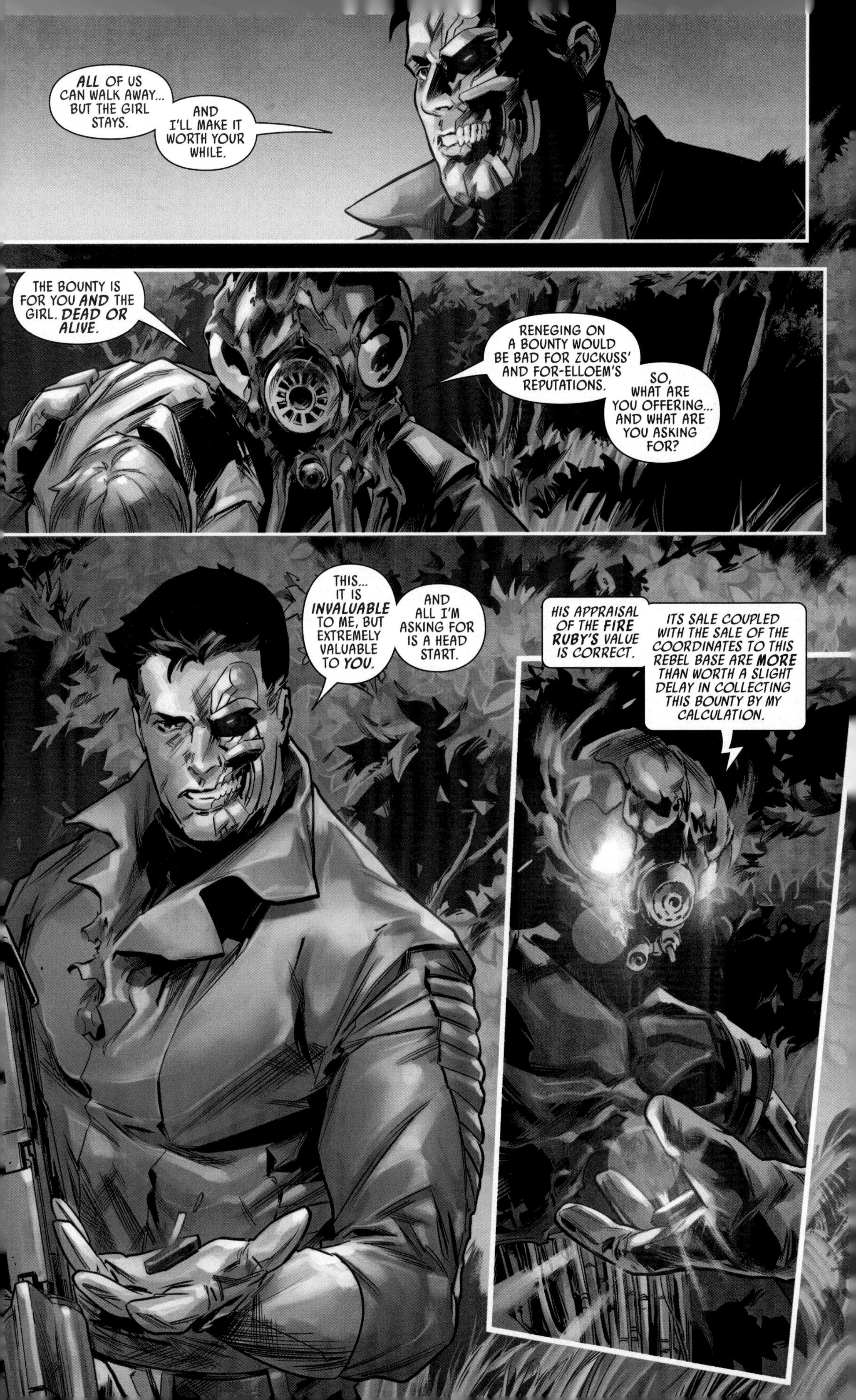

ALL OF US CAN WALK AWAY... BUT THE GIRL STAYS.
AND I'LL MAKE IT WORTH YOUR WHILE.
THE BOUNTY IS FOR YOU AND THE GIRL. DEAD OR ALIVE.
RENEGING ON A BOUNTY WOULD BE BAD FOR ZUCKUSS' AND FOR-ELLOEM'S REPUTATIONS.
SO, WHAT ARE YOU OFFERING... AND WHAT ARE YOU ASKING FOR?
THIS... IT IS INVALUABLE TO ME, BUT EXTREMELY VALUABLE TO YOU.
AND ALL I'M ASKING FOR IS A HEAD START.
HIS APPRAISAL OF THE FIRE RUBY'S VALUE IS CORRECT.
ITS SALE COUPLED WITH THE SALE OF THE COORDINATES TO THIS REBEL BASE ARE MORE THAN WORTH A SLIGHT DELAY IN COLLECTING THIS BOUNTY BY MY CALCULATION.

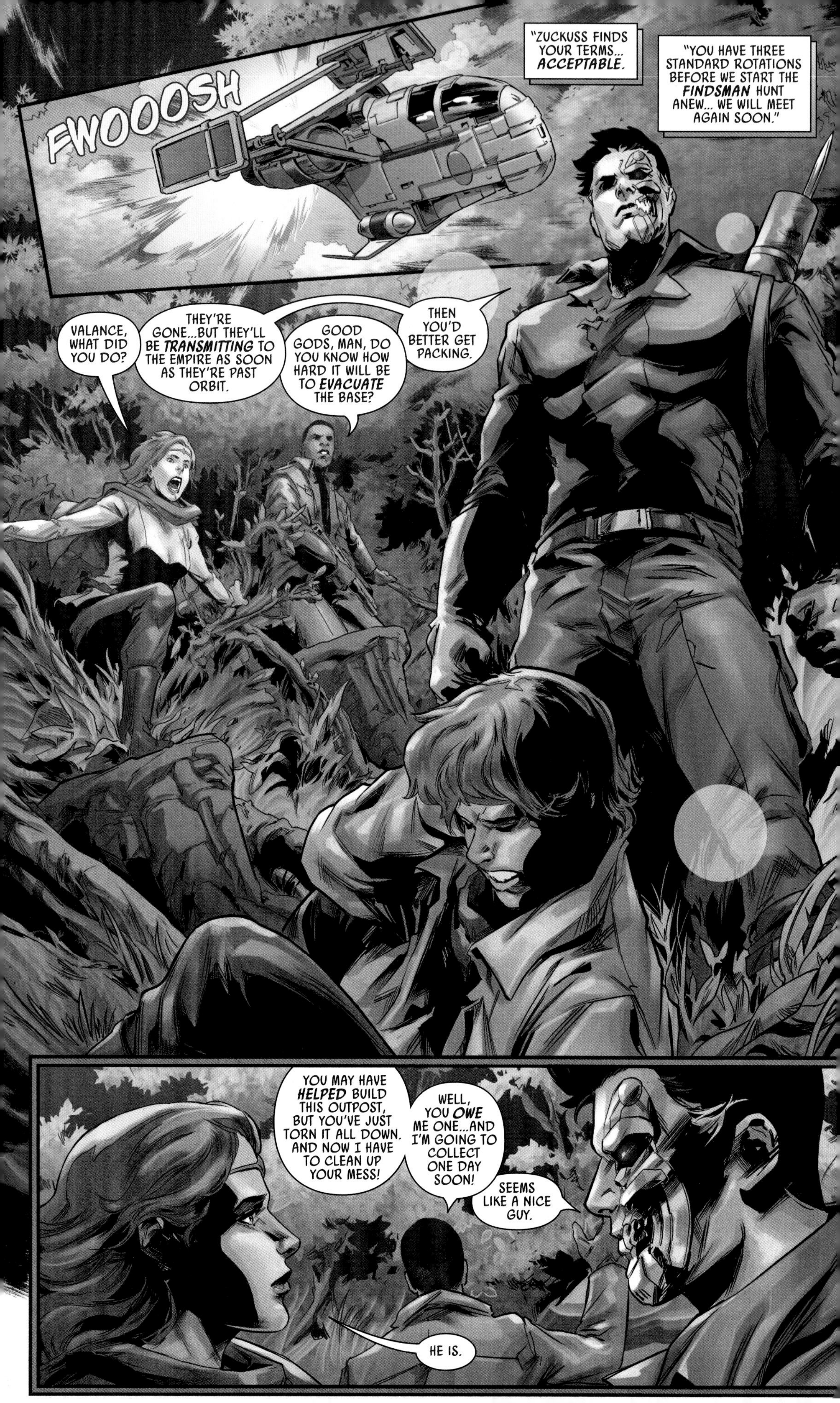
FWOOOSH
"ZUCKUSS FINDS YOUR TERMS... ACCEPTABLE.
"YOU HAVE THREE STANDARD ROTATIONS BEFORE WE START THE FINDSMAN HUNT ANEW... WE WILL MEET AGAIN SOON."
VALANCE, WHAT DID YOU DO?
THEY'RE GONE...BUT THEY'LL BE TRANSMITTING TO THE EMPIRE AS SOON AS THEY'RE PAST ORBIT.
GOOD GODS, MAN, DO YOU KNOW HOW HARD IT WILL BE TO EVACUATE THE BASE?
THEN YOU'D BETTER GET PACKING.
YOU MAY HAVE HELPED BUILD THIS OUTPOST, BUT YOU'VE JUST TORN IT ALL DOWN. AND NOW I HAVE TO CLEAN UP YOUR MESS!
WELL, YOU OWE ME ONE...AND I'M GOING TO COLLECT ONE DAY SOON!
SEEMS LIKE A NICE GUY.
HE IS.

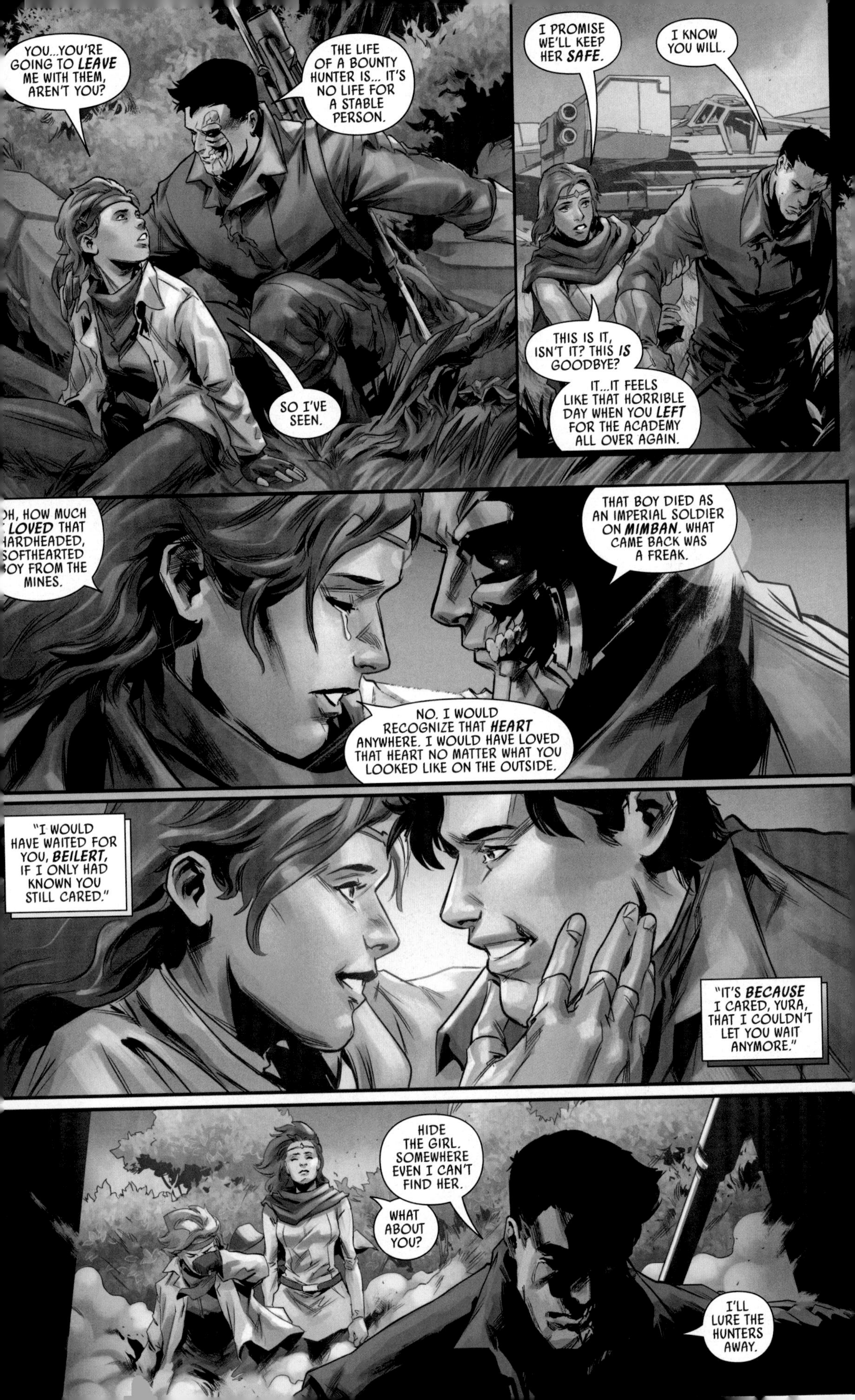
YOU...YOU'RE GOING TO LEAVE ME WITH THEM, AREN'T YOU?
THE LIFE OF A BOUNTY HUNTER IS... IT'S NO LIFE FOR A STABLE PERSON.
SO I'VE SEEN.
I PROMISE WE'LL KEEP HER SAFE.
I KNOW YOU WILL.
THIS IS IT, ISN'T IT? THIS IS GOODBYE?
IT...IT FEELS LIKE THAT HORRIBLE DAY WHEN YOU LEFT FOR THE ACADEMY ALL OVER AGAIN.
H, HOW MUCH LOVED THAT HARDHEADED, SOFTHEARTED OY FROM THE MINES.
THAT BOY DIED AS AN IMPERIAL SOLDIER ON MIMBAN. WHAT CAME BACK WAS A FREAK.
NO. I WOULD RECOGNIZE THAT HEART ANYWHERE. I WOULD HAVE LOVED THAT HEART NO MATTER WHAT YOU LOOKED LIKE ON THE OUTSIDE.
"I WOULD HAVE WAITED FOR YOU, BEILERT, IF I ONLY HAD KNOWN YOU STILL CARED."
"IT'S BECAUSE I CARED, YURA, THAT I COULDN'T LET YOU WAIT ANYMORE."
HIDE THE GIRL. SOMEWHERE EVEN I CAN'T FIND HER.
WHAT ABOUT YOU?
I'LL LURE THE HUNTERS AWAY.

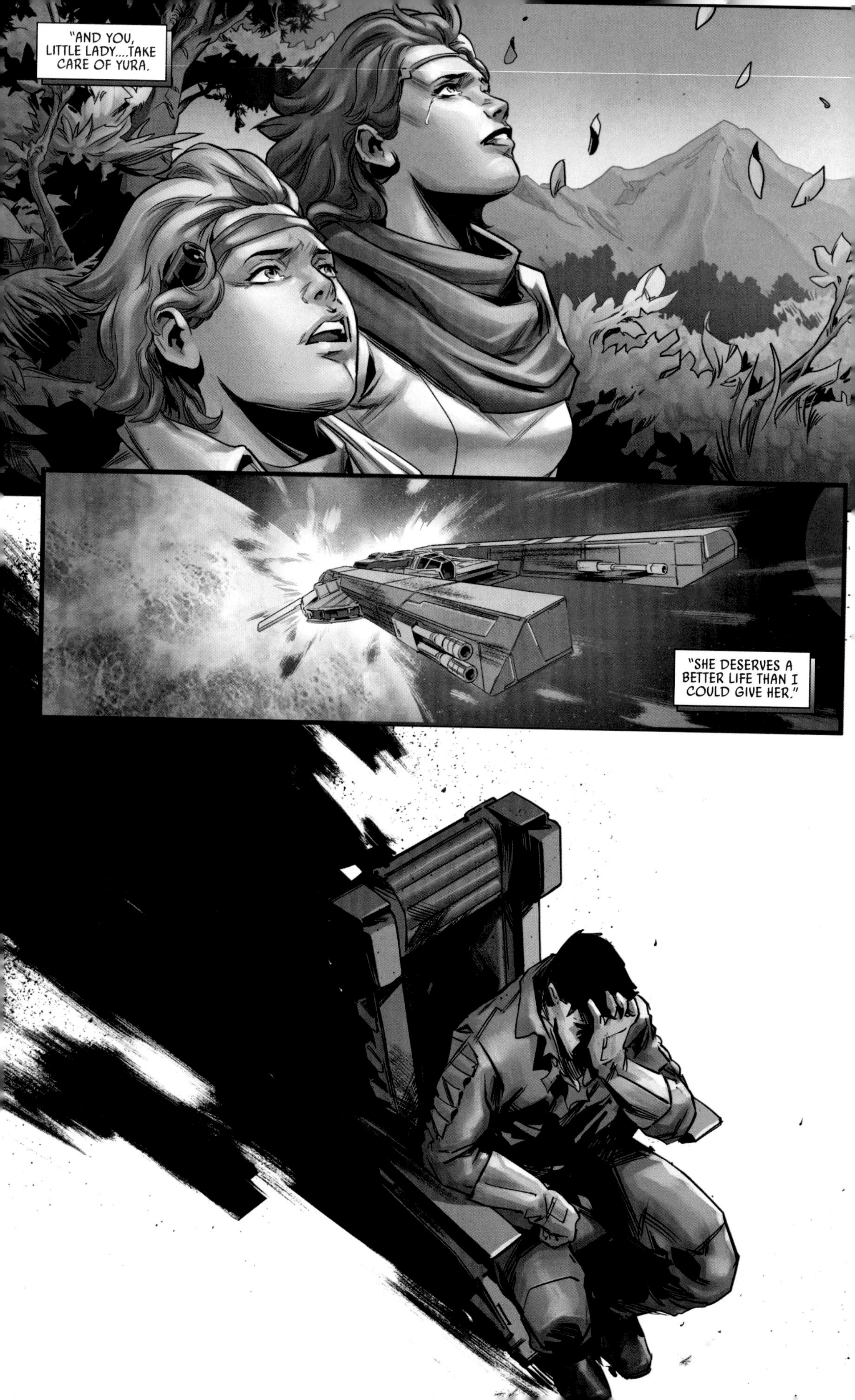
"AND YOU, LITTLE LADY....TAKE CARE OF YURA.
"SHE DESERVES A BETTER LIFE THAN I COULD GIVE HER."

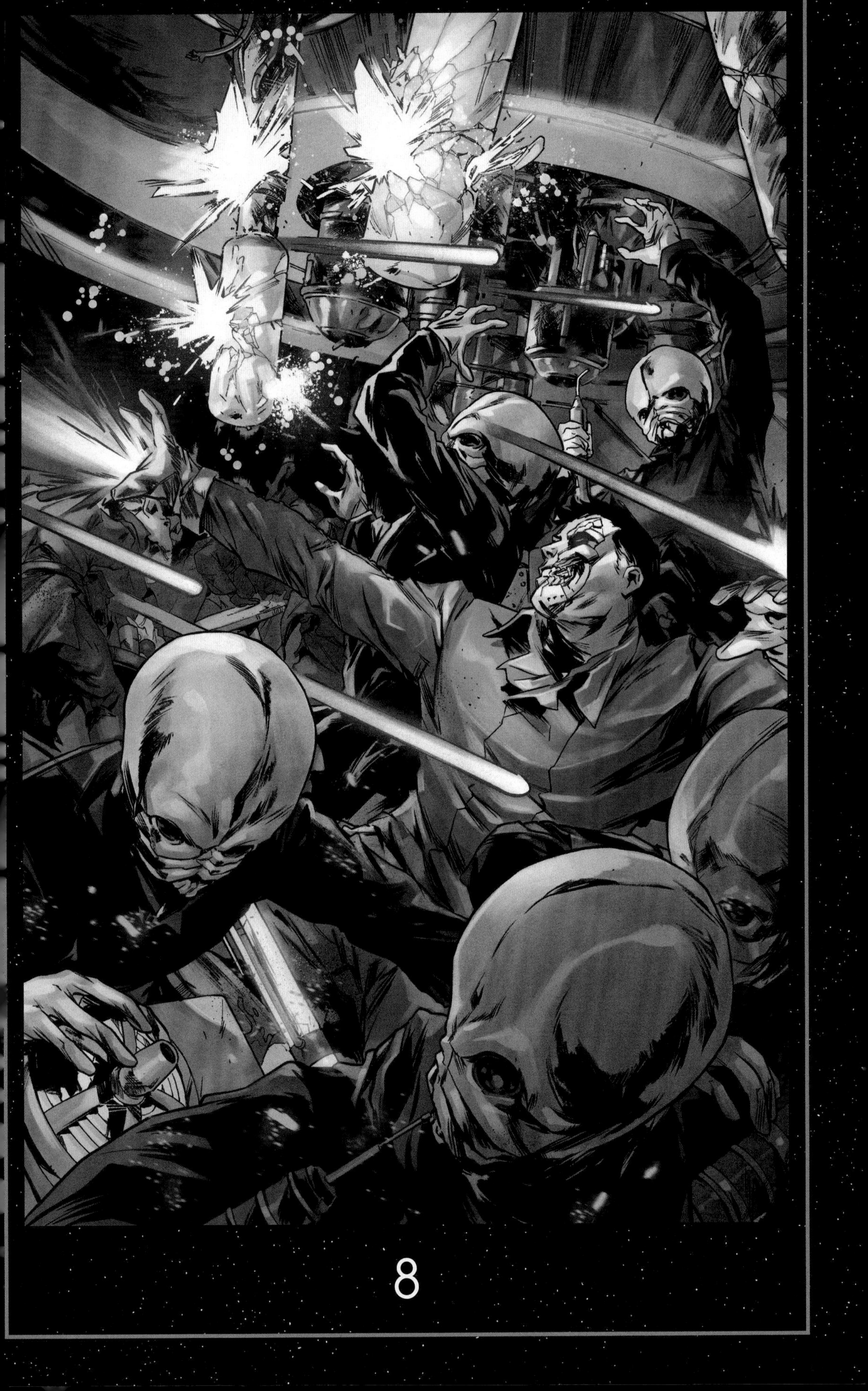

8

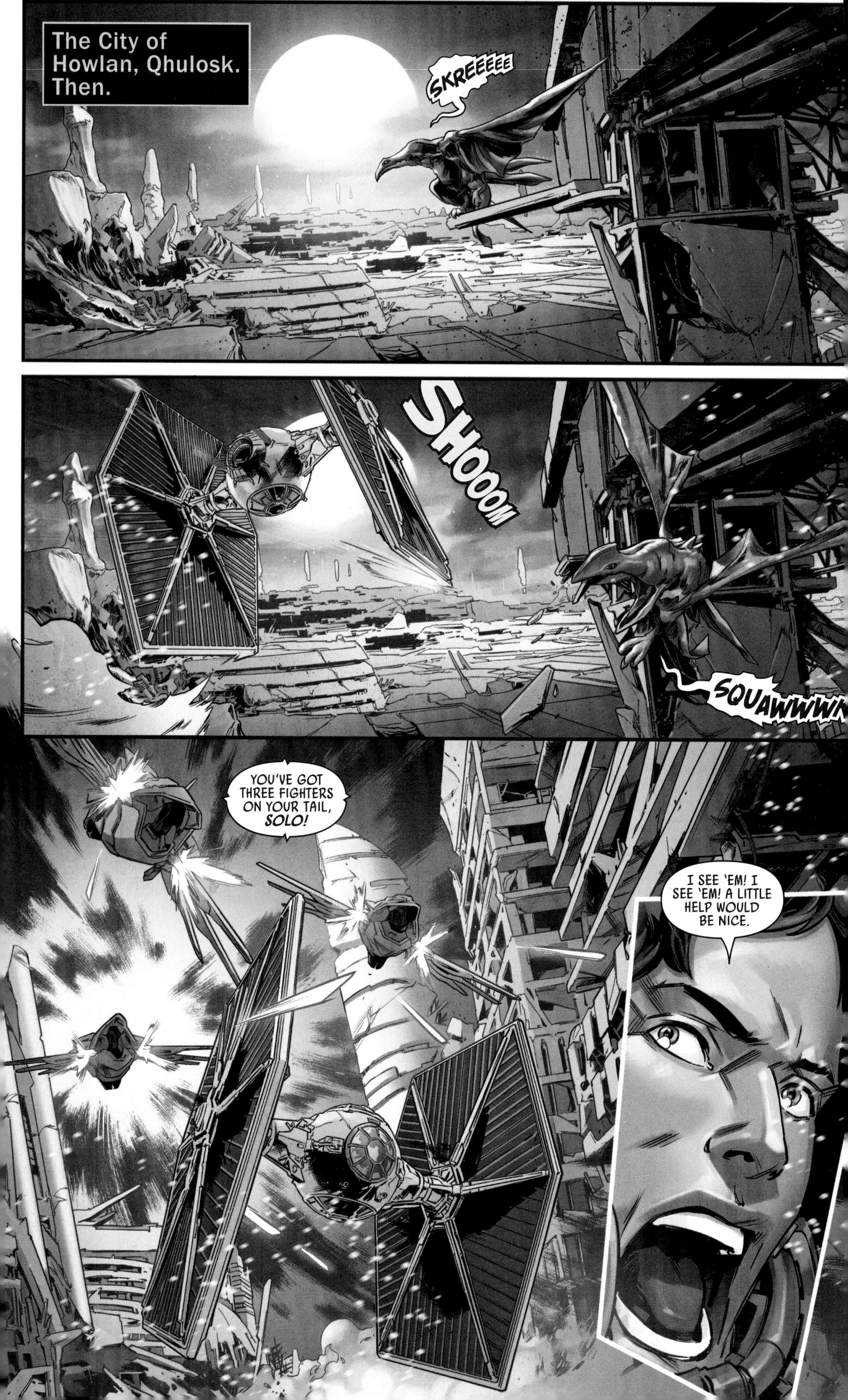
The City of Howlan, Qhulosk. Then.
SKREEEEEE
SHOOOM
SQUAWWW
YOU'VE GOT THREE FIGHTERS ON YOUR TAIL, SOLO!
I SEE 'EM! I SEE 'EM! A LITTLE HELP WOULD BE NICE.

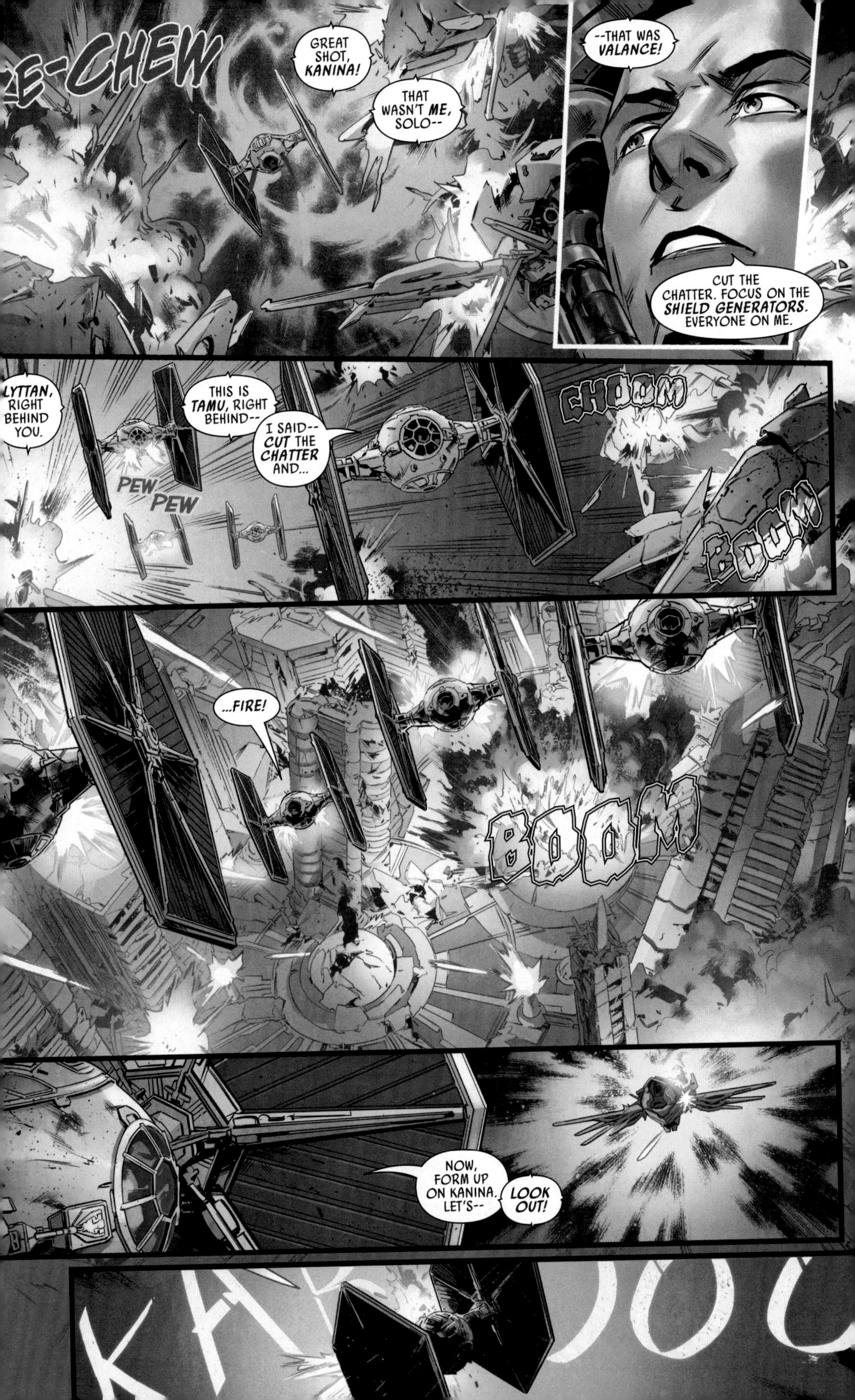

KE-CHEW
GREAT SHOT, KANINA!
THAT WASN'T ME, SOLO--
--THAT WAS VALANCE!
CUT THE CHATTER. FOCUS ON THE SHIELD GENERATORS. EVERYONE ON ME.
LYTTAN, RIGHT BEHIND YOU.
THIS IS TAMU, RIGHT BEHIND--
I SAID--CUT THE CHATTER AND...
PEW
PEW
CHOOM
BOOM
...FIRE!
BOOM
NOW, FORM UP ON KANINA. LET'S--
LOOK OUT!

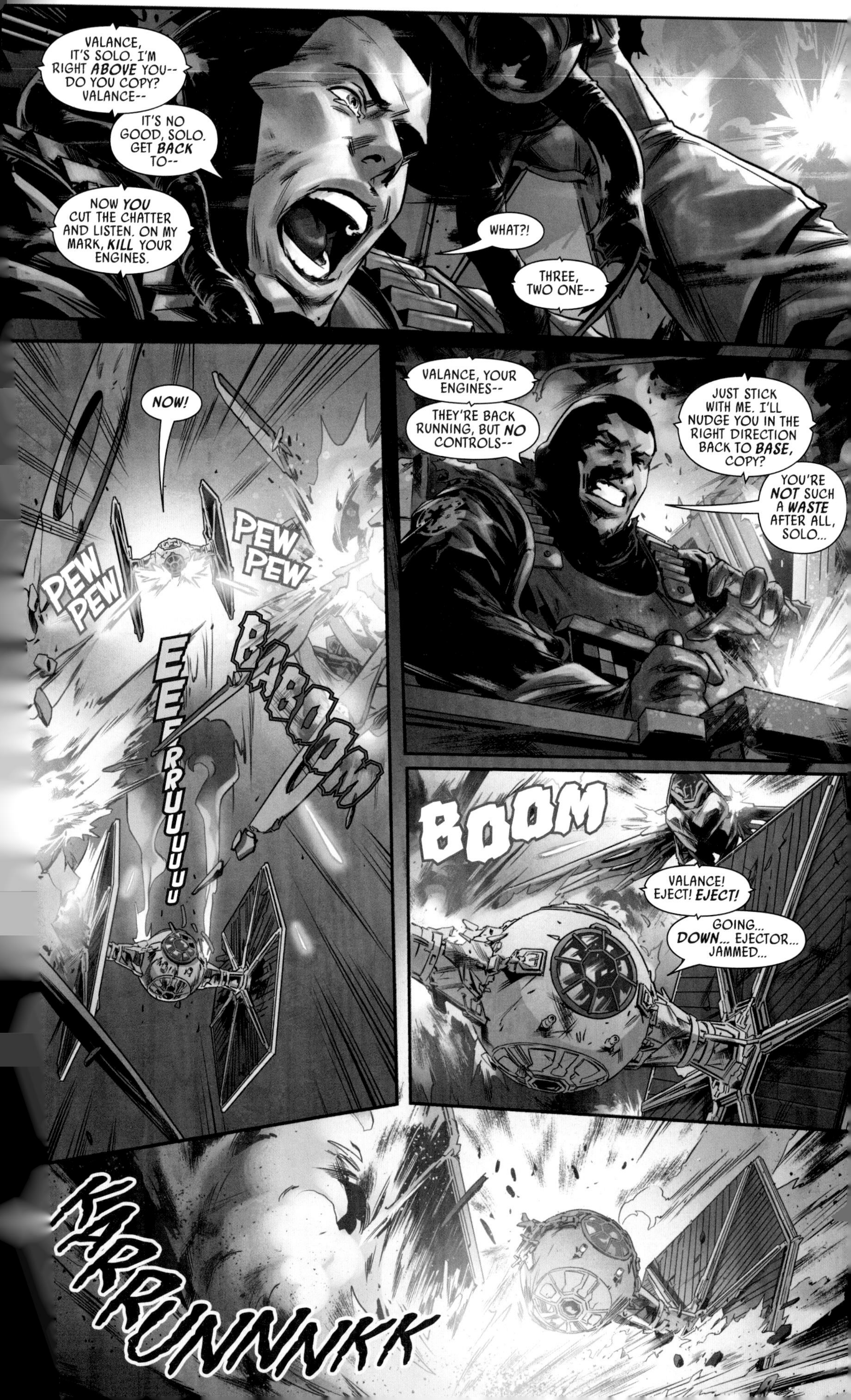
VALANCE, IT'S SOLO. I'M RIGHT ABOVE YOU-- DO YOU COPY? VALANCE--
IT'S NO GOOD, SOLO. GET BACK TO--
NOW YOU CUT THE CHATTER AND LISTEN. ON MY MARK, KILL YOUR ENGINES.
WHAT?!
THREE, TWO ONE--
NOW!
PEW PEW
PEW PEW
BABOOM
EEERRUUUUUU
VALANCE, YOUR ENGINES--
THEY'RE BACK RUNNING, BUT NO CONTROLS--
JUST STICK WITH ME. I'LL NUDGE YOU IN THE RIGHT DIRECTION BACK TO BASE, COPY?
YOU'RE NOT SUCH A WASTE AFTER ALL, SOLO...
BOOM
VALANCE! EJECT! EJECT!
GOING... DOWN... EJECTOR... JAMMED...
KARRUNNNKK

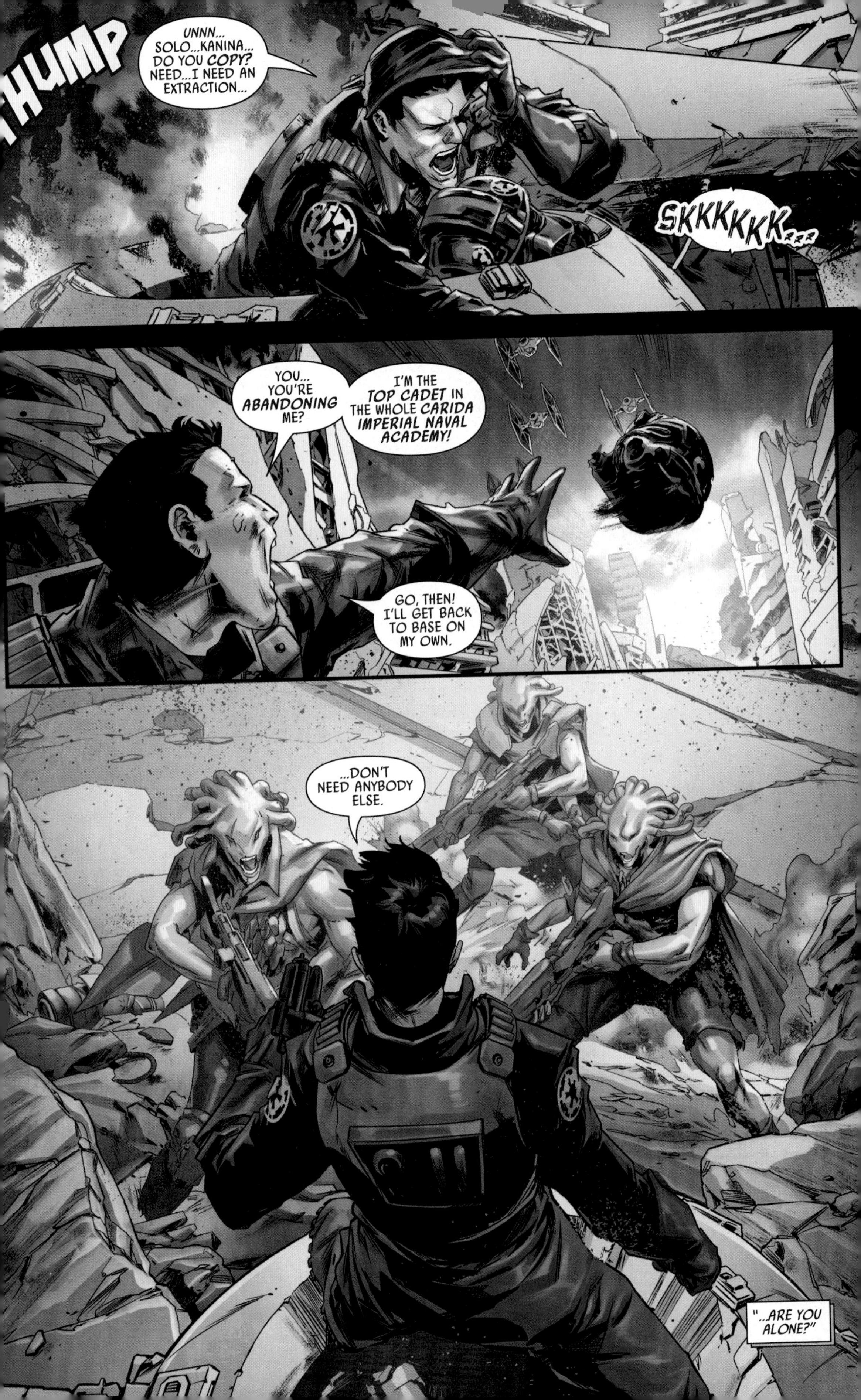
THUMP
UNNN... SOLO...KANINA... DO YOU COPY? NEED...I NEED AN EXTRACTION...
SKKKKKK...
YOU... YOU'RE ABANDONING ME?
I'M THE TOP CADET IN THE WHOLE CARIDA IMPERIAL NAVAL ACADEMY!
GO, THEN! I'LL GET BACK TO BASE ON MY OWN.
...DON'T NEED ANYBODY ELSE.
"...ARE YOU ALONE?"

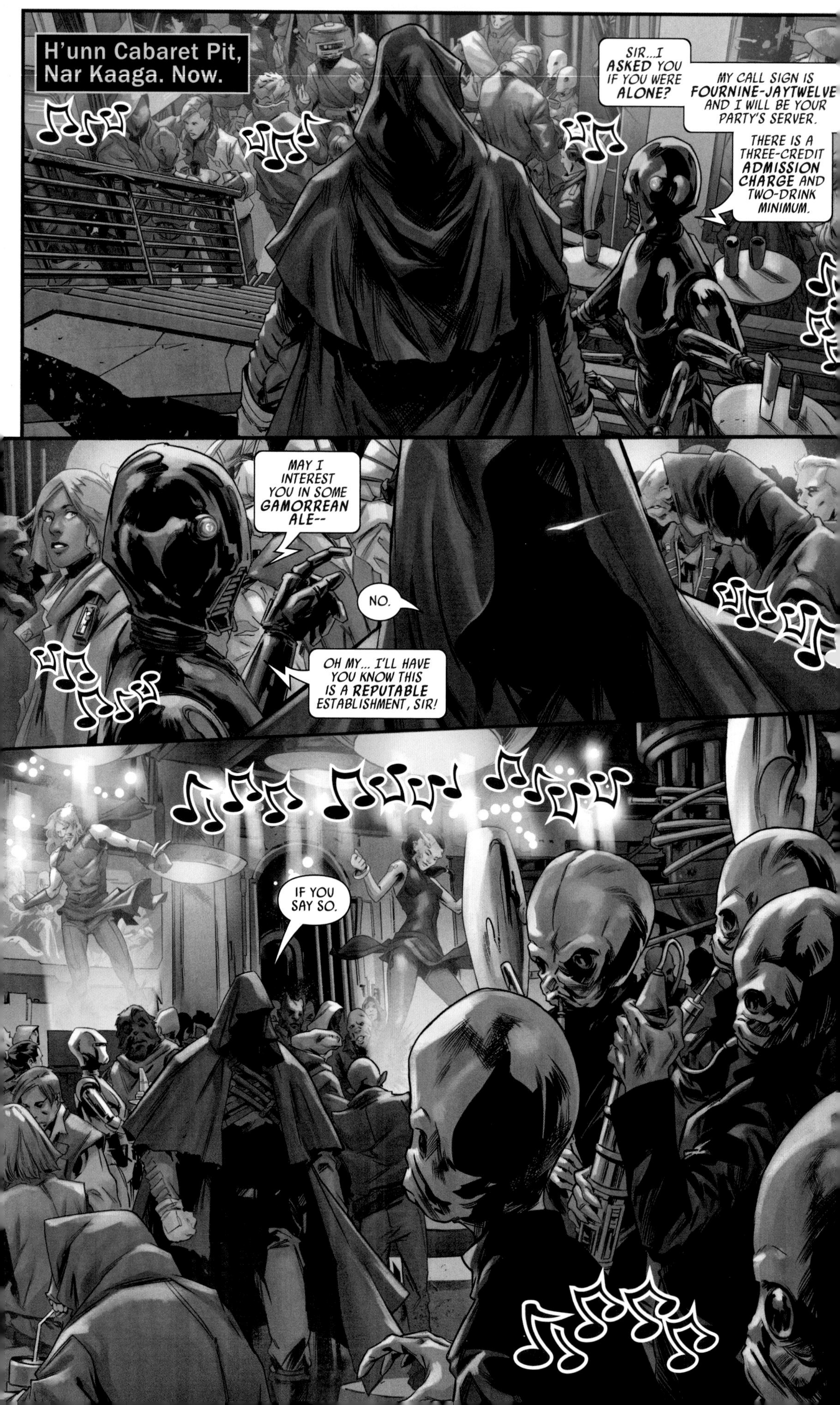

H'unn Cabaret Pit, Nar Kaaga. Now.
SIR...I ASKED YOU IF YOU WERE ALONE?
MY CALL SIGN IS FOURNINE-JAYTWELVE AND I WILL BE YOUR PARTY'S SERVER.
THERE IS A THREE-CREDIT ADMISSION CHARGE AND TWO-DRINK MINIMUM.
MAY I INTEREST YOU IN SOME GAMORREAN ALE--
NO.
OH MY... I'LL HAVE YOU KNOW THIS IS A REPUTABLE ESTABLISHMENT, SIR!
IF YOU SAY SO.

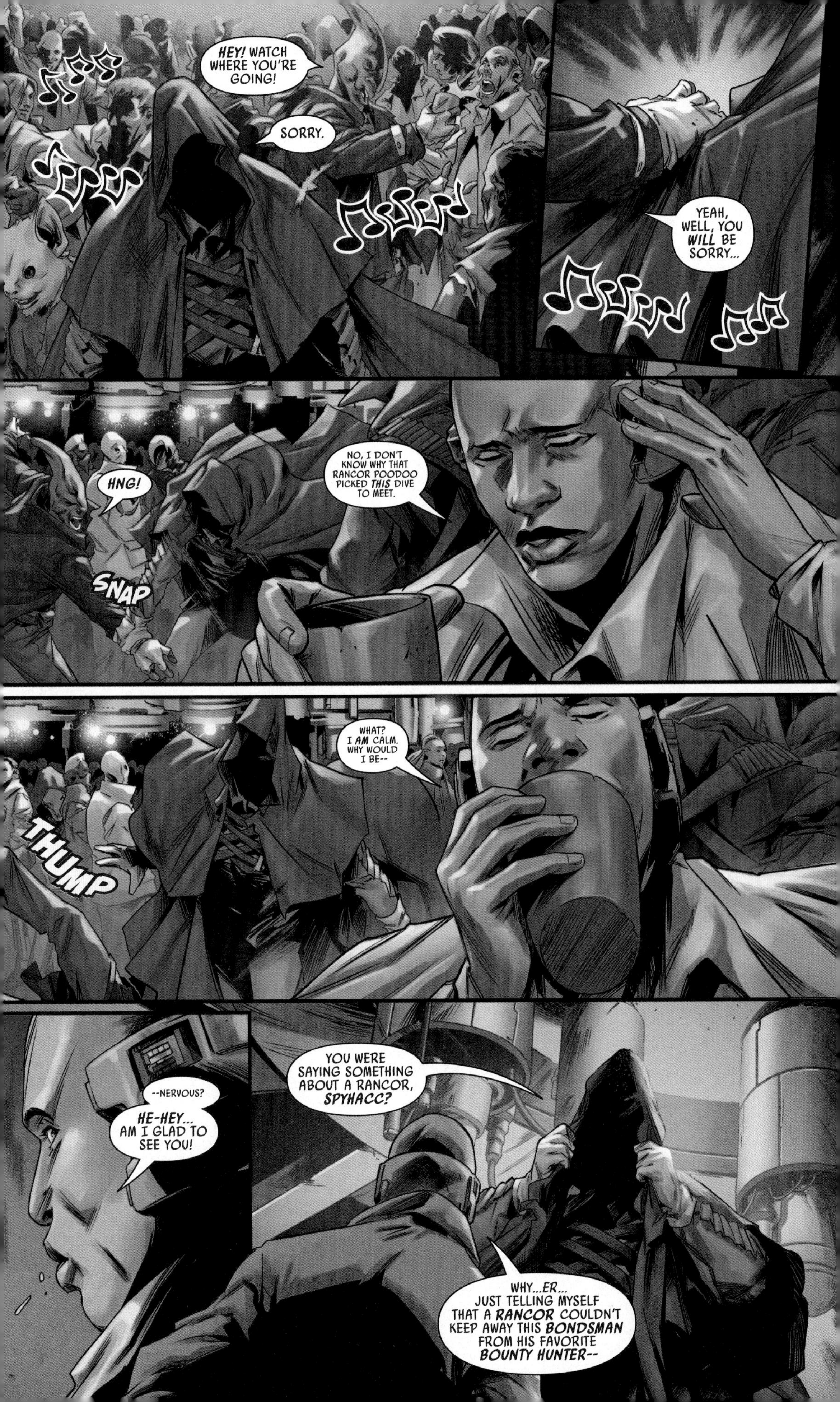

HEY! WATCH WHERE YOU'RE GOING!
SORRY.
YEAH, WELL, YOU WILL BE SORRY...
HNG!
NO, I DON'T KNOW WHY THAT RANCOR POODOO PICKED THIS DIVE TO MEET.
SNAP
WHAT? I AM CALM. WHY WOULD I BE--
THUMP
--NERVOUS?
HE-HEY... AM I GLAD TO SEE YOU!
YOU WERE SAYING SOMETHING ABOUT A RANCOR, SPYHACC?
WHY...ER... JUST TELLING MYSELF THAT A RANCOR COULDN'T KEEP AWAY THIS BONDSMAN FROM HIS FAVORITE BOUNTY HUNTER--

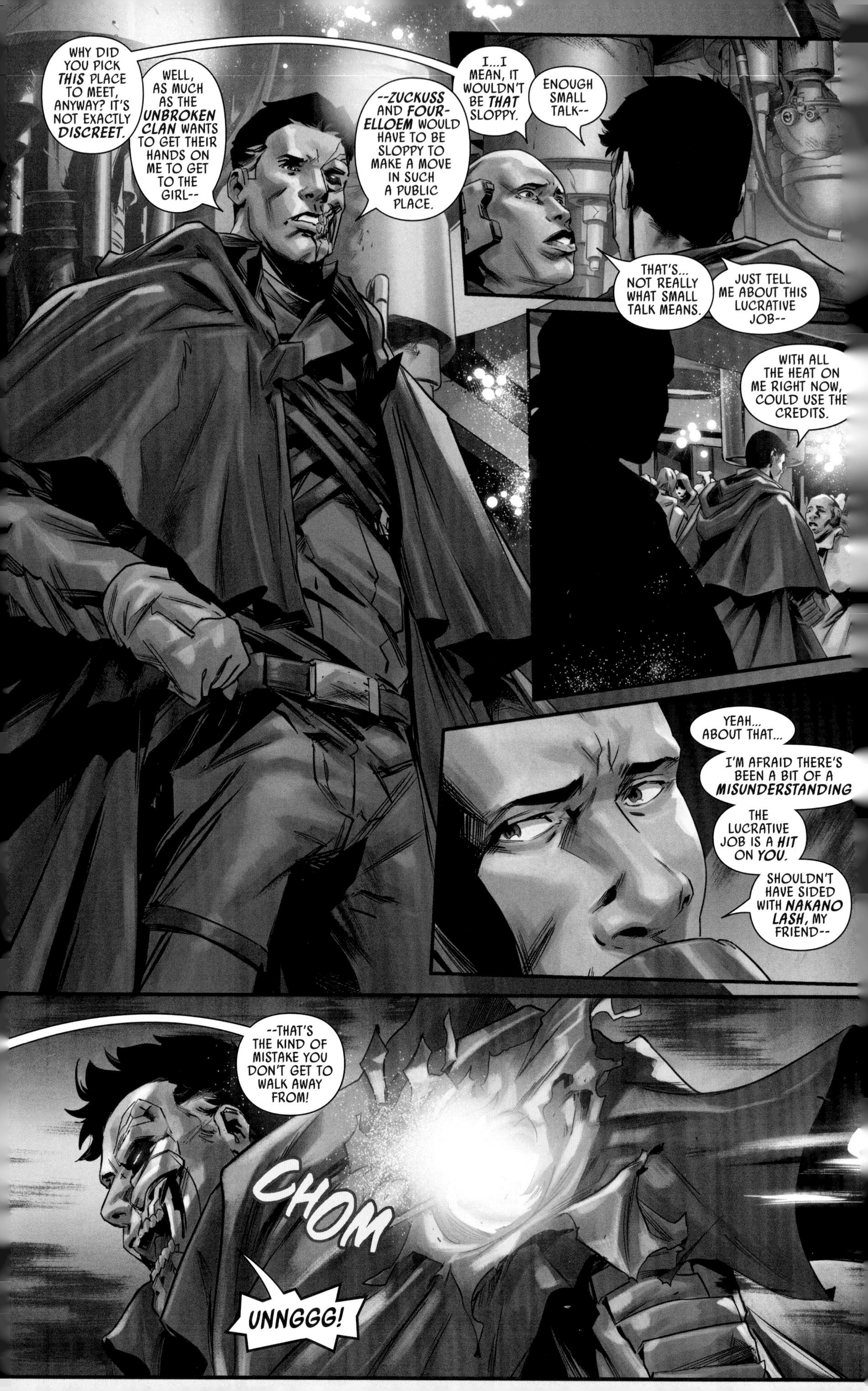
WHY DID YOU PICK THIS PLACE TO MEET, ANYWAY? IT'S NOT EXACTLY DISCREET.
I...I MEAN, IT WOULDN'T BE THAT SLOPPY.
WELL, AS MUCH AS THE UNBROKEN CLAN WANTS TO GET THEIR HANDS ON ME TO GET TO THE GIRL--
--ZUCKUSS AND FOUR-ELLOEM WOULD HAVE TO BE SLOPPY TO MAKE A MOVE IN SUCH A PUBLIC PLACE.
ENOUGH SMALL TALK--
THAT'S... NOT REALLY WHAT SMALL TALK MEANS.
JUST TELL ME ABOUT THIS LUCRATIVE JOB--
WITH ALL THE HEAT ON ME RIGHT NOW, COULD USE THE CREDITS.
YEAH... ABOUT THAT...
I'M AFRAID THERE'S BEEN A BIT OF A MISUNDERSTANDING
THE LUCRATIVE JOB IS A HIT ON YOU.
SHOULDN'T HAVE SIDED WITH NAKANO LASH, MY FRIEND--
--THAT'S THE KIND OF MISTAKE YOU DON'T GET TO WALK AWAY FROM!
CHOM
UNNGGG!

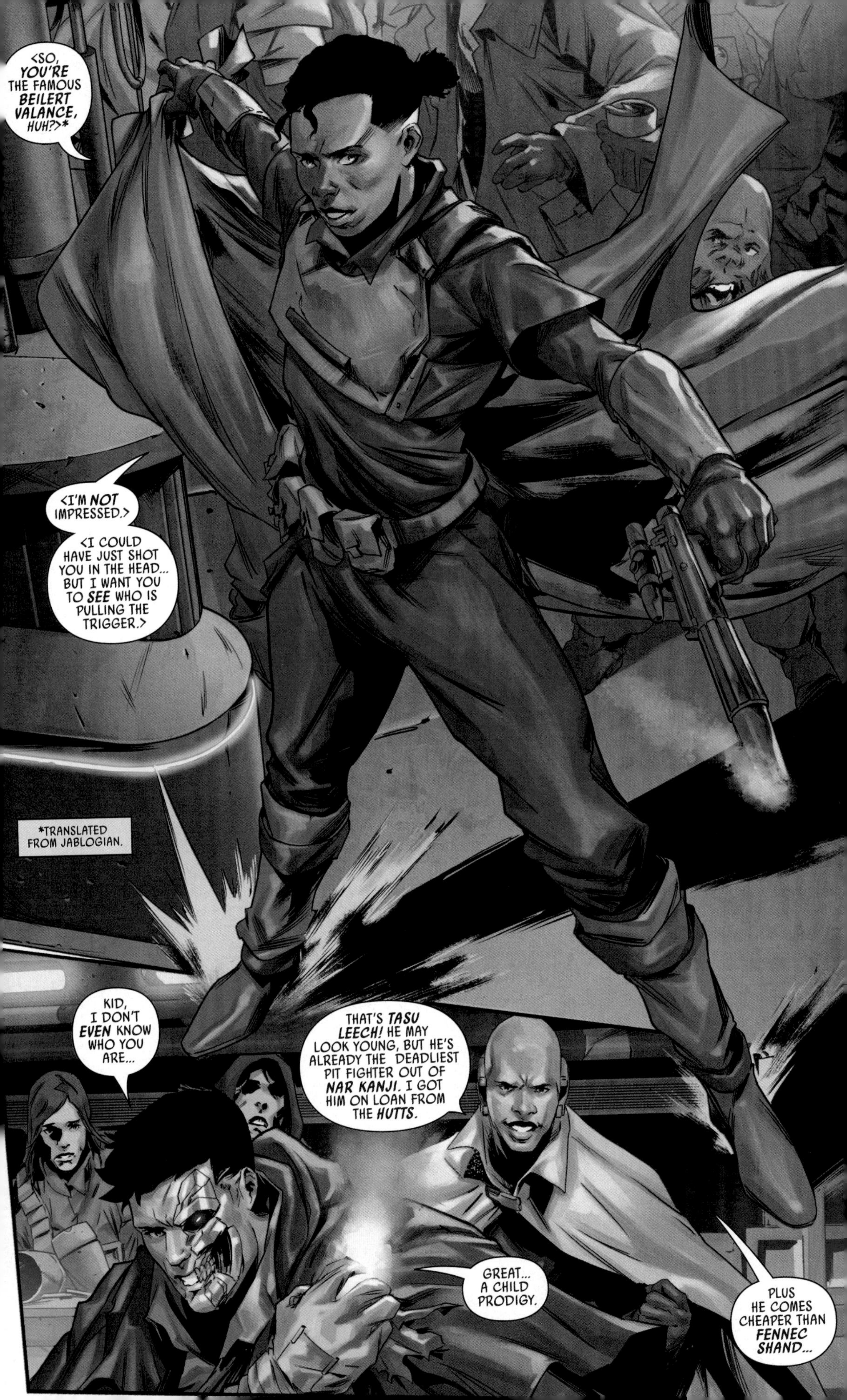

<SO, YOU'RE THE FAMOUS BEILERT VALANCE, HUH?>*
<I'M NOT IMPRESSED.>
<I COULD HAVE JUST SHOT YOU IN THE HEAD... BUT I WANT YOU TO SEE WHO IS PULLING THE TRIGGER.>
*TRANSLATED FROM JABLOGIAN.
KID, I DON'T EVEN KNOW WHO YOU ARE...
THAT'S TASU LEECH! HE MAY LOOK YOUNG, BUT HE'S ALREADY THE DEADLIEST PIT FIGHTER OUT OF NAR KANJI. I GOT HIM ON LOAN FROM THE HUTTS.
GREAT... A CHILD PRODIGY.
PLUS HE COMES CHEAPER THAN FENNEC SHAND...

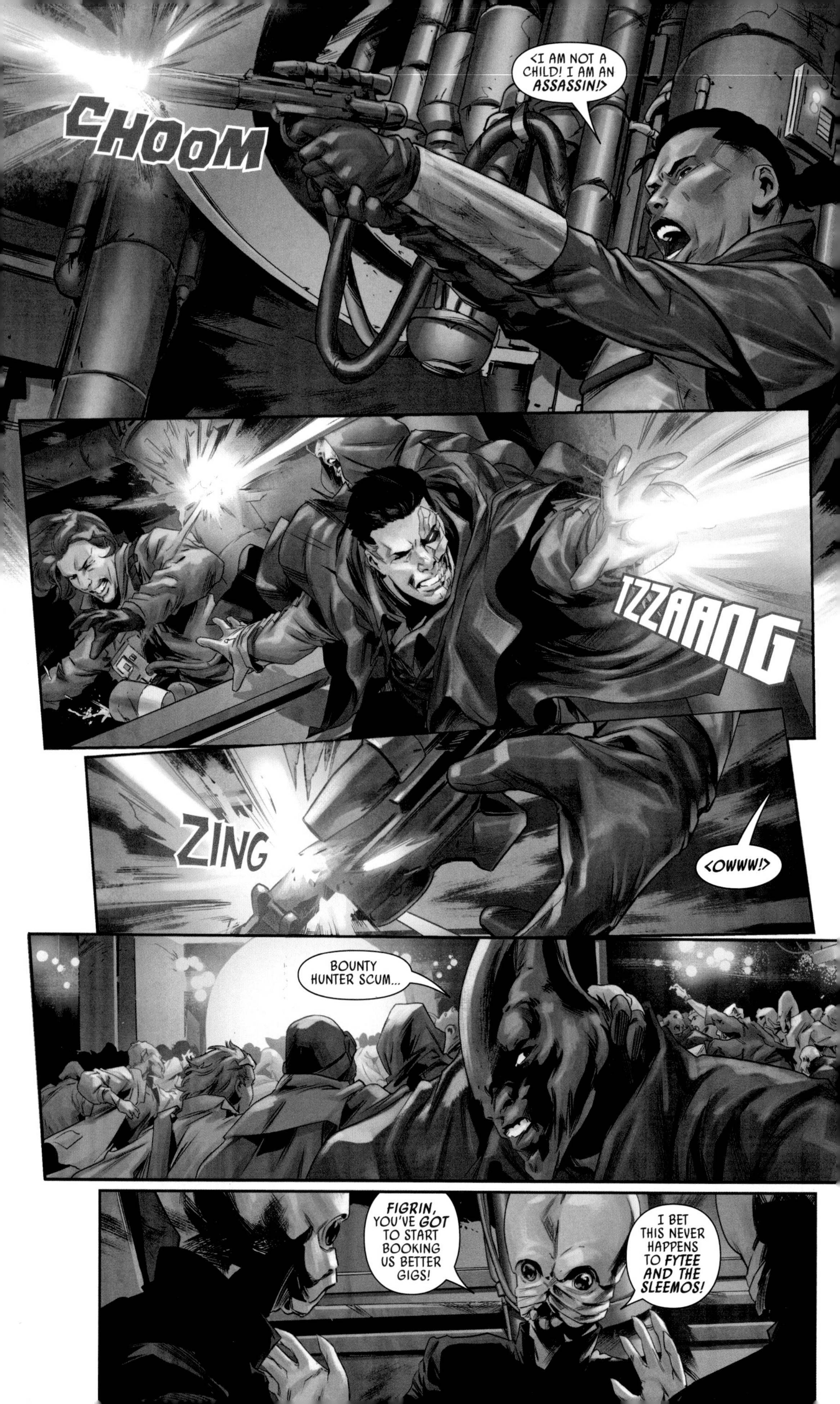
CHOOM
<I AM NOT A CHILD! I AM AN ASSASSIN!>
TZZAANG
ZING
<OWWW!>
BOUNTY HUNTER SCUM...
FIGRIN, YOU'VE GOT TO START BOOKING US BETTER GIGS!
I BET THIS NEVER HAPPENS TO FYTEE AND THE SLEEMOS!

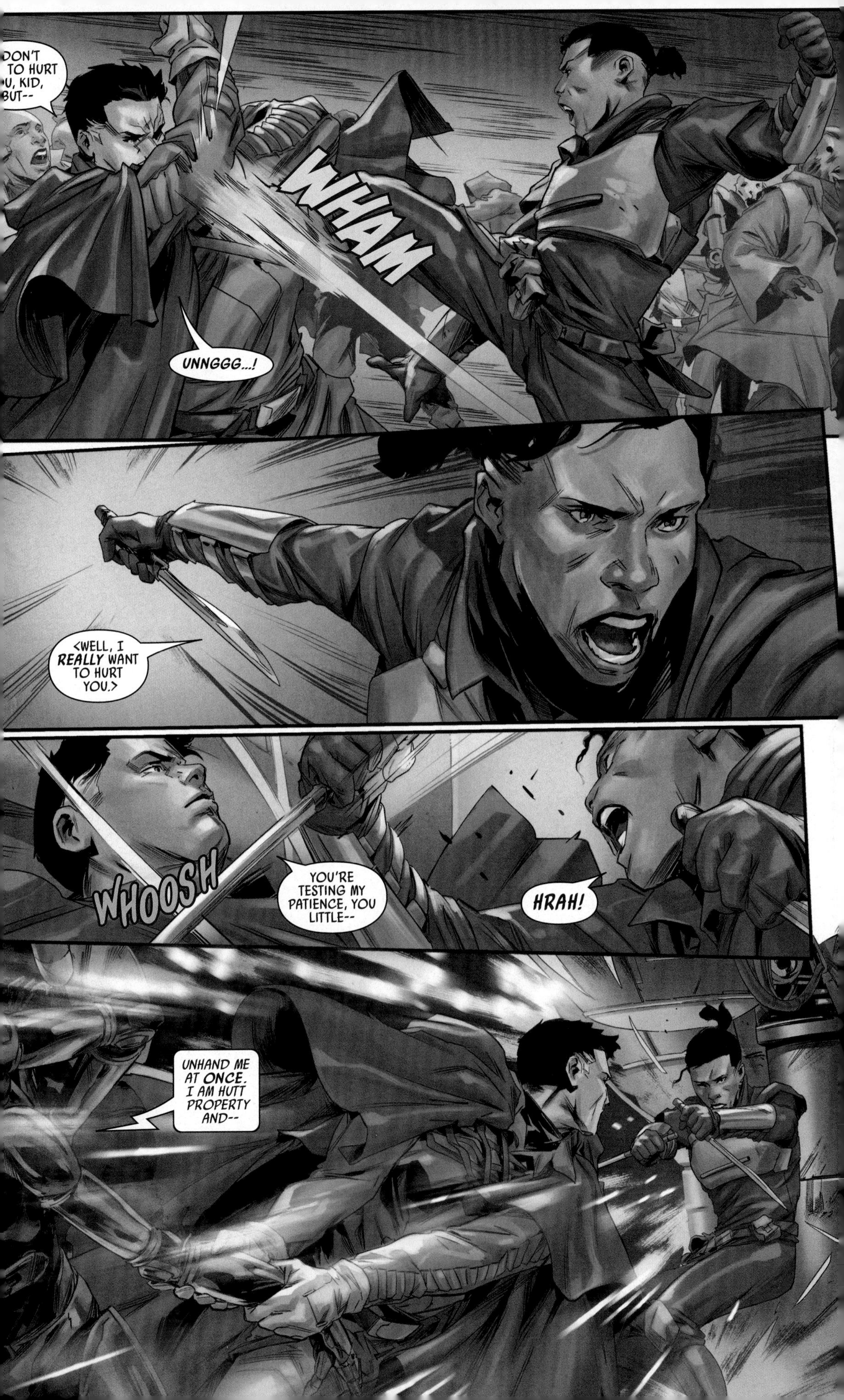
DON'T TO HURT U, KID, BUT--
WHAM
UNNGGG...!
<WELL, I REALLY WANT TO HURT YOU.>
WHOOSH
YOU'RE TESTING MY PATIENCE, YOU LITTLE--
HRAH!
UNHAND ME AT ONCE. I AM HUTT PROPERTY AND--

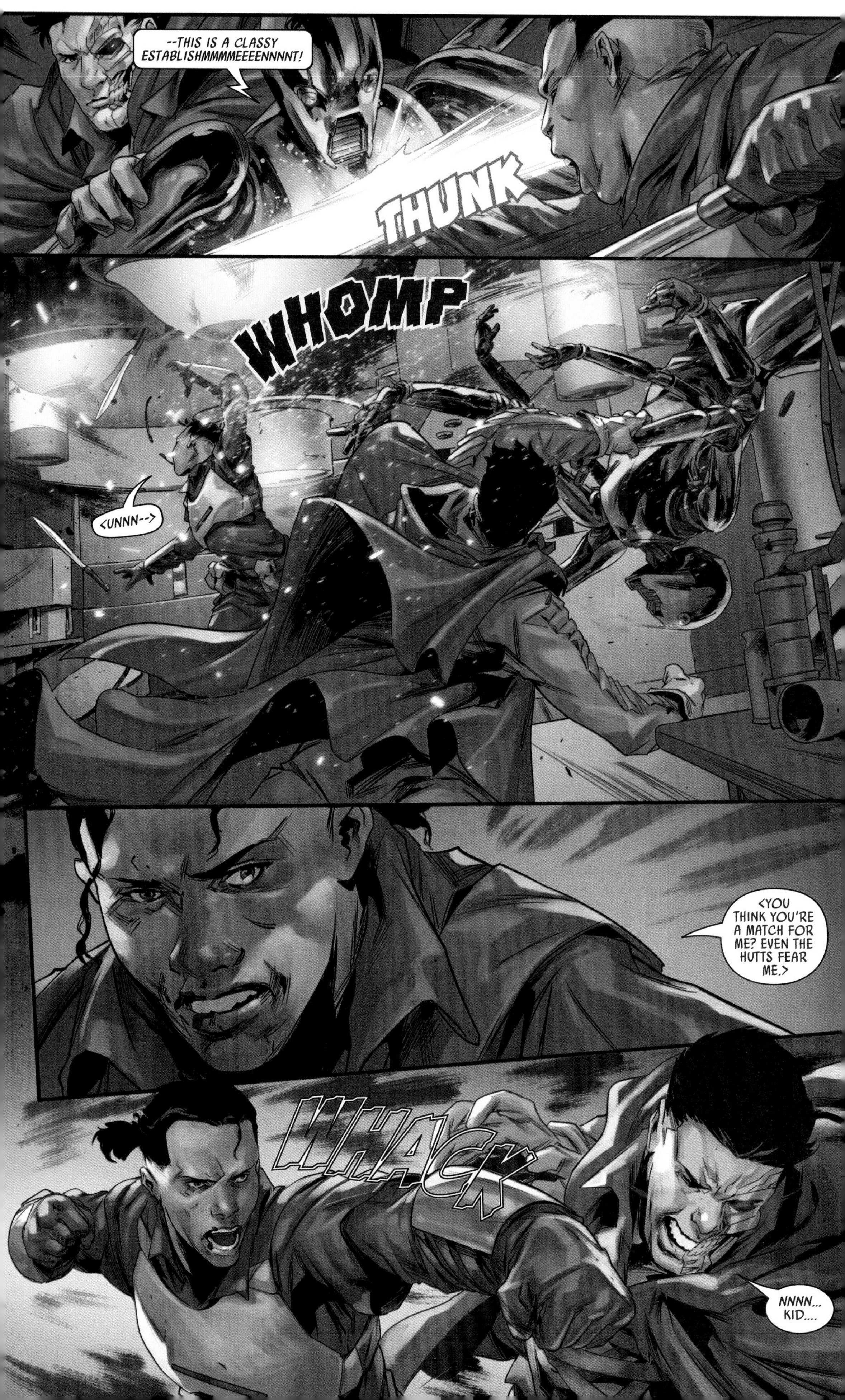
--THIS IS A CLASSY ESTABLISHMMMMEEEENNNNT!
THUNK
WHOMP
<UNNN-->
<YOU THINK YOU'RE A MATCH FOR ME? EVEN THE HUTTS FEAR ME.>
WHACK
NNNN... KID....

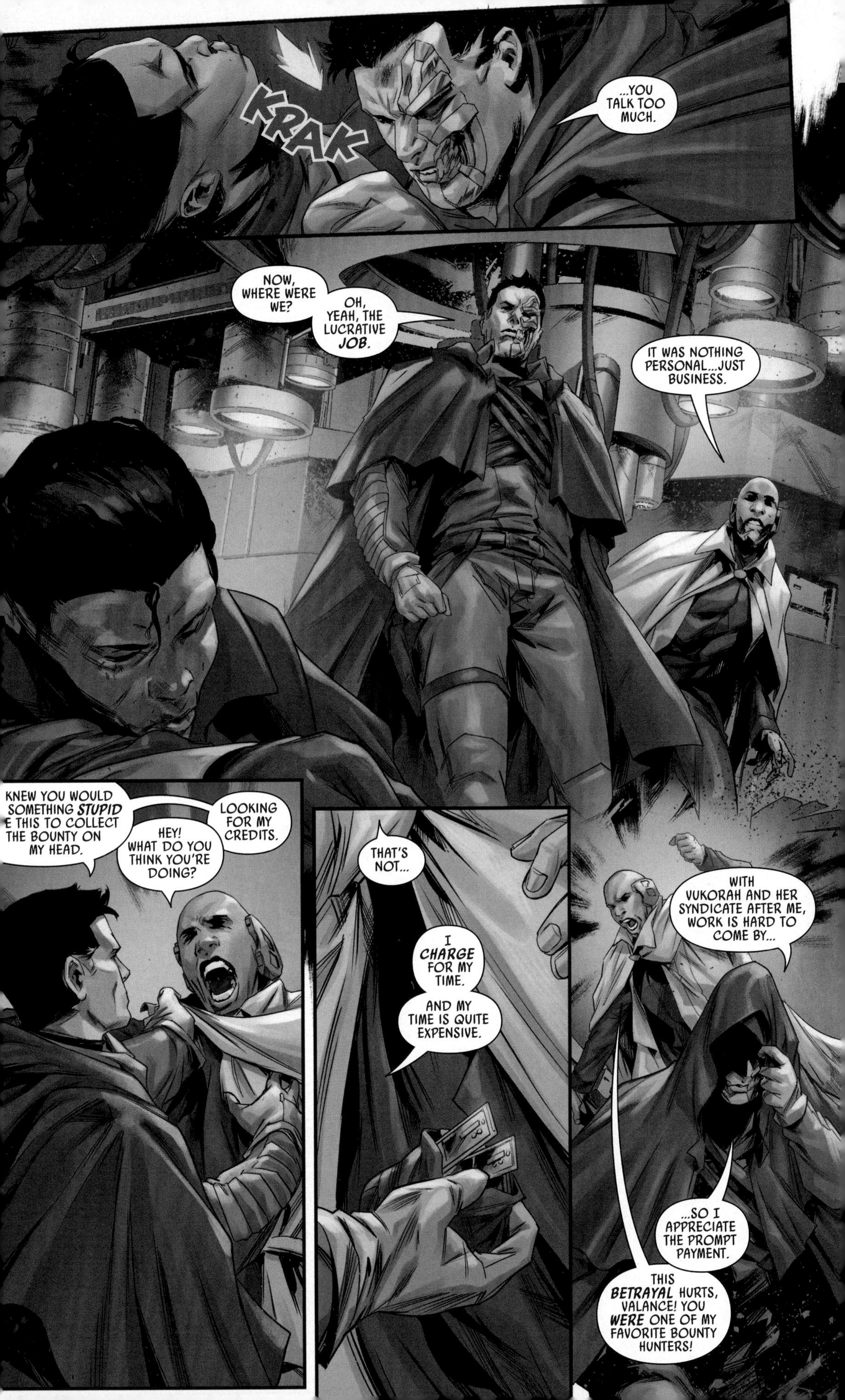
KRAK
...YOU TALK TOO MUCH.
NOW, WHERE WERE WE?
OH, YEAH, THE LUCRATIVE JOB.
IT WAS NOTHING PERSONAL...JUST BUSINESS.
KNEW YOU WOULD SOMETHING STUPID E THIS TO COLLECT THE BOUNTY ON MY HEAD.
HEY! WHAT DO YOU THINK YOU'RE DOING?
LOOKING FOR MY CREDITS.
THAT'S NOT...
I CHARGE FOR MY TIME.
AND MY TIME IS QUITE EXPENSIVE.
WITH VUKORAH AND HER SYNDICATE AFTER ME, WORK IS HARD TO COME BY...
...SO I APPRECIATE THE PROMPT PAYMENT.
THIS BETRAYAL HURTS, VALANCE! YOU WERE ONE OF MY FAVORITE BOUNTY HUNTERS!

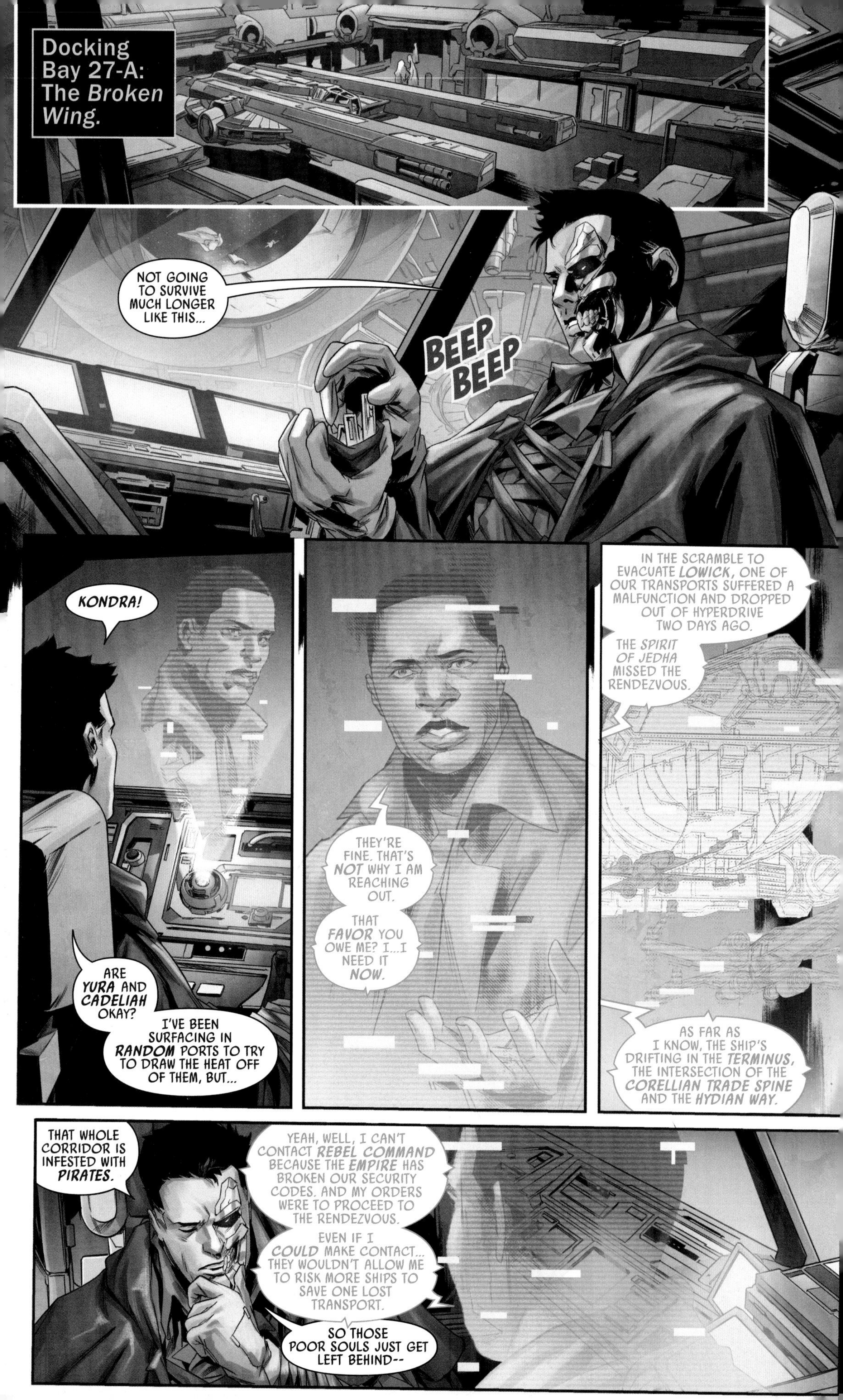
Docking Bay 27-A: The Broken Wing.
NOT GOING TO SURVIVE MUCH LONGER LIKE THIS...
BEEP BEEP
KONDRA!
ARE YURA AND CADELIAH OKAY?
I'VE BEEN SURFACING IN RANDOM PORTS TO TRY TO DRAW THE HEAT OFF OF THEM, BUT...
THEY'RE FINE. THAT'S NOT WHY I AM REACHING OUT.
THAT FAVOR YOU OWE ME? I...I NEED IT NOW.
IN THE SCRAMBLE TO EVACUATE LOWICK, ONE OF OUR TRANSPORTS SUFFERED A MALFUNCTION AND DROPPED OUT OF HYPERDRIVE TWO DAYS AGO.
THE SPIRIT OF JEDHA MISSED THE RENDEZVOUS.
AS FAR AS I KNOW, THE SHIP'S DRIFTING IN THE TERMINUS, THE INTERSECTION OF THE CORELLIAN TRADE SPINE AND THE HYDIAN WAY.
THAT WHOLE CORRIDOR IS INFESTED WITH PIRATES.
YEAH, WELL, I CAN'T CONTACT REBEL COMMAND BECAUSE THE EMPIRE HAS BROKEN OUR SECURITY CODES. AND MY ORDERS WERE TO PROCEED TO THE RENDEZVOUS.
EVEN IF I COULD MAKE CONTACT... THEY WOULDN'T ALLOW ME TO RISK MORE SHIPS TO SAVE ONE LOST TRANSPORT.
SO THOSE POOR SOULS JUST GET LEFT BEHIND--

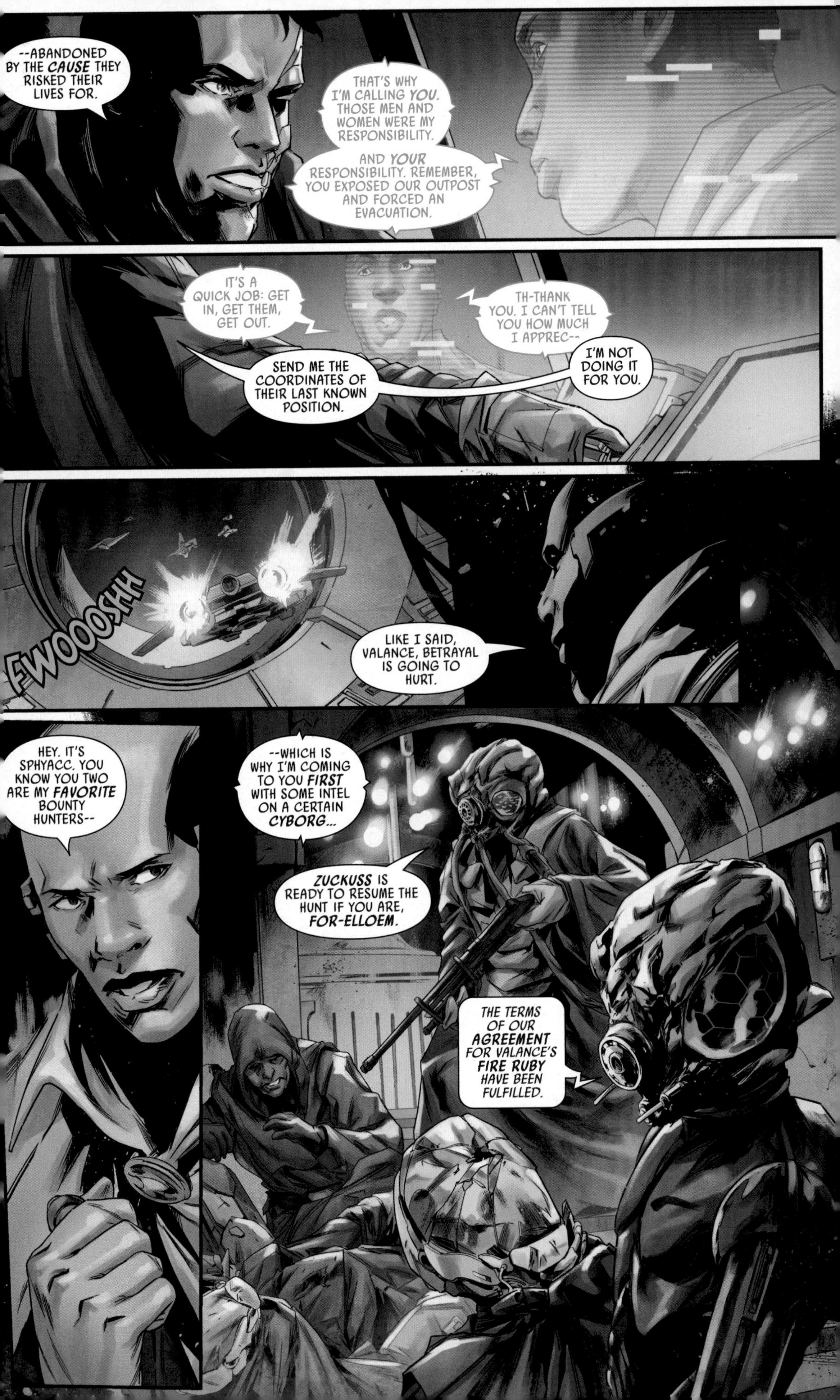
--ABANDONED BY THE CAUSE THEY RISKED THEIR LIVES FOR.
THAT'S WHY I'M CALLING YOU. THOSE MEN AND WOMEN WERE MY RESPONSIBILITY.
AND YOUR RESPONSIBILITY. REMEMBER, YOU EXPOSED OUR OUTPOST AND FORCED AN EVACUATION.
IT'S A QUICK JOB: GET IN, GET THEM, GET OUT.
TH-THANK YOU. I CAN'T TELL YOU HOW MUCH I APPREC--
SEND ME THE COORDINATES OF THEIR LAST KNOWN POSITION.
I'M NOT DOING IT FOR YOU.
FWOOOSHH
LIKE I SAID, VALANCE, BETRAYAL IS GOING TO HURT.
HEY. IT'S SPHYACC. YOU KNOW YOU TWO ARE MY FAVORITE BOUNTY HUNTERS--
--WHICH IS WHY I'M COMING TO YOU FIRST WITH SOME INTEL ON A CERTAIN CYBORG...
ZUCKUSS IS READY TO RESUME THE HUNT IF YOU ARE, FOR-ELLOEM.
THE TERMS OF OUR AGREEMENT FOR VALANCE'S FIRE RUBY HAVE BEEN FULFILLED.

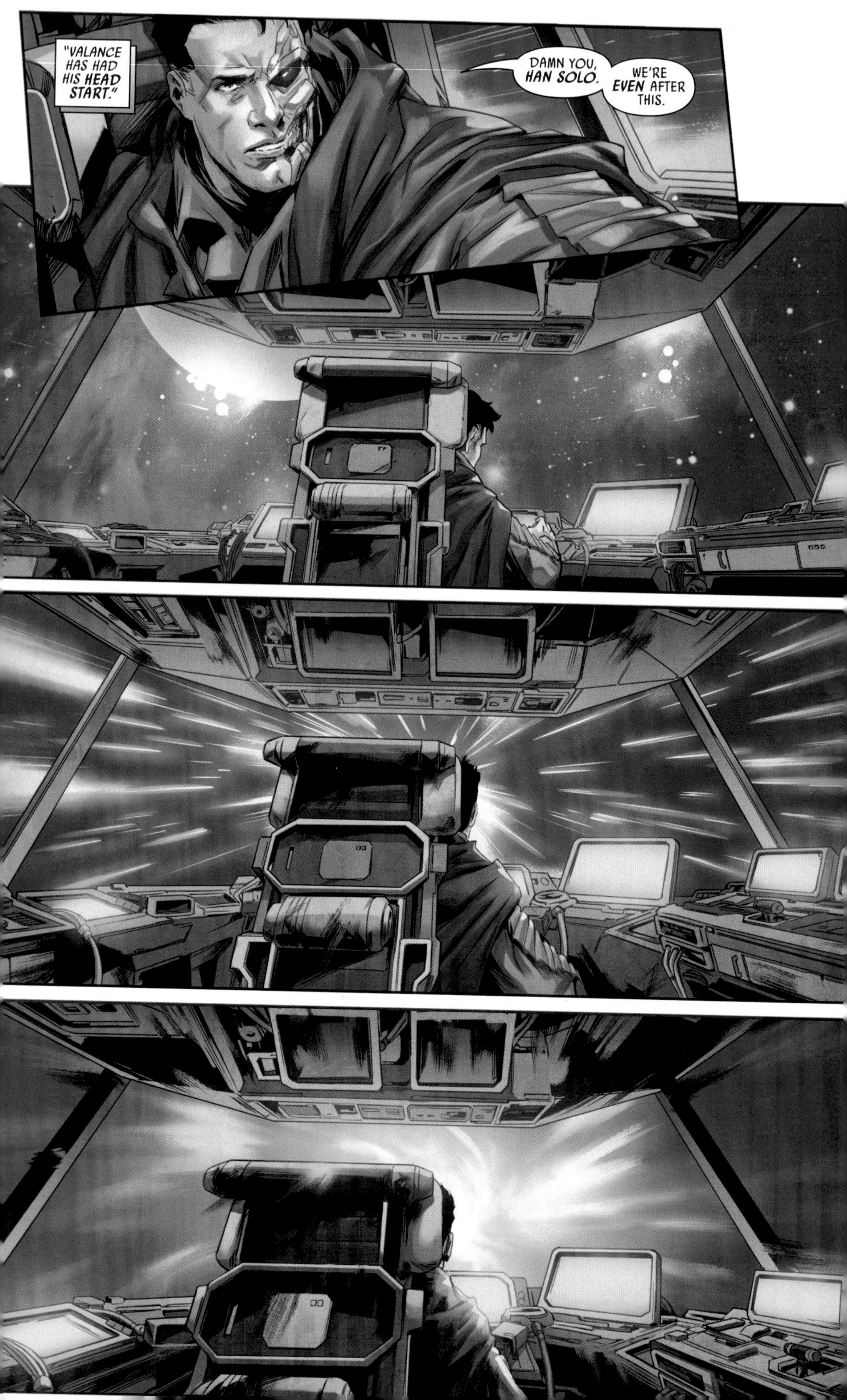
"VALANCE HAS HAD HIS HEAD START."
DAMN YOU, HAN SOLO.
WE'RE EVEN AFTER THIS.

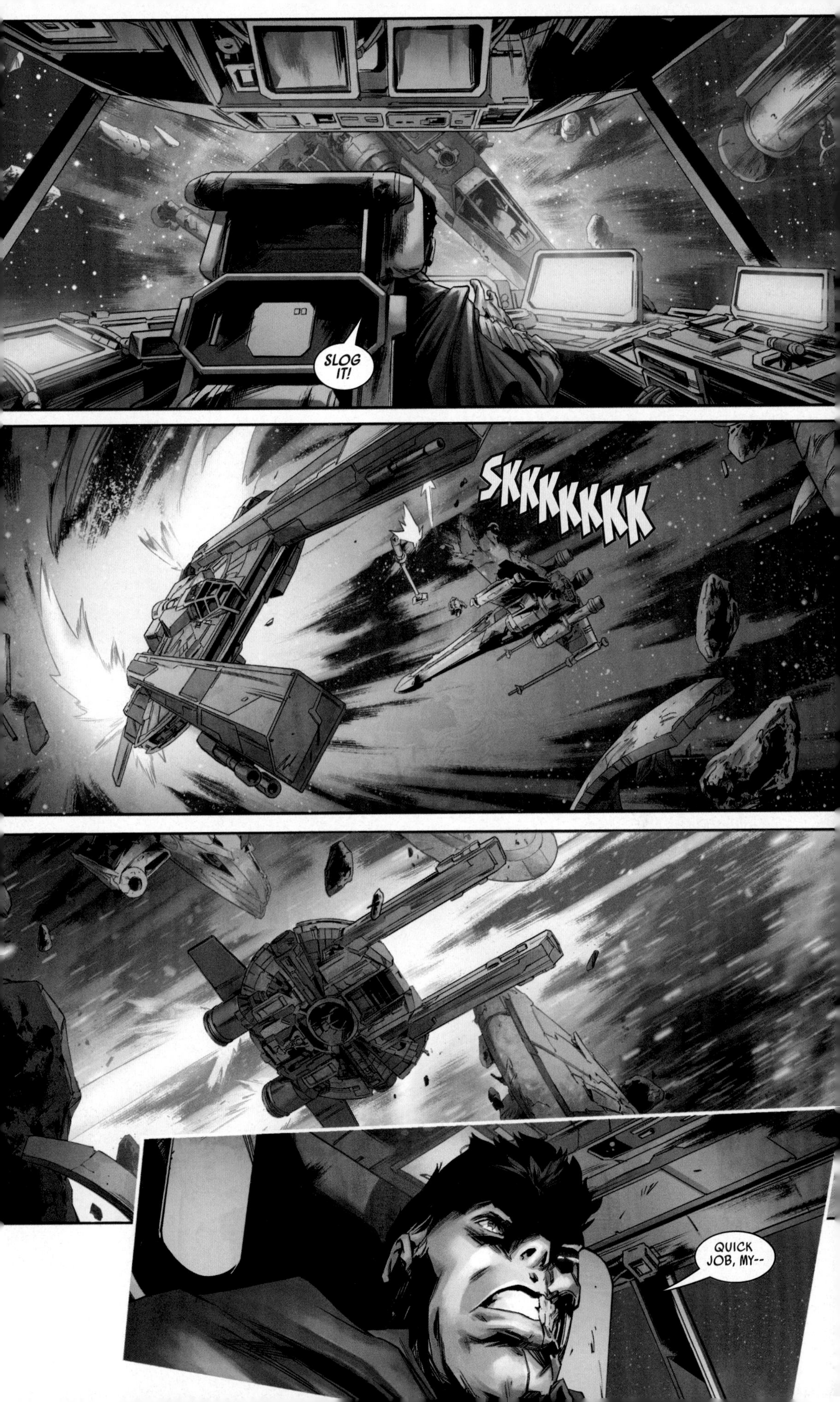
SLOG IT!
SKKKKKKK
QUICK JOB, MY--

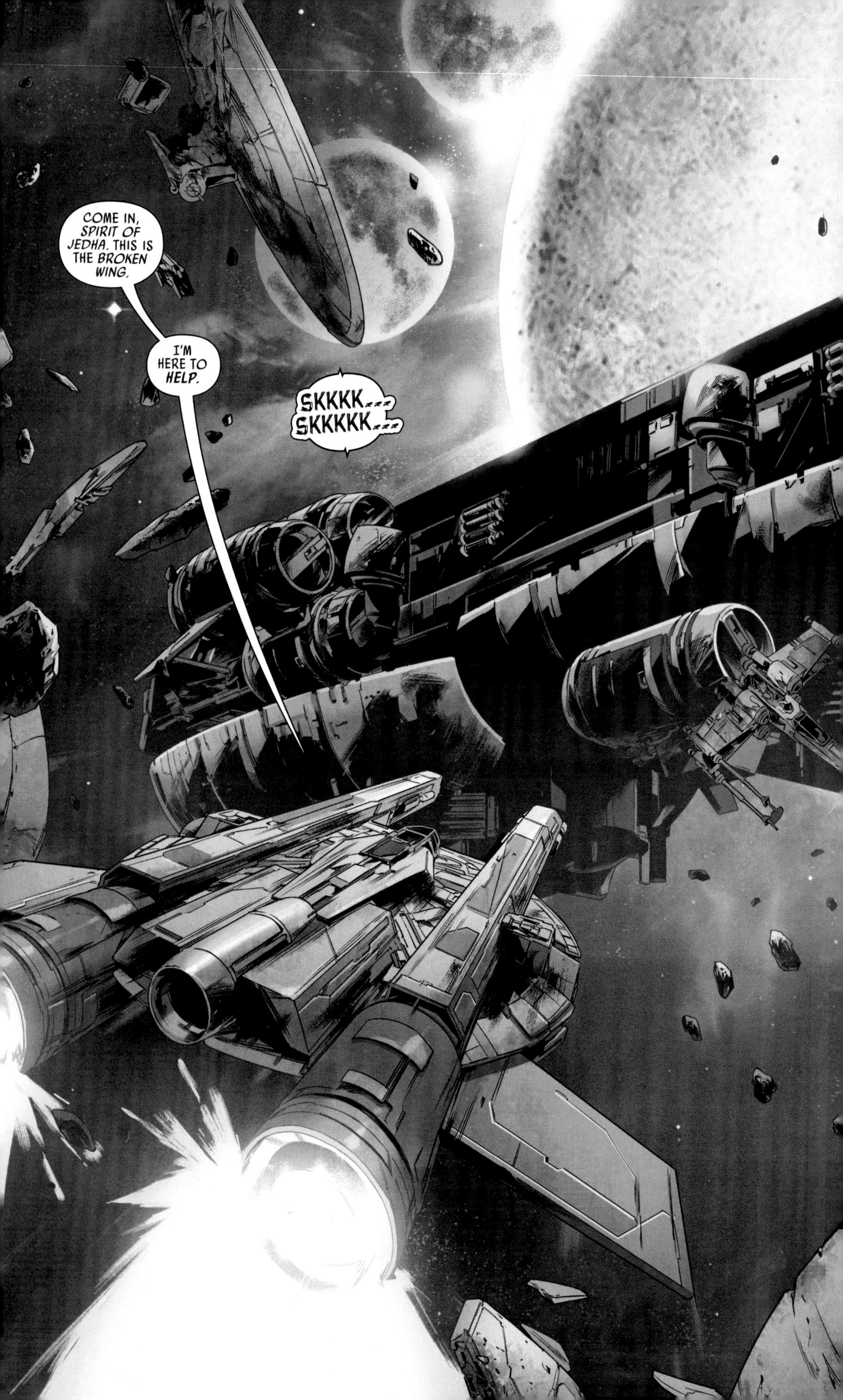
COME IN, SPIRIT OF JEDHA. THIS IS THE BROKEN WING.
I'M HERE TO HELP.
SKKKK... SKKKKK...

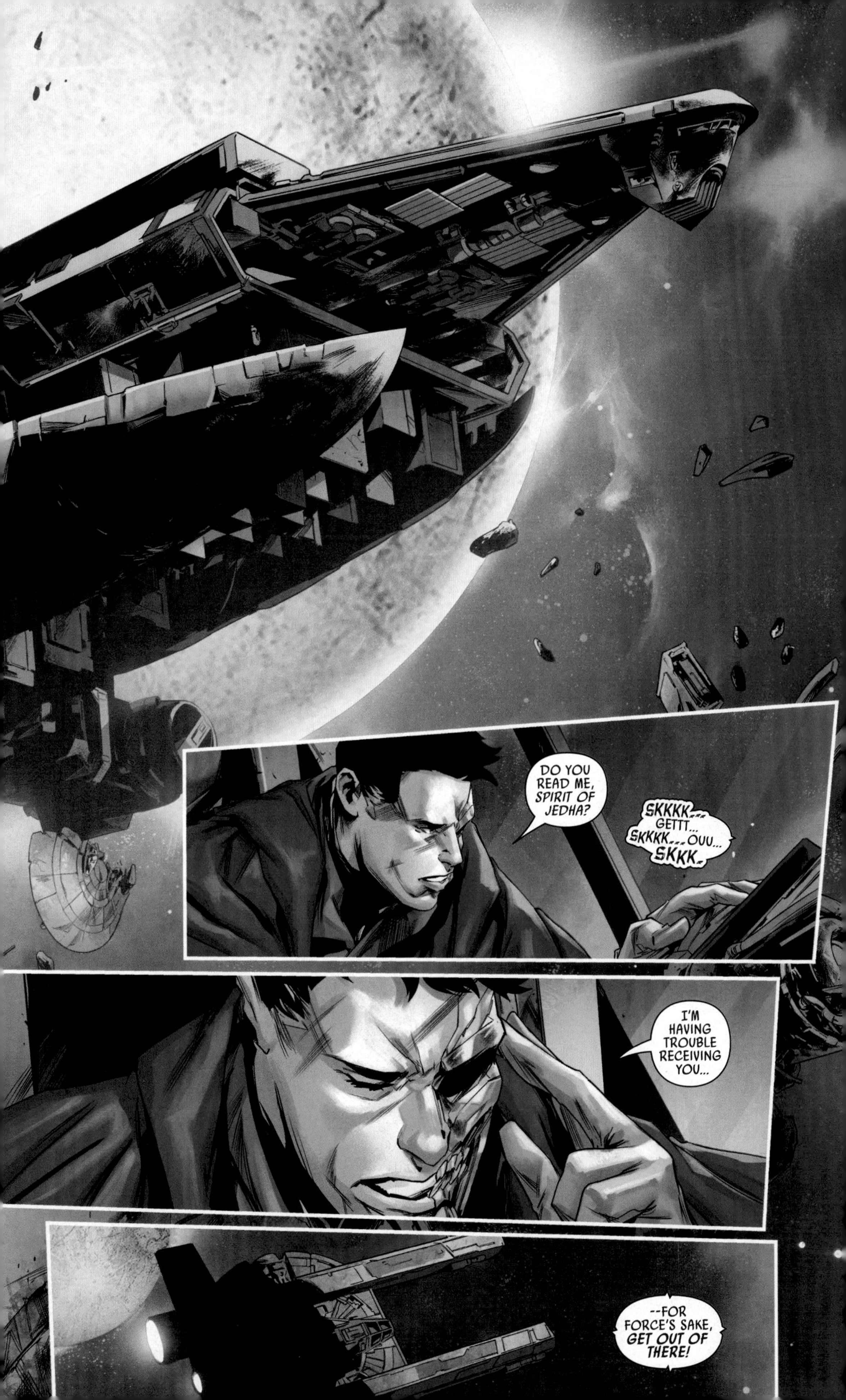
DO YOU READ ME, SPIRIT OF JEDHA?
SKKKK... GETTT... SKKKK... OUU... SKKK.
I'M HAVING TROUBLE RECEIVING YOU...
--FOR FORCE'S SAKE, GET OUT OF THERE!

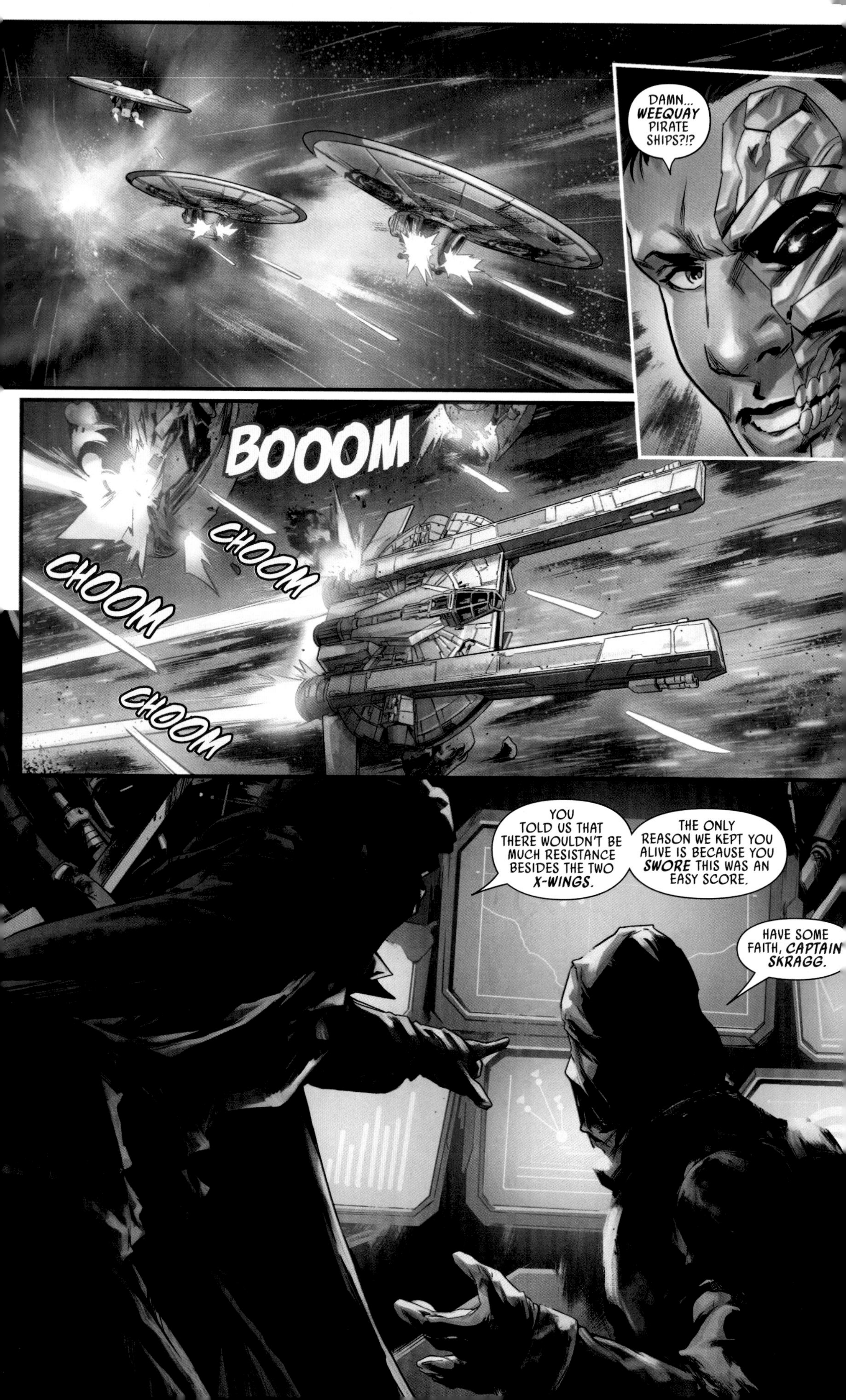
DAMN... WEEQUAY PIRATE SHIPS?!?
BOOOM
CHOOM
CHOOM
CHOOM
YOU TOLD US THAT THERE WOULDN'T BE MUCH RESISTANCE BESIDES THE TWO X-WINGS.
THE ONLY REASON WE KEPT YOU ALIVE IS BECAUSE YOU SWORE THIS WAS AN EASY SCORE.
HAVE SOME FAITH, CAPTAIN SKRAGG.

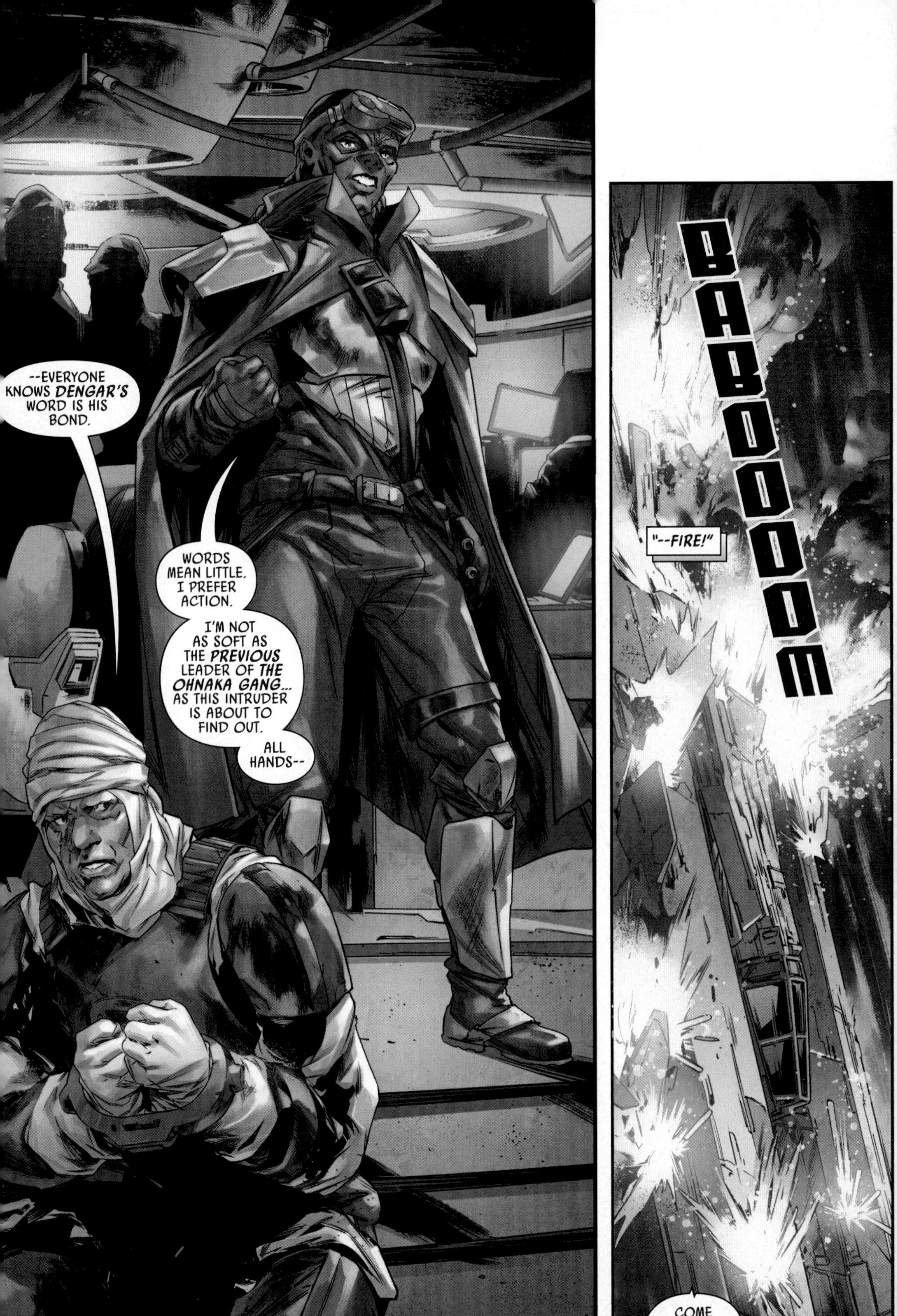
--EVERYONE KNOWS *DENGAR'S* WORD IS HIS BOND.
WORDS MEAN LITTLE. I PREFER ACTION.
I'M NOT AS SOFT AS THE *PREVIOUS* LEADER OF *THE OHNAKA GANG*... AS THIS INTRUDER IS ABOUT TO FIND OUT.
ALL HANDS--
"--*FIRE!*"
BABOOOOM
COME IN, *BROKEN WING*... COME IN, *BROKEN WING*...

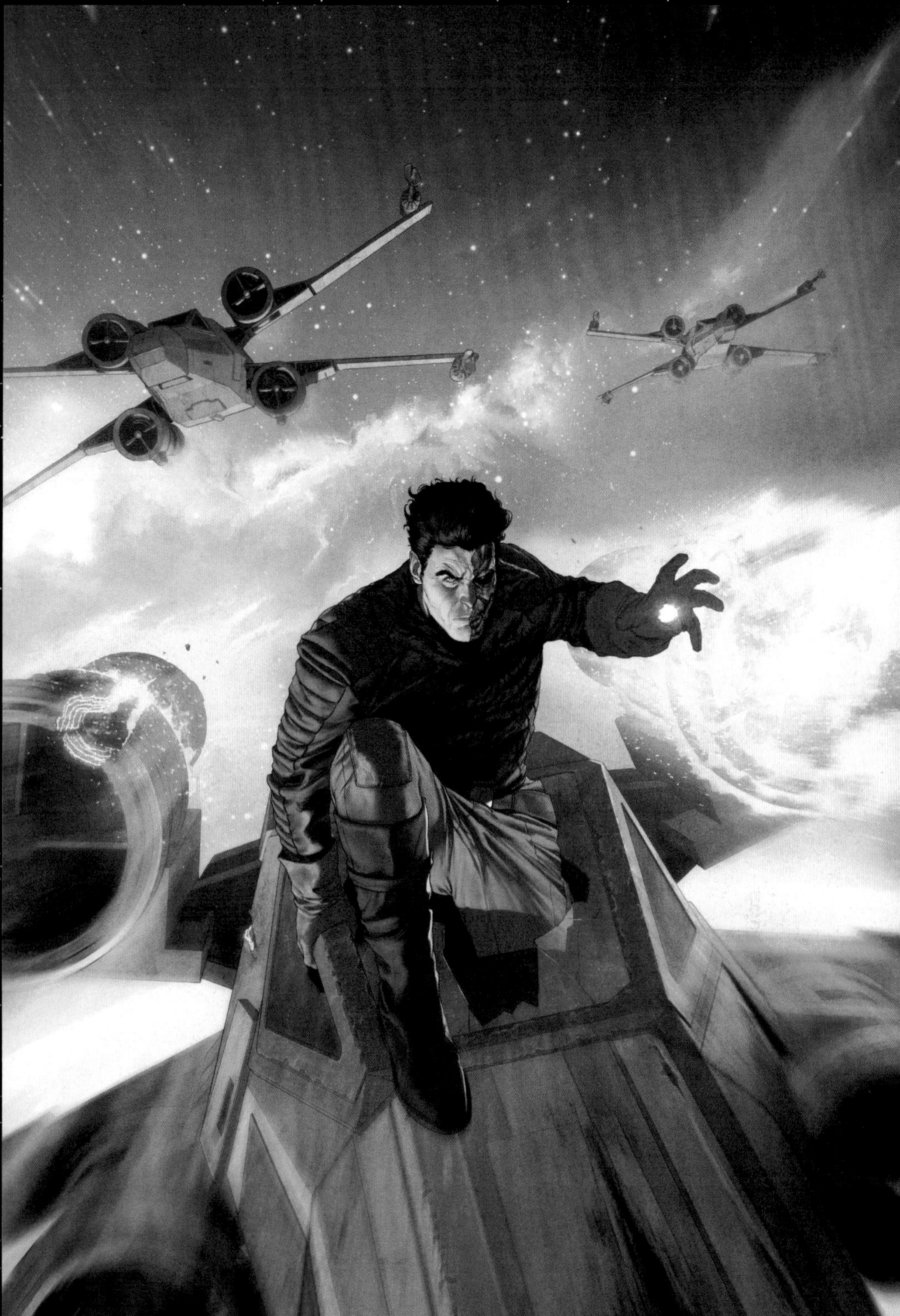

9

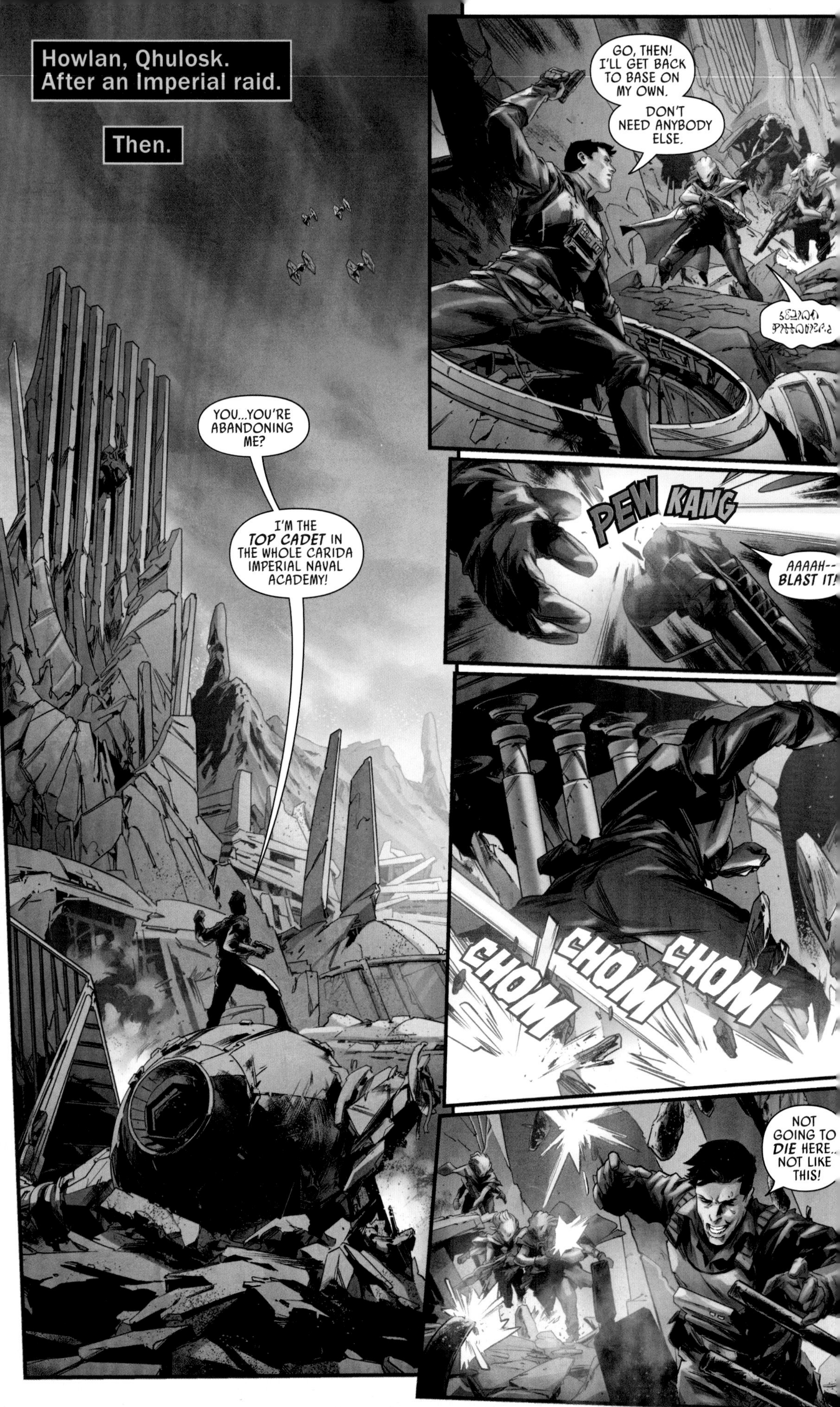
Howlan, Qhulosk.
After an Imperial raid.
Then.
YOU...YOU'RE ABANDONING ME?
I'M THE TOP CADET IN THE WHOLE CARIDA IMPERIAL NAVAL ACADEMY!
GO, THEN! I'LL GET BACK TO BASE ON MY OWN.
DON'T NEED ANYBODY ELSE.
PEW KANG
AAAAH-- BLAST IT!
CHOM CHOM CHOM
NOT GOING TO DIE HERE.. NOT LIKE THIS!

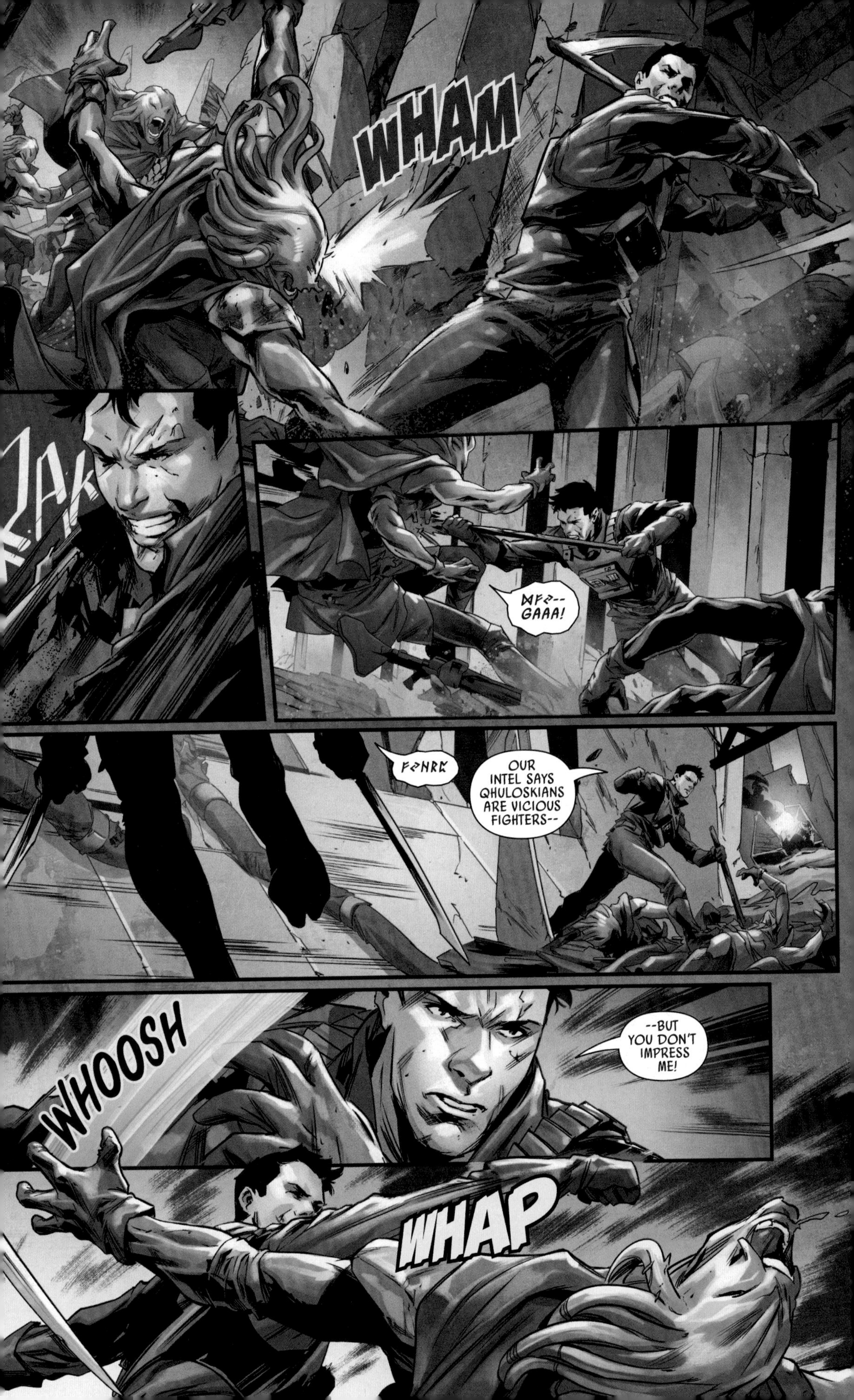
WHAM
ZAK
GAAA!
OUR INTEL SAYS QHULOSKIANS ARE VICIOUS FIGHTERS--
WHOOSH
--BUT YOU DON'T IMPRESS ME!
WHAP

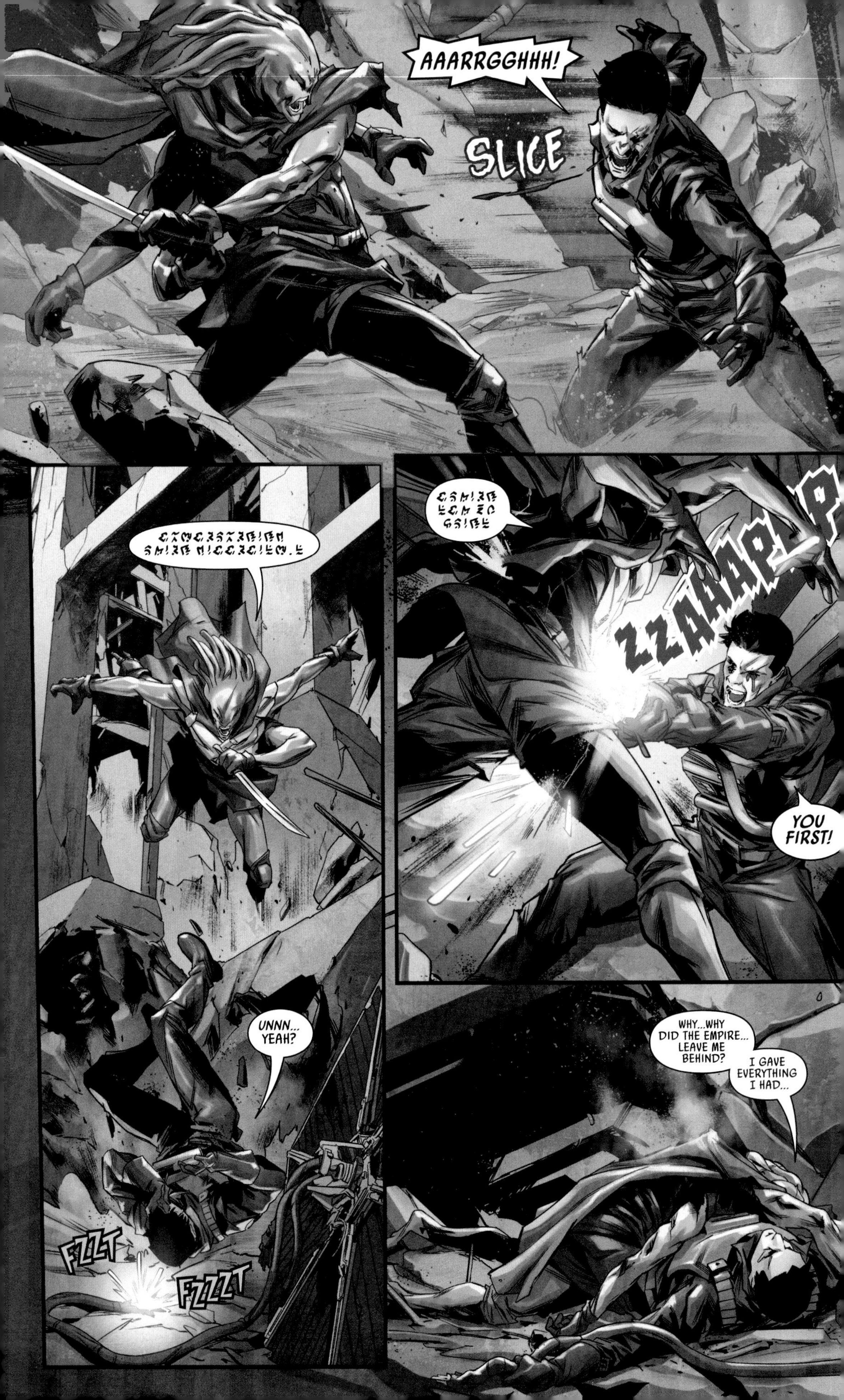
AAARRGGHHH!
SLICE
UNNN... YEAH?
ZZAAAPP
YOU FIRST!
FZZZT
FZZZT
WHY...WHY DID THE EMPIRE... LEAVE ME BEHIND?
I GAVE EVERYTHING I HAD...

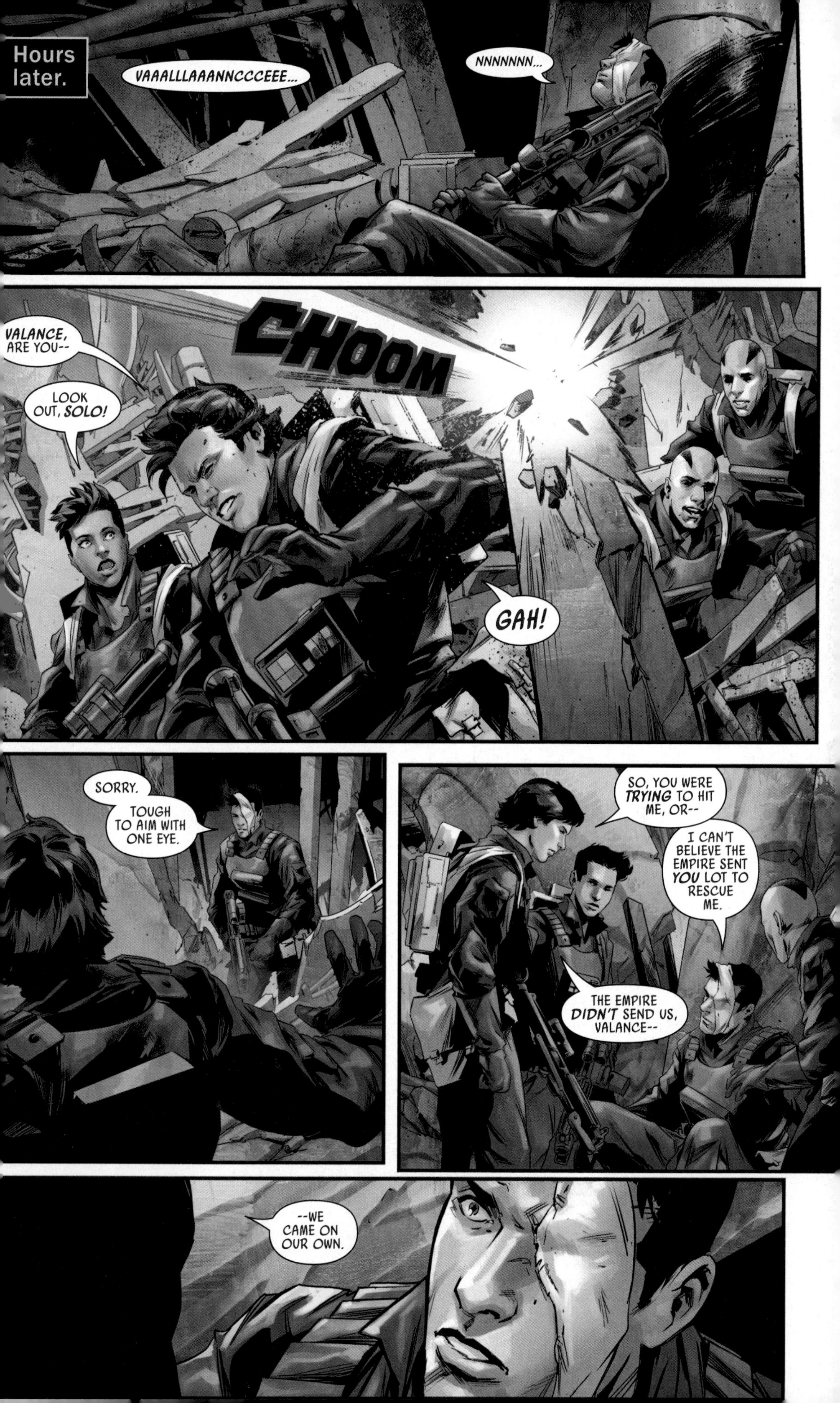
Hours later.
VAAALLLAAANNCCCEEE...
NNNNNNN...
VALANCE, ARE YOU--
LOOK OUT, SOLO!
CHOOM
GAH!
SORRY.
TOUGH TO AIM WITH ONE EYE.
SO, YOU WERE TRYING TO HIT ME, OR--
I CAN'T BELIEVE THE EMPIRE SENT YOU LOT TO RESCUE ME.
THE EMPIRE DIDN'T SEND US, VALANCE--
--WE CAME ON OUR OWN.

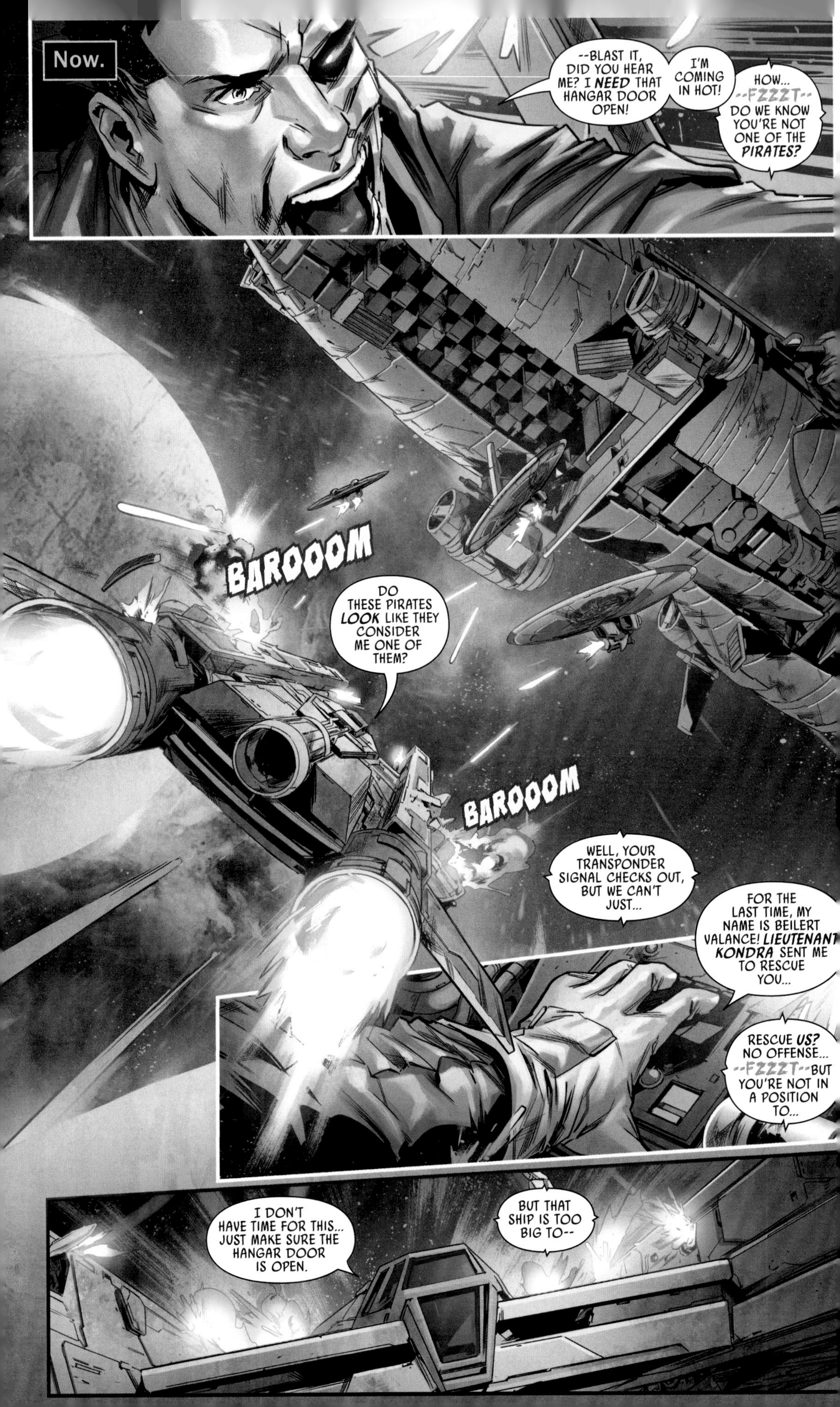
Now.
--BLAST IT, DID YOU HEAR ME? I NEED THAT HANGAR DOOR OPEN!
I'M COMING IN HOT!
HOW... --FZZZT-- DO WE KNOW YOU'RE NOT ONE OF THE PIRATES?
BAROOOM
DO THESE PIRATES LOOK LIKE THEY CONSIDER ME ONE OF THEM?
BAROOOM
WELL, YOUR TRANSPONDER SIGNAL CHECKS OUT, BUT WE CAN'T JUST...
FOR THE LAST TIME, MY NAME IS BEILERT VALANCE! LIEUTENANT KONDRA SENT ME TO RESCUE YOU...
RESCUE US? NO OFFENSE... --FZZZT-- BUT YOU'RE NOT IN A POSITION TO...
I DON'T HAVE TIME FOR THIS... JUST MAKE SURE THE HANGAR DOOR IS OPEN.
BUT THAT SHIP IS TOO BIG TO--

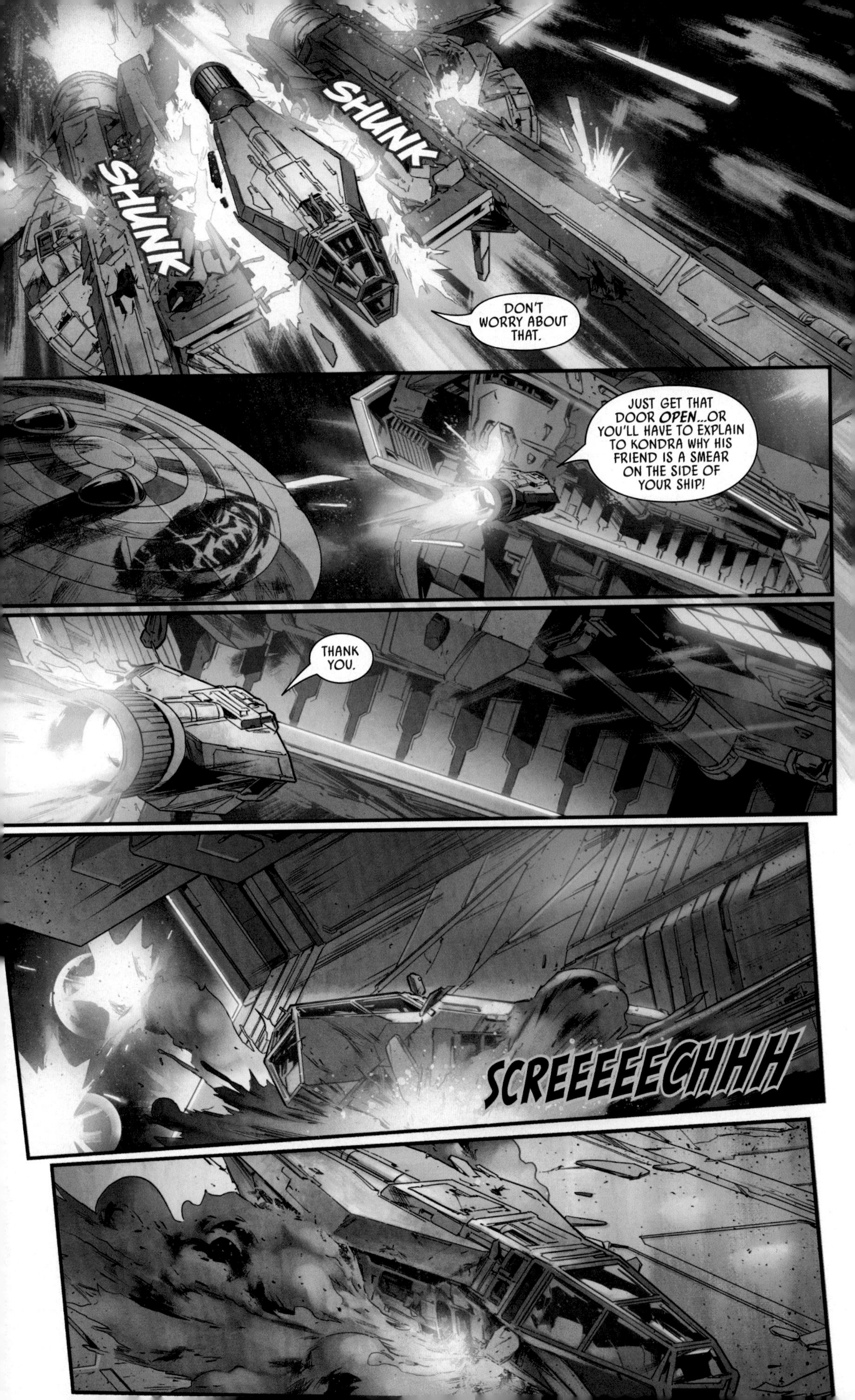
SHUNK
SHUNK
DON'T WORRY ABOUT THAT.
JUST GET THAT DOOR OPEN...OR YOU'LL HAVE TO EXPLAIN TO KONDRA WHY HIS FRIEND IS A SMEAR ON THE SIDE OF YOUR SHIP!
THANK YOU.
SCREEEEEECHHH

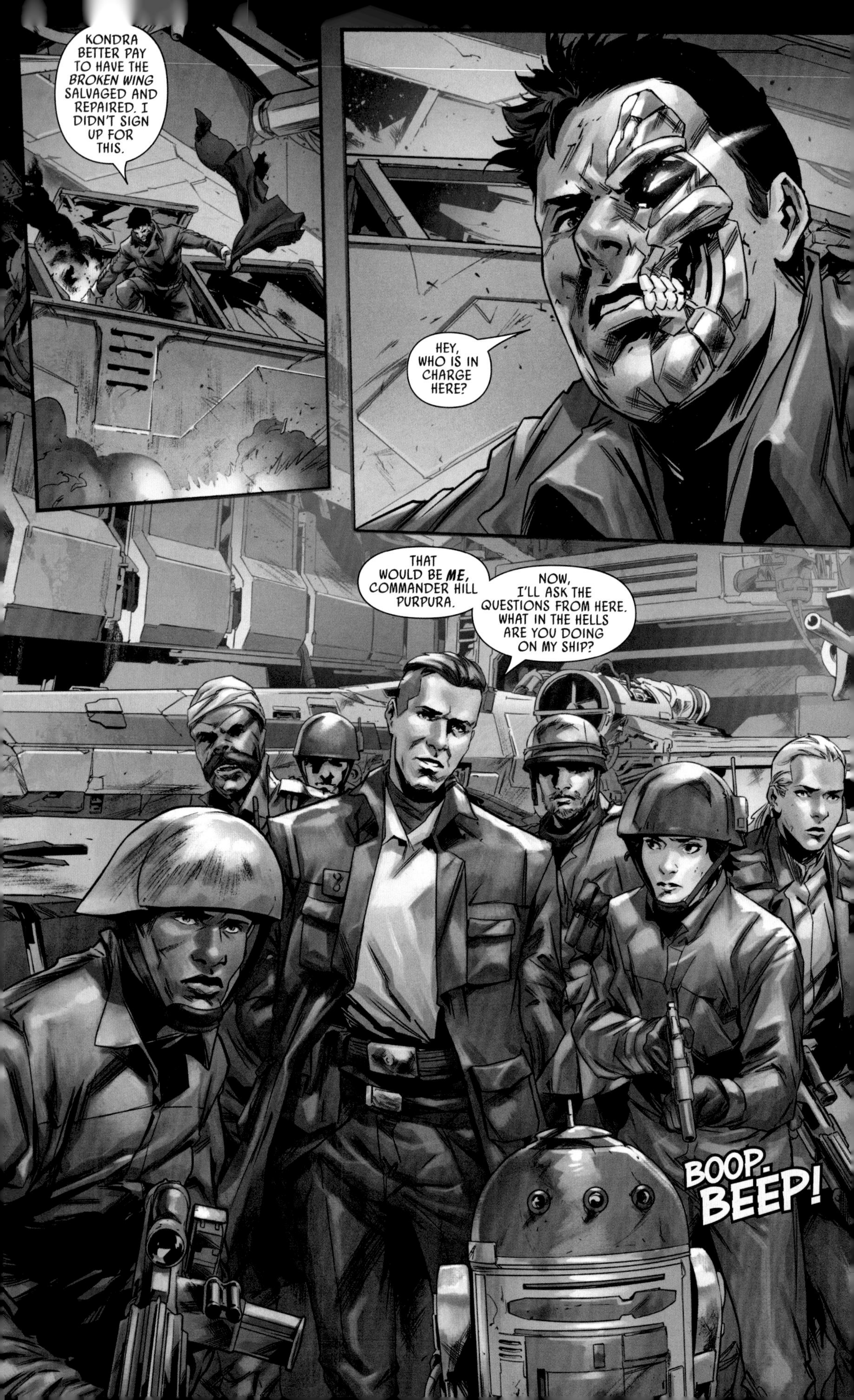
KONDRA BETTER PAY TO HAVE THE *BROKEN WING* SALVAGED AND REPAIRED. I DIDN'T SIGN UP FOR THIS.
HEY, WHO IS IN CHARGE HERE?
THAT WOULD BE ***ME***, COMMANDER HILL PURPURA.
NOW, I'LL ASK THE QUESTIONS FROM HERE. WHAT IN THE HELLS ARE YOU DOING ON MY SHIP?
BOOP. BEEP!

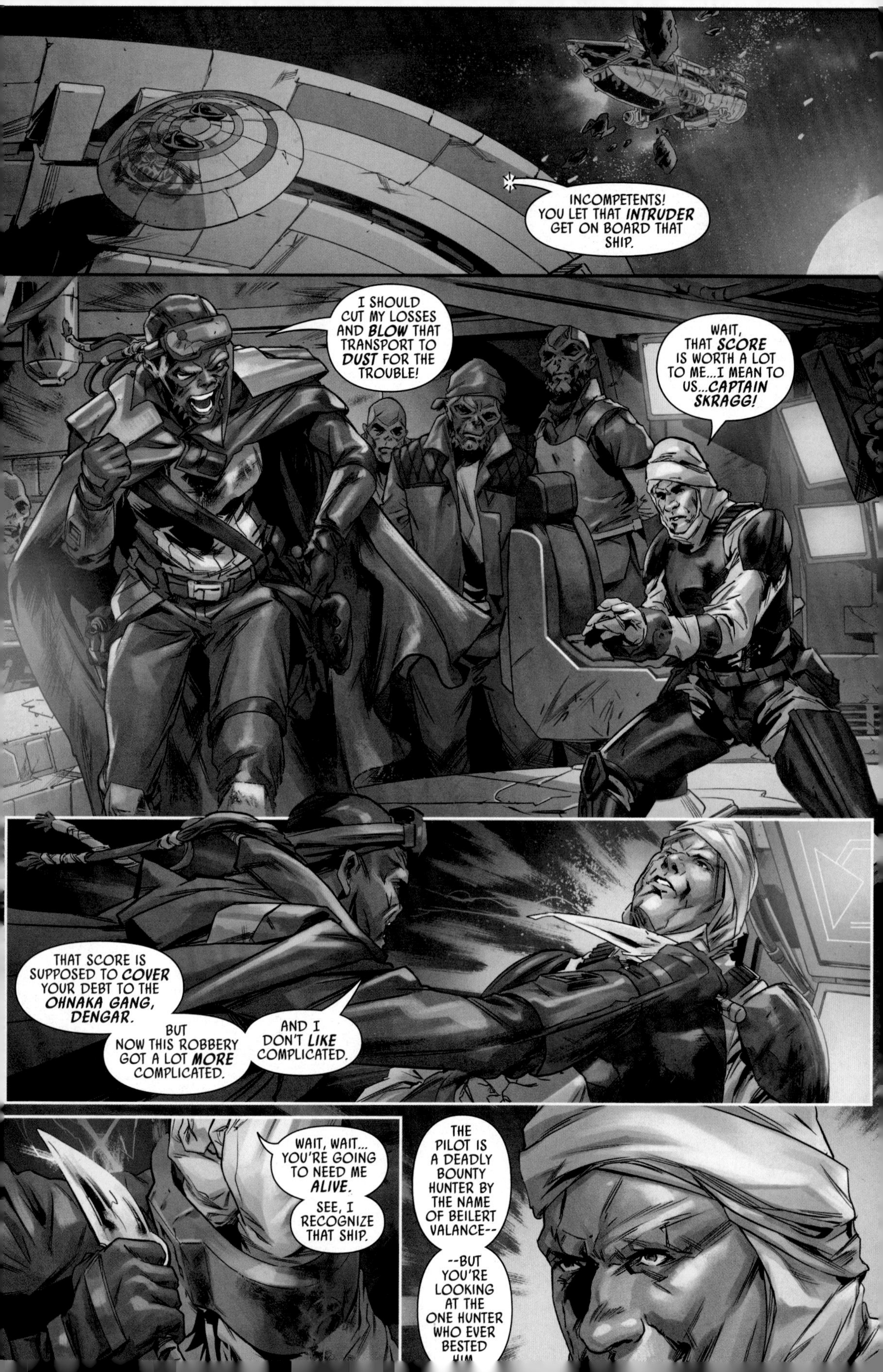

INCOMPETENTS! YOU LET THAT INTRUDER GET ON BOARD THAT SHIP.
I SHOULD CUT MY LOSSES AND BLOW THAT TRANSPORT TO DUST FOR THE TROUBLE!
WAIT, THAT SCORE IS WORTH A LOT TO ME...I MEAN TO US...CAPTAIN SKRAGG!
THAT SCORE IS SUPPOSED TO COVER YOUR DEBT TO THE OHNAKA GANG, DENGAR.
BUT NOW THIS ROBBERY GOT A LOT MORE COMPLICATED.
AND I DON'T LIKE COMPLICATED.
WAIT, WAIT... YOU'RE GOING TO NEED ME ALIVE.
SEE, I RECOGNIZE THAT SHIP.
THE PILOT IS A DEADLY BOUNTY HUNTER BY THE NAME OF BEILERT VALANCE--
--BUT YOU'RE LOOKING AT THE ONE HUNTER WHO EVER BESTED

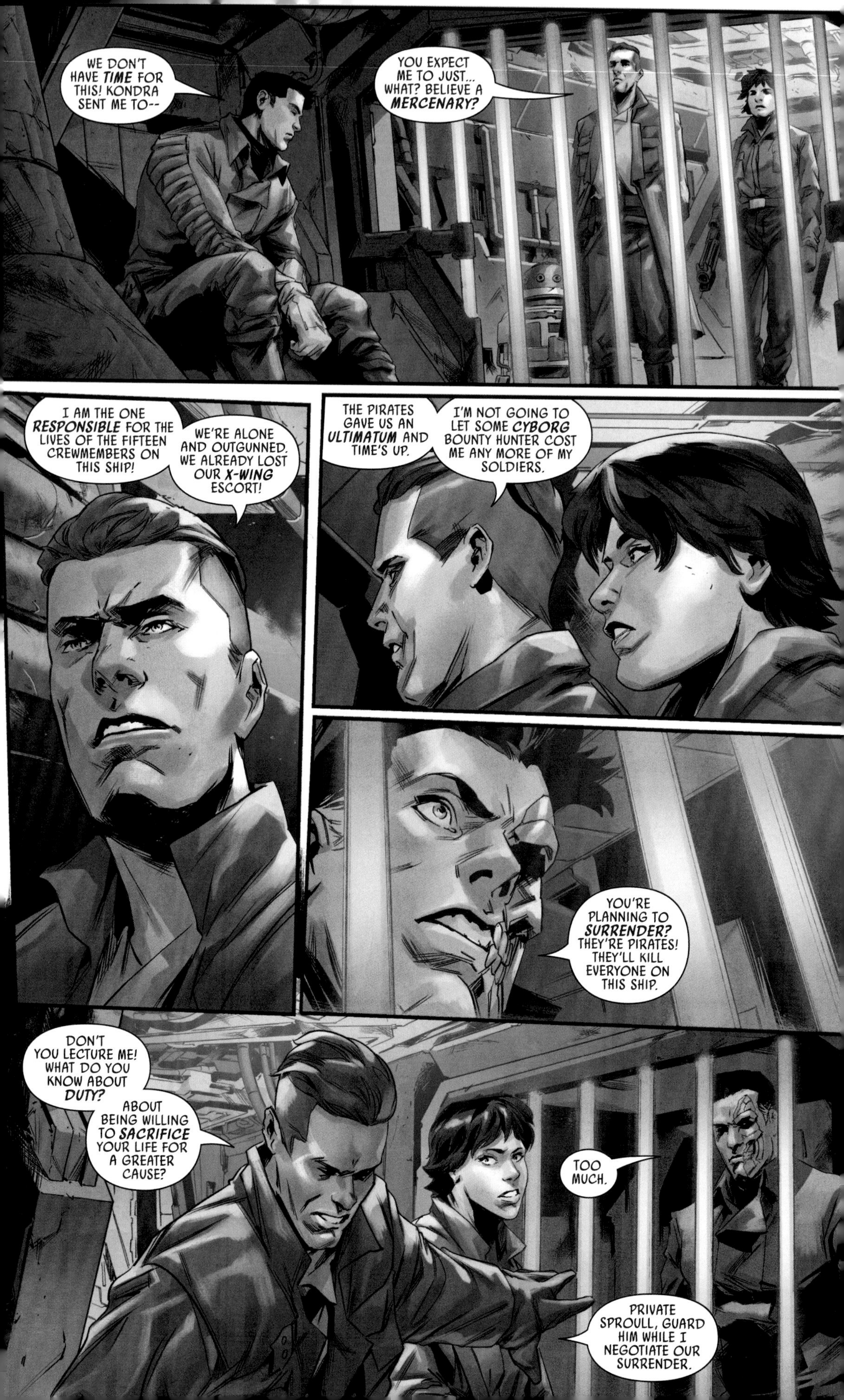
WE DON'T HAVE TIME FOR THIS! KONDRA SENT ME TO--
YOU EXPECT ME TO JUST... WHAT? BELIEVE A MERCENARY?
I AM THE ONE RESPONSIBLE FOR THE LIVES OF THE FIFTEEN CREWMEMBERS ON THIS SHIP!
WE'RE ALONE AND OUTGUNNED. WE ALREADY LOST OUR X-WING ESCORT!
THE PIRATES GAVE US AN ULTIMATUM AND TIME'S UP.
I'M NOT GOING TO LET SOME CYBORG BOUNTY HUNTER COST ME ANY MORE OF MY SOLDIERS.
YOU'RE PLANNING TO SURRENDER? THEY'RE PIRATES! THEY'LL KILL EVERYONE ON THIS SHIP.
DON'T YOU LECTURE ME! WHAT DO YOU KNOW ABOUT DUTY?
ABOUT BEING WILLING TO SACRIFICE YOUR LIFE FOR A GREATER CAUSE?
TOO MUCH.
PRIVATE SPROULL, GUARD HIM WHILE I NEGOTIATE OUR SURRENDER.

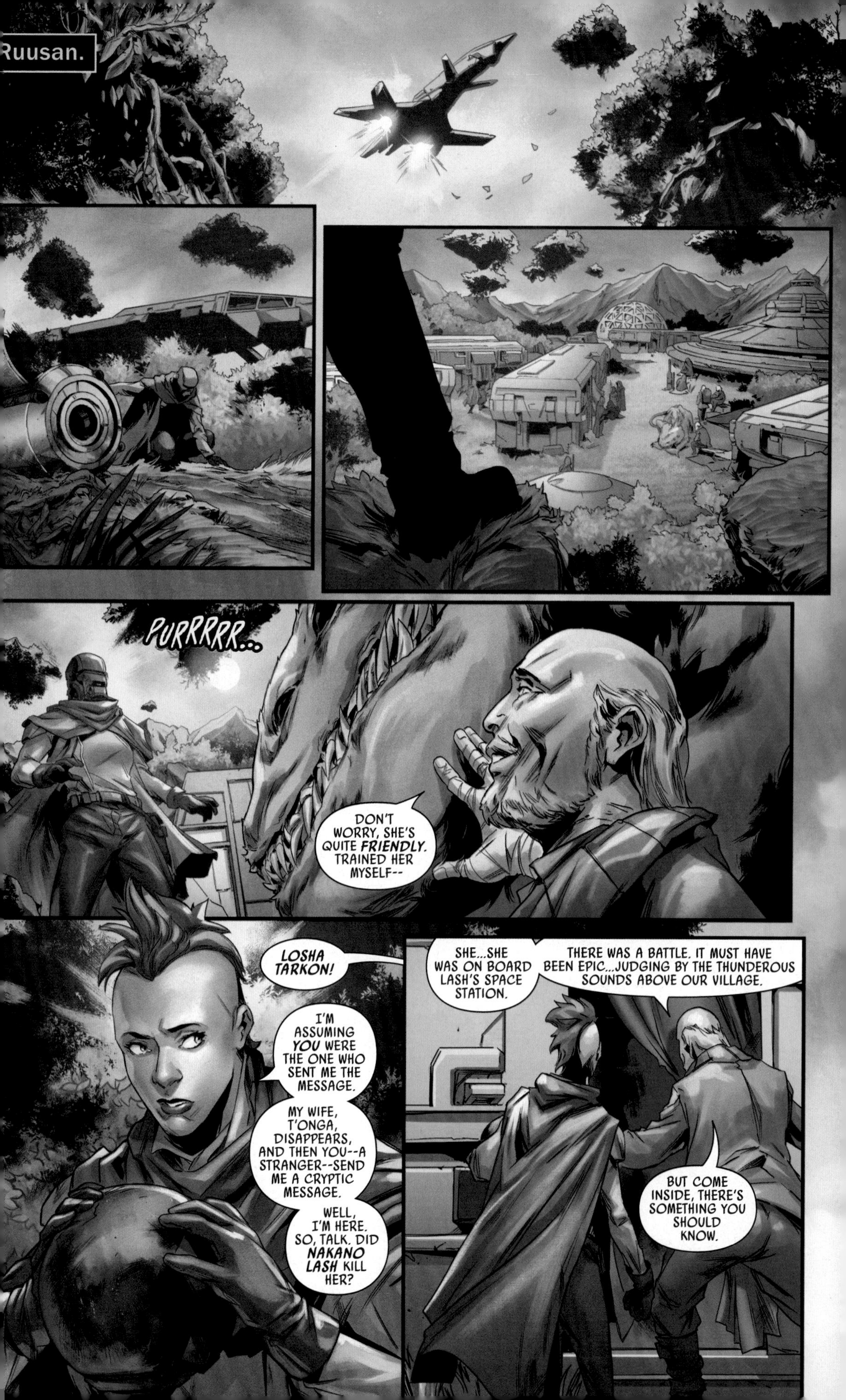

Ruusan.
PURRRRR...
DON'T WORRY, SHE'S QUITE FRIENDLY. TRAINED HER MYSELF--
LOSHA TARKON!
I'M ASSUMING YOU WERE THE ONE WHO SENT ME THE MESSAGE.
MY WIFE, T'ONGA, DISAPPEARS, AND THEN YOU--A STRANGER--SEND ME A CRYPTIC MESSAGE.
WELL, I'M HERE. SO, TALK. DID NAKANO LASH KILL HER?
SHE...SHE WAS ON BOARD LASH'S SPACE STATION.
THERE WAS A BATTLE. IT MUST HAVE BEEN EPIC...JUDGING BY THE THUNDEROUS SOUNDS ABOVE OUR VILLAGE.
BUT COME INSIDE, THERE'S SOMETHING YOU SHOULD KNOW.

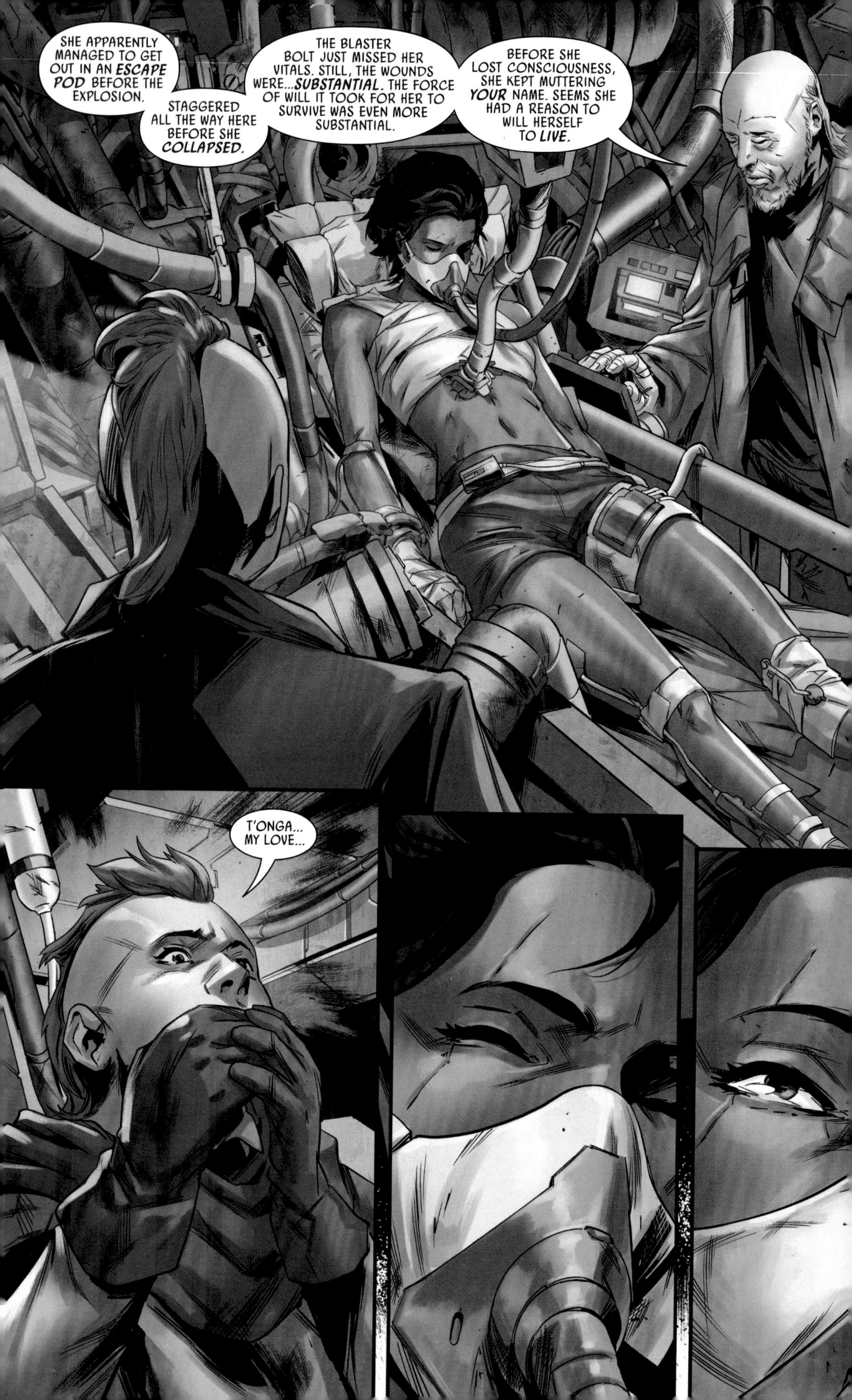
SHE APPARENTLY MANAGED TO GET OUT IN AN ESCAPE POD BEFORE THE EXPLOSION.
STAGGERED ALL THE WAY HERE BEFORE SHE COLLAPSED.
THE BLASTER BOLT JUST MISSED HER VITALS. STILL, THE WOUNDS WERE...SUBSTANTIAL. THE FORCE OF WILL IT TOOK FOR HER TO SURVIVE WAS EVEN MORE SUBSTANTIAL.
BEFORE SHE LOST CONSCIOUSNESS, SHE KEPT MUTTERING YOUR NAME. SEEMS SHE HAD A REASON TO WILL HERSELF TO LIVE.
T'ONGA... MY LOVE...

WHAT'S YOUR NAME, *SOLDIER?*

BLANCH... *BLANCH SPROULL.*

YOU SEEM A LITTLE YOUNG TO BE A *COMBAT* SOLDIER.

NO OFFENSE.

I'M NOT A FIGHTER. I'M JUST A MECHANIC.

I JOINED THE [R]ELLION BECAUSE *BELIEVED* IN THE CAUSE...

WELL, [T]HAT AND WANTED TO [G]ET OFF MY MINING PLANET.

EH, YOU WOULDN'T UNDERSTAND.

YOU'D BE SURPRISED.

SOME MECHANIC I AM. I CHECKED THE [HY]PERDRIVE CONVERTER [B]EFORE WE LEFT...BUT WE STALLED MID-JUMP.

[TH]OSE PIRATES [A]RE RIGHT HERE WAITING.

NOT THAT THERE'S ANYTHING ON THIS [R]UST BUCKET WORTH STEALING--

ALERT. ALERT. PREPARE FOR BOARDING.

[DI]D [I] MEAN [T] YOU [A]BOUT [PI]RATES [BOAR]DING [EVERY]BODY [OFF] THE [SH]IP?

YES, BUT I CAN STILL STOP THEM...

BEEP BEEP BEEEEP!

DON'T PANIC, TEE-SIX--FREEING HIM MAY SEEM LIKE A BAD IDEA, BUT WE'RE OUT OF *GOOD* OPTIONS.

THANK YOU...NOW, IS THERE *ANYTHING* ON BOARD I CAN USE TO FIGHT THEM?

MINING SUPPLIES MOSTLY...I MEAN, *THERE IS* ONE HALF-WORKING FIGHTER IN THE HANGAR, BUT NO ONE LEFT WHO CAN FLY IT.

WHAT *KIND* OF FIGHTER?

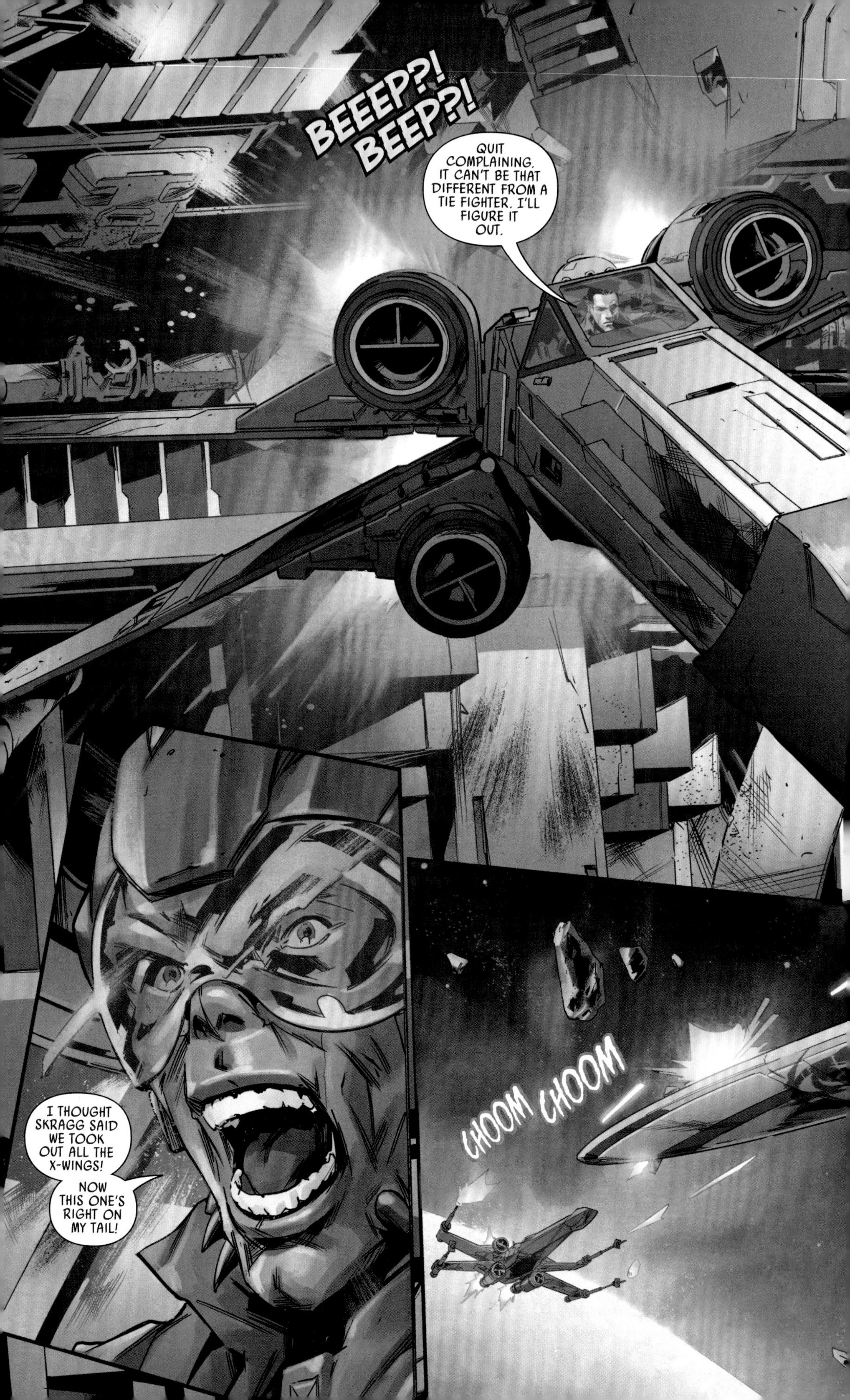
BEEEEP?! BEEP?!
QUIT COMPLAINING. IT CAN'T BE THAT DIFFERENT FROM A TIE FIGHTER. I'LL FIGURE IT OUT.
I THOUGHT SKRAGG SAID WE TOOK OUT ALL THE X-WINGS!
NOW THIS ONE'S RIGHT ON MY TAIL!
CHOOM CHOOM

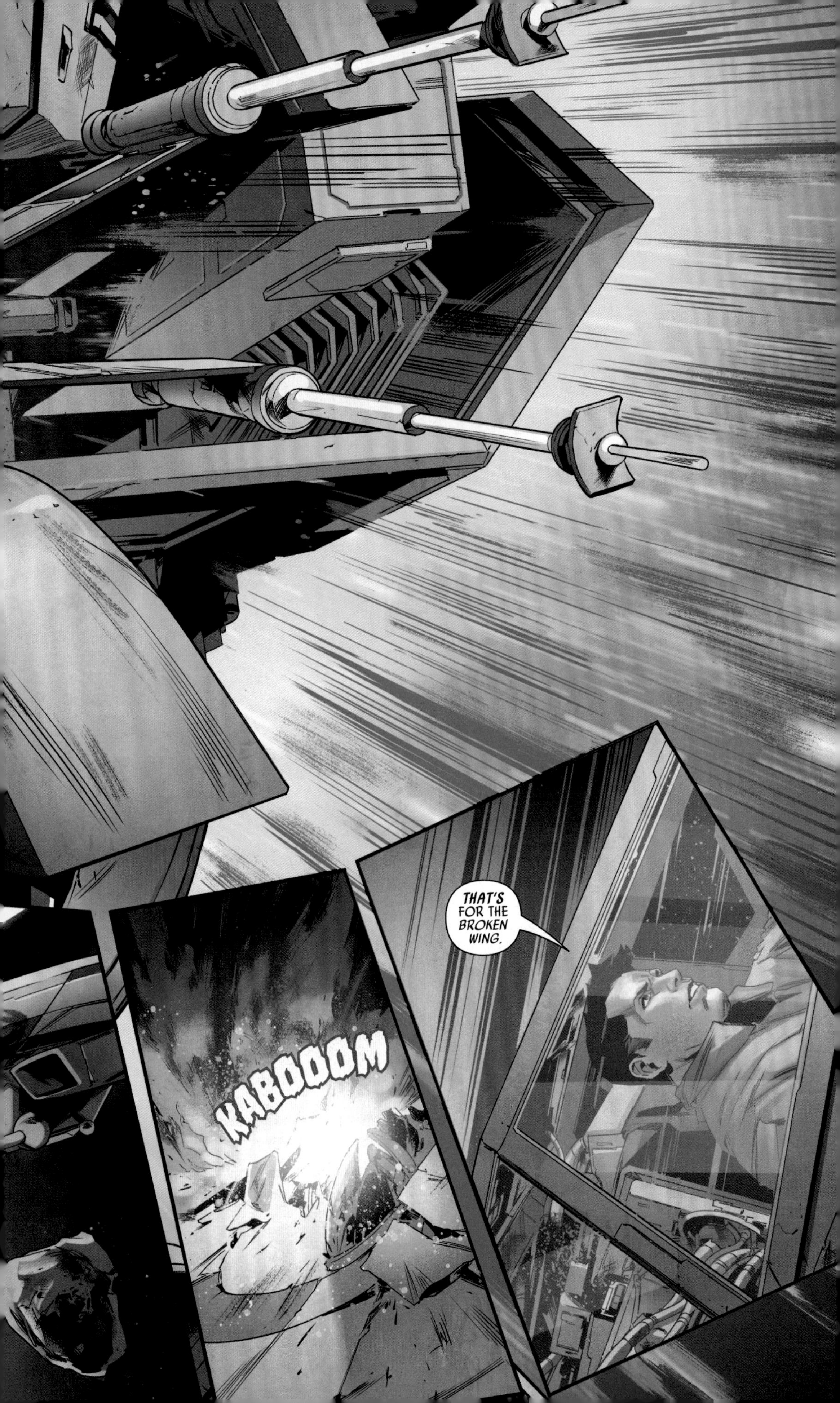
THAT'S FOR THE BROKEN WING.
KABOOOM

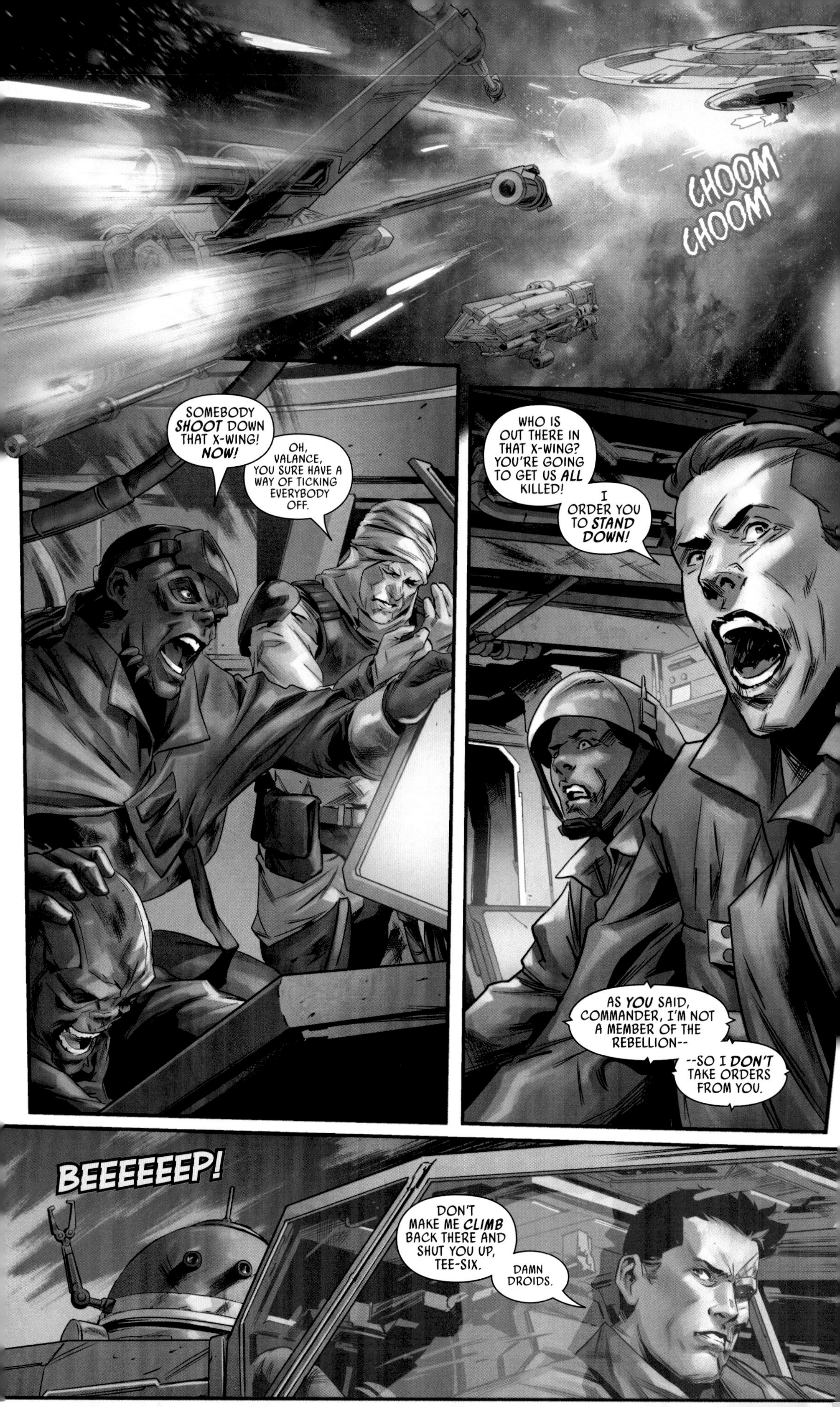

CHOOM CHOOM
SOMEBODY SHOOT DOWN THAT X-WING! NOW!
OH, VALANCE, YOU SURE HAVE A WAY OF TICKING EVERYBODY OFF.
WHO IS OUT THERE IN THAT X-WING? YOU'RE GOING TO GET US ALL KILLED!
I ORDER YOU TO STAND DOWN!
AS YOU SAID, COMMANDER, I'M NOT A MEMBER OF THE REBELLION--
--SO I DON'T TAKE ORDERS FROM YOU.
BEEEEEEP!
DON'T MAKE ME CLIMB BACK THERE AND SHUT YOU UP, TEE-SIX.
DAMN DROIDS.

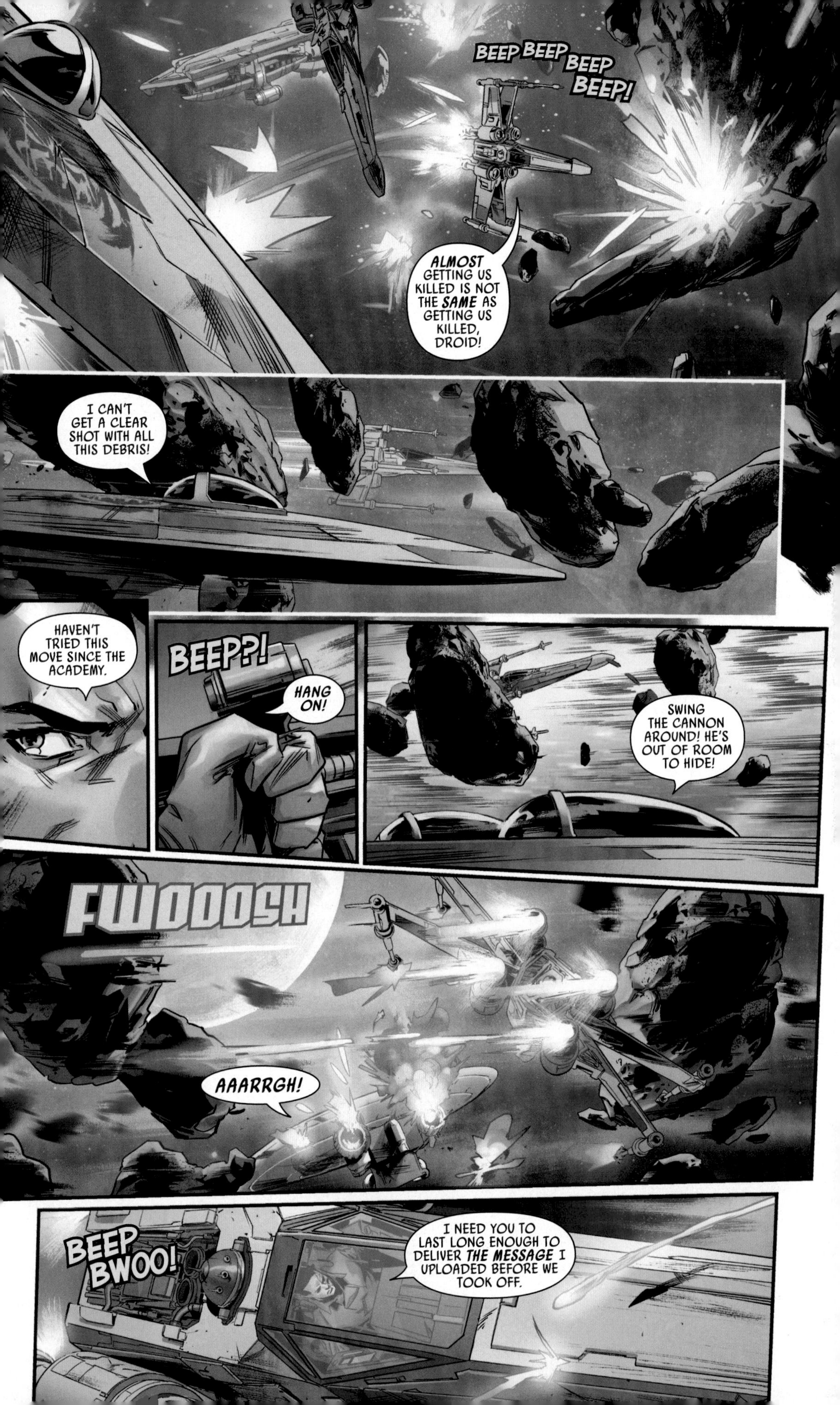
BEEP BEEP BEEP BEEP!
ALMOST GETTING US KILLED IS NOT THE SAME AS GETTING US KILLED, DROID!
I CAN'T GET A CLEAR SHOT WITH ALL THIS DEBRIS!
HAVEN'T TRIED THIS MOVE SINCE THE ACADEMY.
BEEP?!
HANG ON!
SWING THE CANNON AROUND! HE'S OUT OF ROOM TO HIDE!
FWOOOSH
AAARRGH!
BEEP BWOO!
I NEED YOU TO LAST LONG ENOUGH TO DELIVER THE MESSAGE I UPLOADED BEFORE WE TOOK OFF.

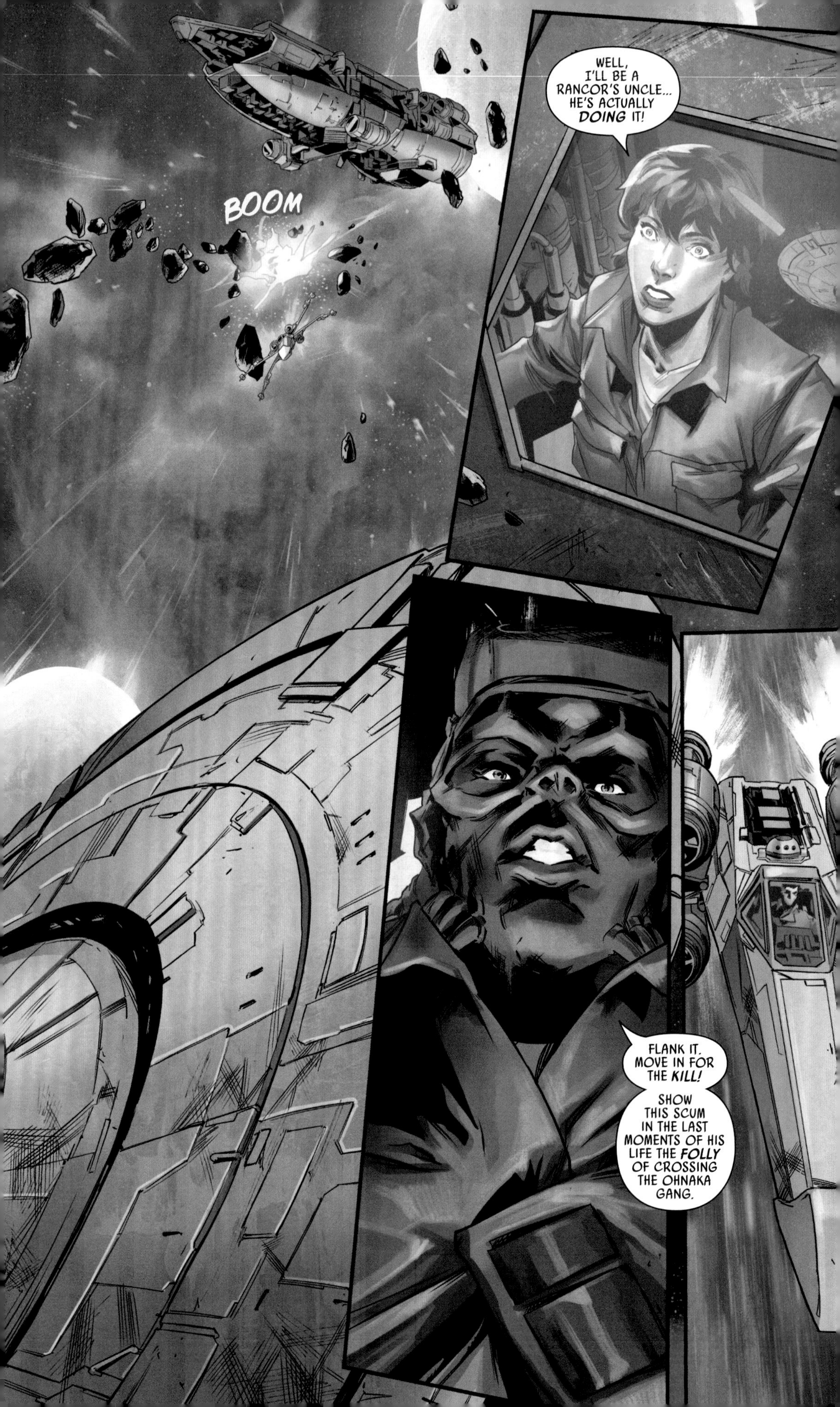
BOOM
WELL, I'LL BE A RANCOR'S UNCLE... HE'S ACTUALLY *DOING* IT!
FLANK IT. MOVE IN FOR THE *KILL!*
SHOW THIS SCUM IN THE LAST MOMENTS OF HIS LIFE THE *FOLLY* OF CROSSING THE OHNAKA GANG.

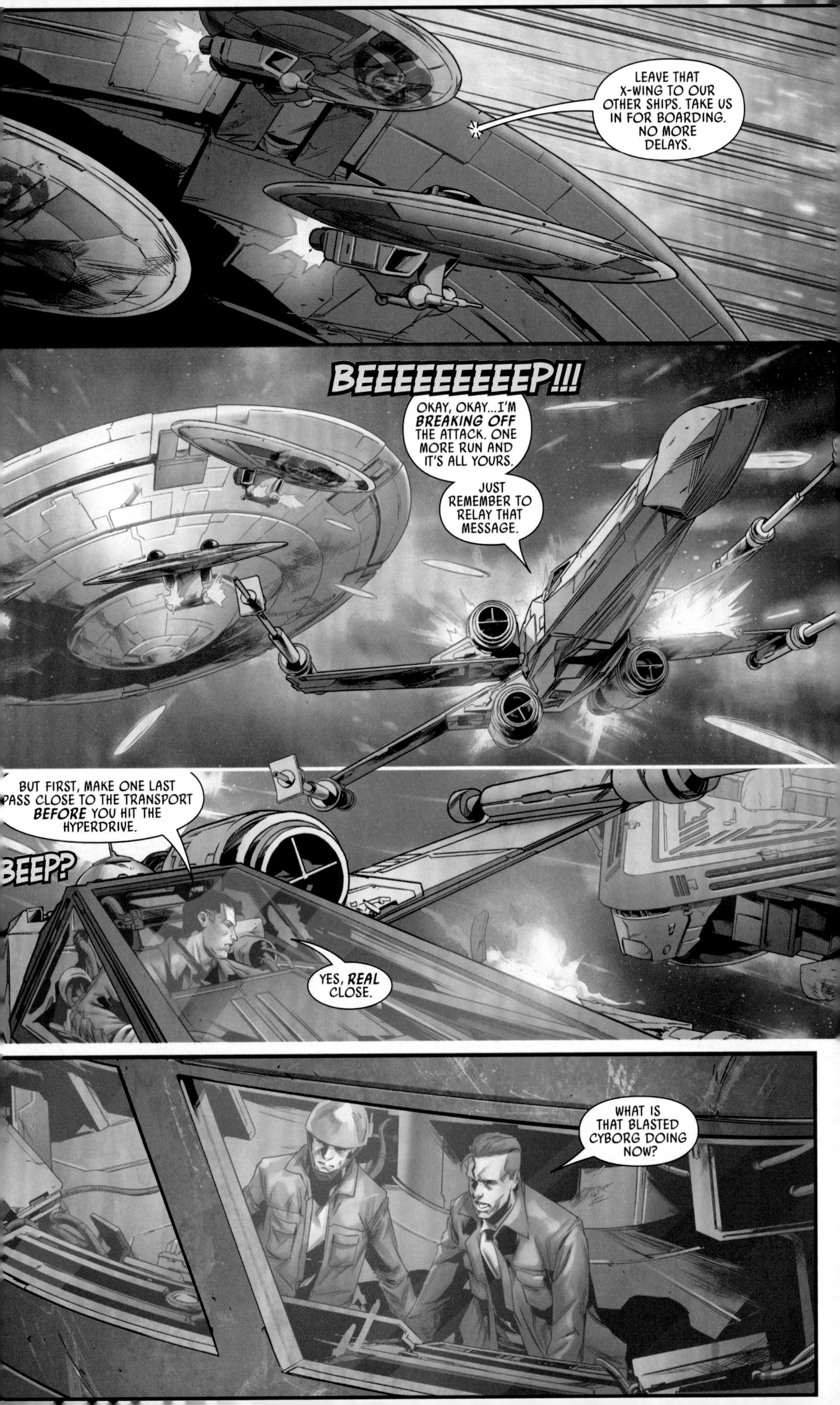
LEAVE THAT X-WING TO OUR OTHER SHIPS. TAKE US IN FOR BOARDING. NO MORE DELAYS.
BEEEEEEEEEEP!!!
OKAY, OKAY...I'M BREAKING OFF THE ATTACK. ONE MORE RUN AND IT'S ALL YOURS.
JUST REMEMBER TO RELAY THAT MESSAGE.
BUT FIRST, MAKE ONE LAST PASS CLOSE TO THE TRANSPORT BEFORE YOU HIT THE HYPERDRIVE.
BEEP?
YES, REAL CLOSE.
WHAT IS THAT BLASTED CYBORG DOING NOW?

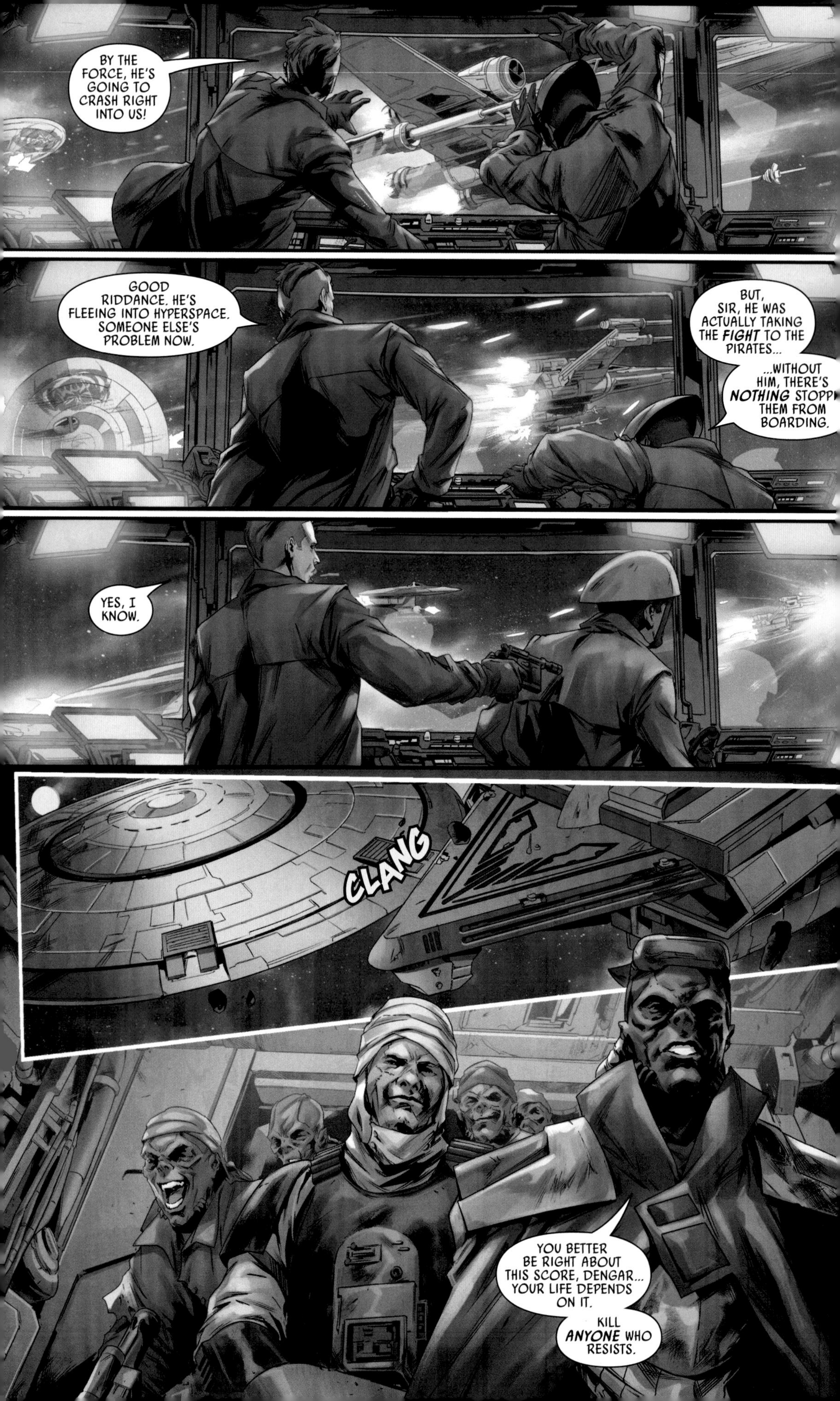

BY THE FORCE, HE'S GOING TO CRASH RIGHT INTO US!
GOOD RIDDANCE. HE'S FLEEING INTO HYPERSPACE. SOMEONE ELSE'S PROBLEM NOW.
BUT, SIR, HE WAS ACTUALLY TAKING THE *FIGHT* TO THE PIRATES...
...WITHOUT HIM, THERE'S *NOTHING* STOPP THEM FROM BOARDING.
YES, I KNOW.
CLANG
YOU BETTER BE RIGHT ABOUT THIS SCORE, DENGAR... YOUR LIFE DEPENDS ON IT.
KILL *ANYONE* WHO RESISTS.

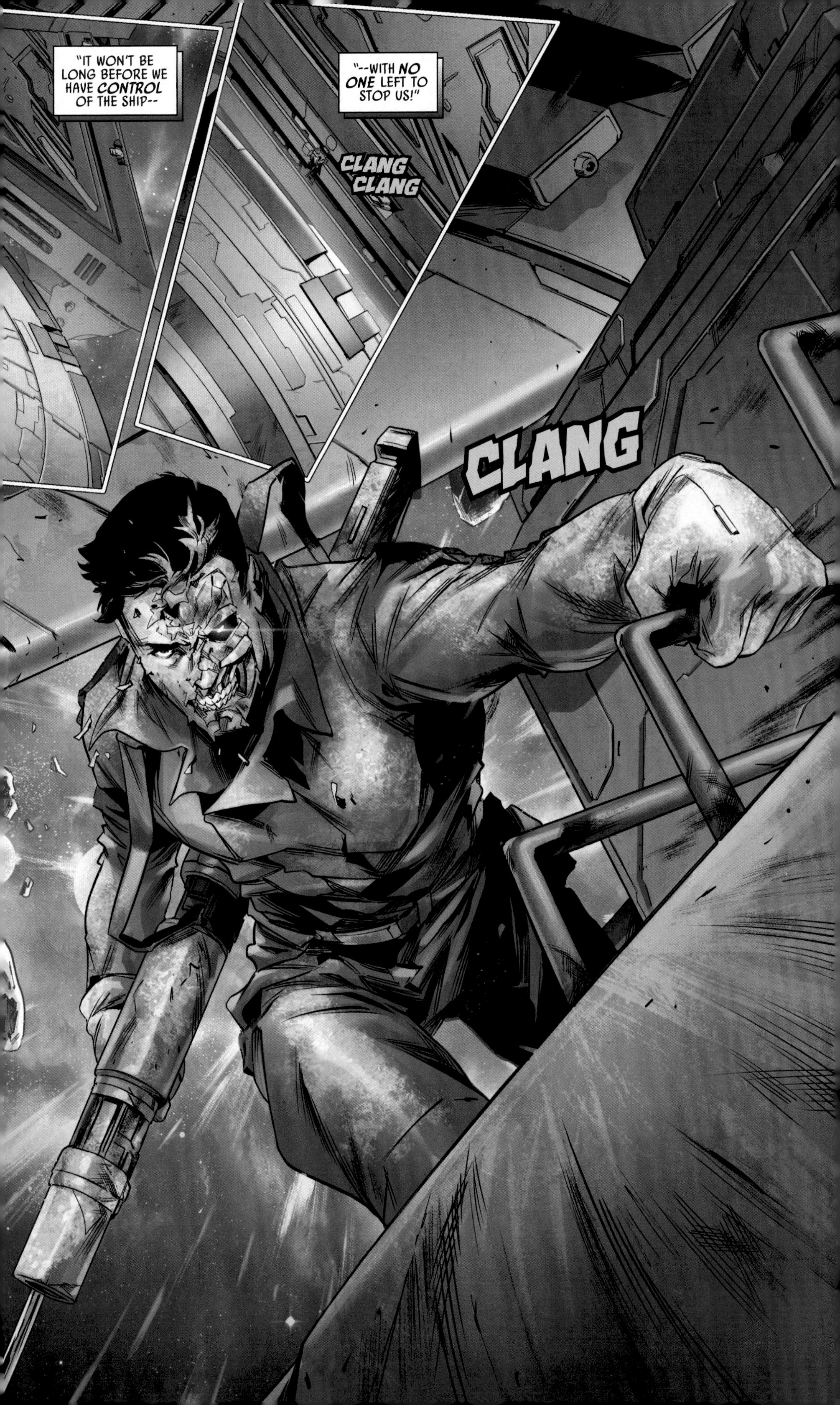
"IT WON'T BE LONG BEFORE WE HAVE CONTROL OF THE SHIP--
"--WITH NO ONE LEFT TO STOP US!"
CLANG CLANG
CLANG

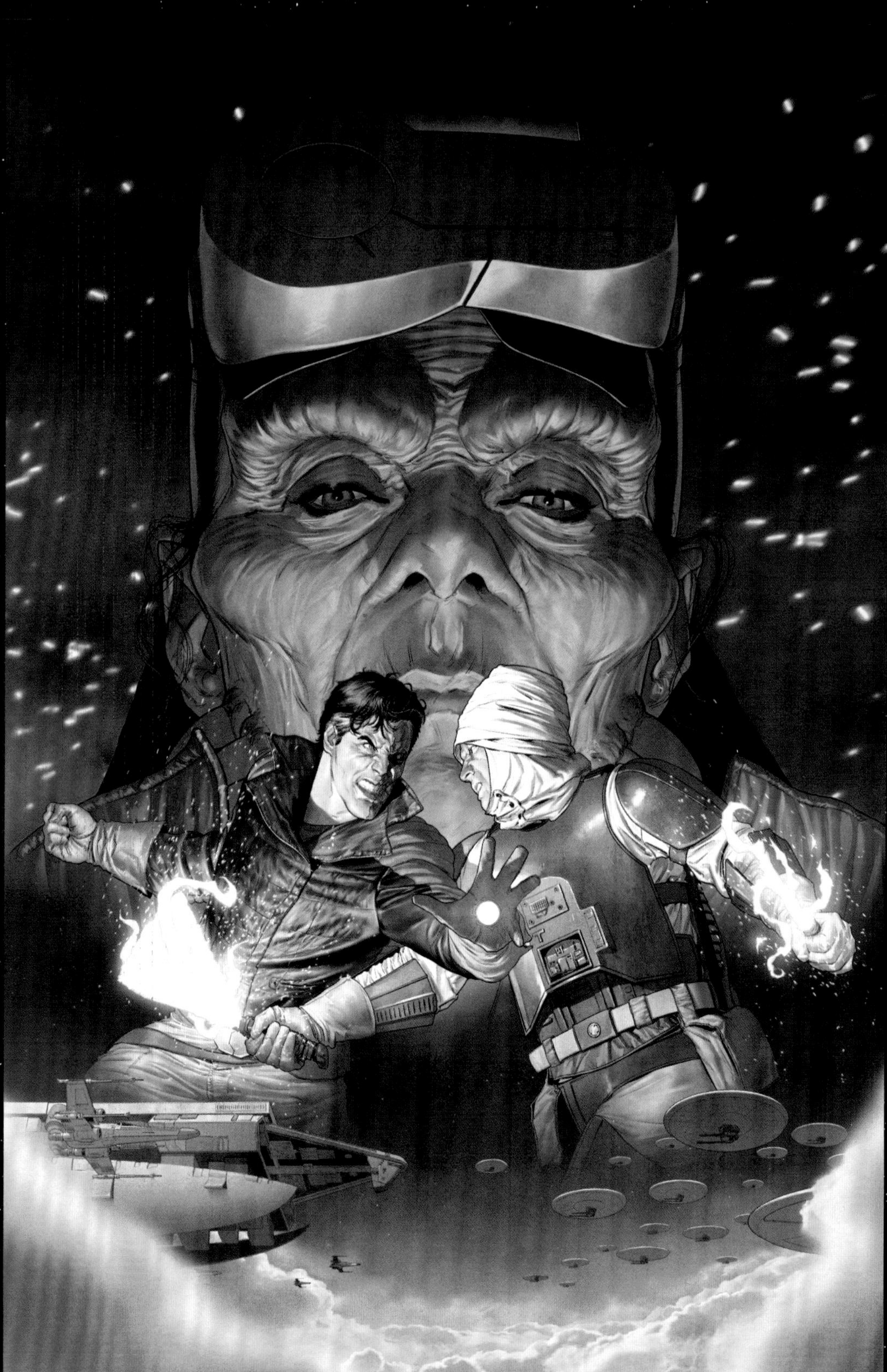

10

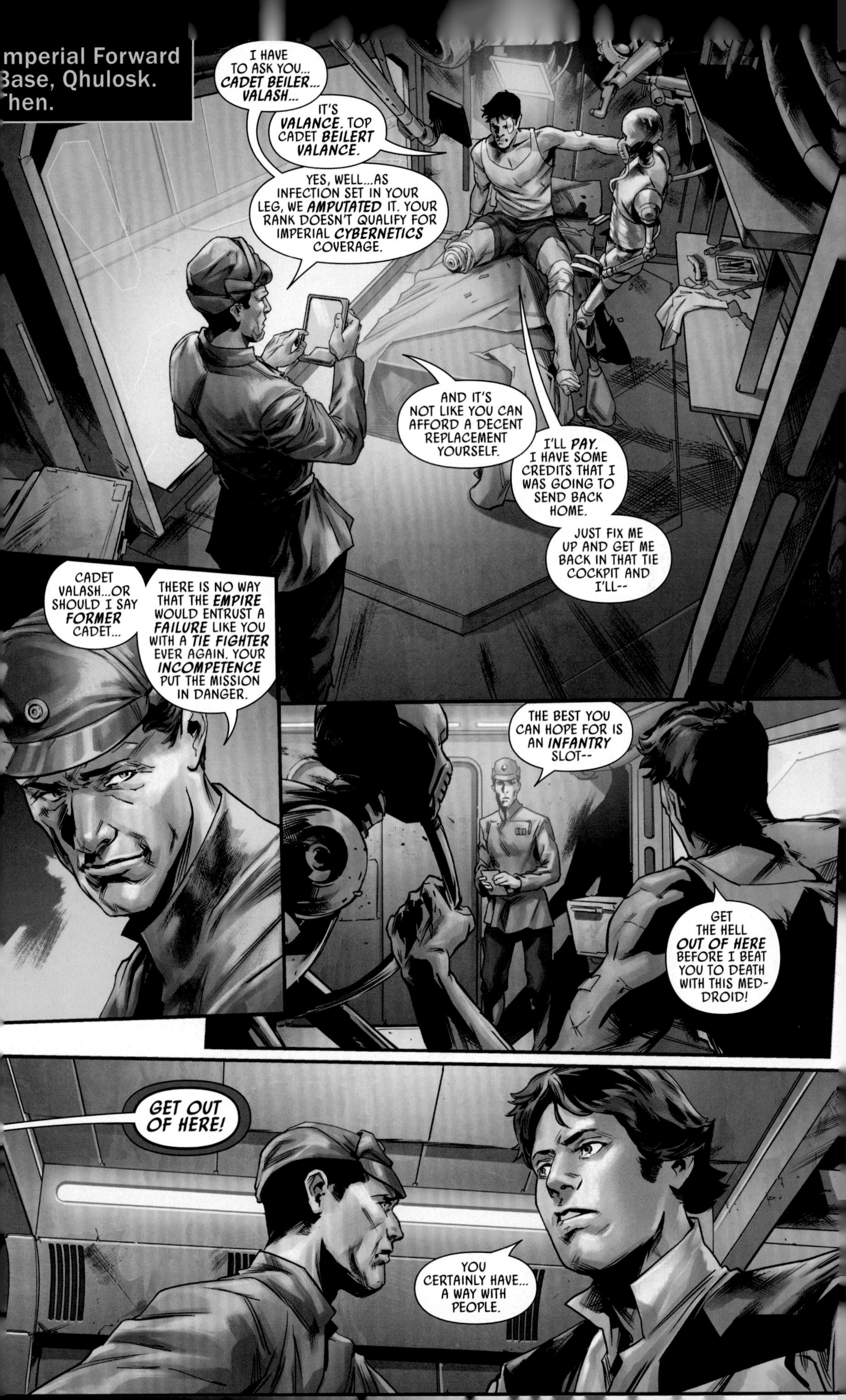

mperial Forward Base, Qhulosk. hen.
I HAVE TO ASK YOU... CADET BEILER... VALASH...
IT'S VALANCE. TOP CADET BEILERT VALANCE.
YES, WELL...AS INFECTION SET IN YOUR LEG, WE AMPUTATED IT. YOUR RANK DOESN'T QUALIFY FOR IMPERIAL CYBERNETICS COVERAGE.
AND IT'S NOT LIKE YOU CAN AFFORD A DECENT REPLACEMENT YOURSELF.
I'LL PAY. I HAVE SOME CREDITS THAT I WAS GOING TO SEND BACK HOME.
JUST FIX ME UP AND GET ME BACK IN THAT TIE COCKPIT AND I'LL--
CADET VALASH...OR SHOULD I SAY FORMER CADET...
THERE IS NO WAY THAT THE EMPIRE WOULD ENTRUST A FAILURE LIKE YOU WITH A TIE FIGHTER EVER AGAIN. YOUR INCOMPETENCE PUT THE MISSION IN DANGER.
THE BEST YOU CAN HOPE FOR IS AN INFANTRY SLOT--
GET THE HELL OUT OF HERE BEFORE I BEAT YOU TO DEATH WITH THIS MED-DROID!
GET OUT OF HERE!
YOU CERTAINLY HAVE... A WAY WITH PEOPLE.

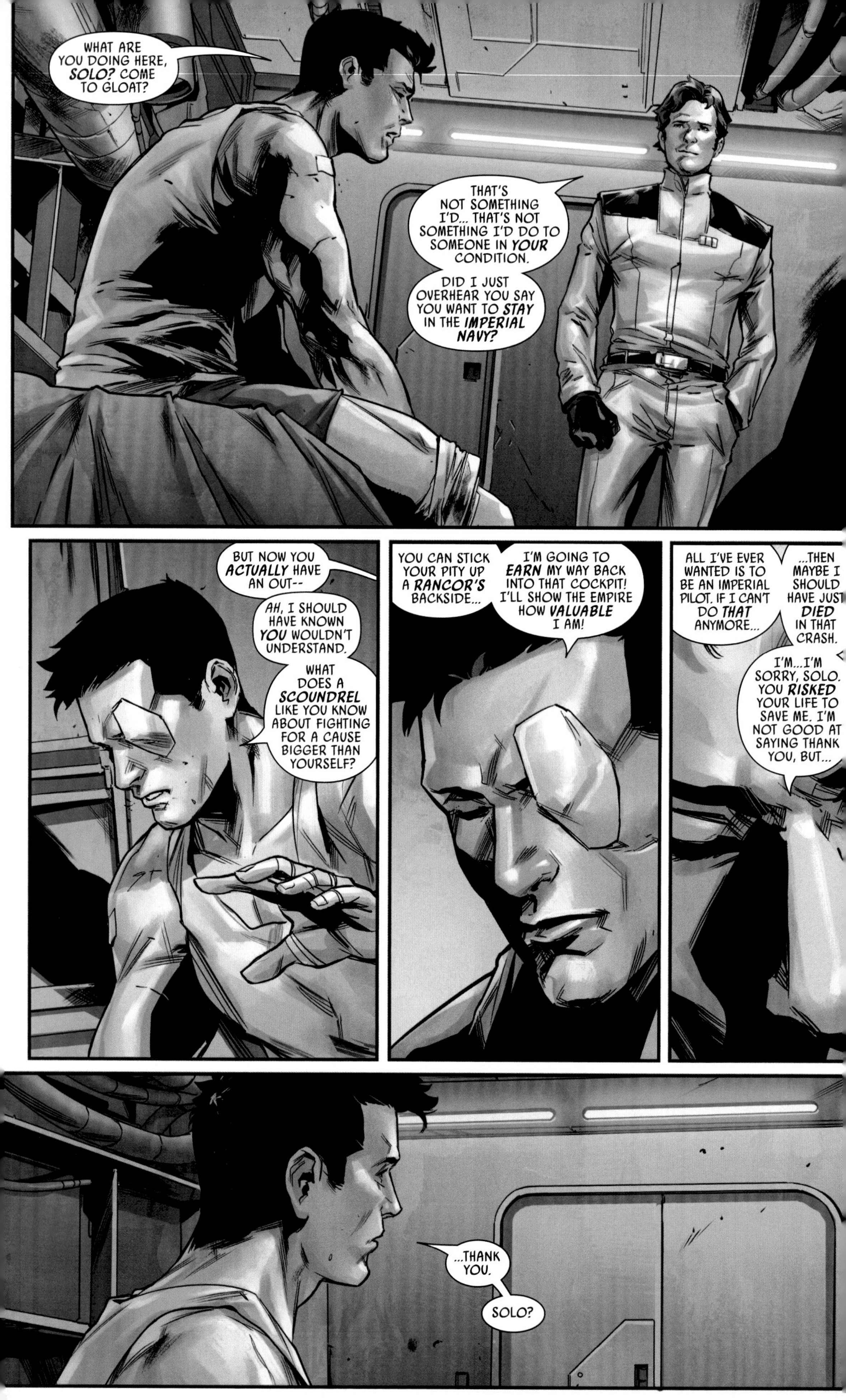
WHAT ARE YOU DOING HERE, SOLO? COME TO GLOAT?
THAT'S NOT SOMETHING I'D... THAT'S NOT SOMETHING I'D DO TO SOMEONE IN YOUR CONDITION.
DID I JUST OVERHEAR YOU SAY YOU WANT TO STAY IN THE IMPERIAL NAVY?
BUT NOW YOU ACTUALLY HAVE AN OUT--
AH, I SHOULD HAVE KNOWN YOU WOULDN'T UNDERSTAND.
WHAT DOES A SCOUNDREL LIKE YOU KNOW ABOUT FIGHTING FOR A CAUSE BIGGER THAN YOURSELF?
YOU CAN STICK YOUR PITY UP A RANCOR'S BACKSIDE...
I'M GOING TO EARN MY WAY BACK INTO THAT COCKPIT! I'LL SHOW THE EMPIRE HOW VALUABLE I AM!
ALL I'VE EVER WANTED IS TO BE AN IMPERIAL PILOT. IF I CAN'T DO THAT ANYMORE...
...THEN MAYBE I SHOULD HAVE JUST DIED IN THAT CRASH.
I'M...I'M SORRY, SOLO. YOU RISKED YOUR LIFE TO SAVE ME. I'M NOT GOOD AT SAYING THANK YOU, BUT...
...THANK YOU.
SOLO?

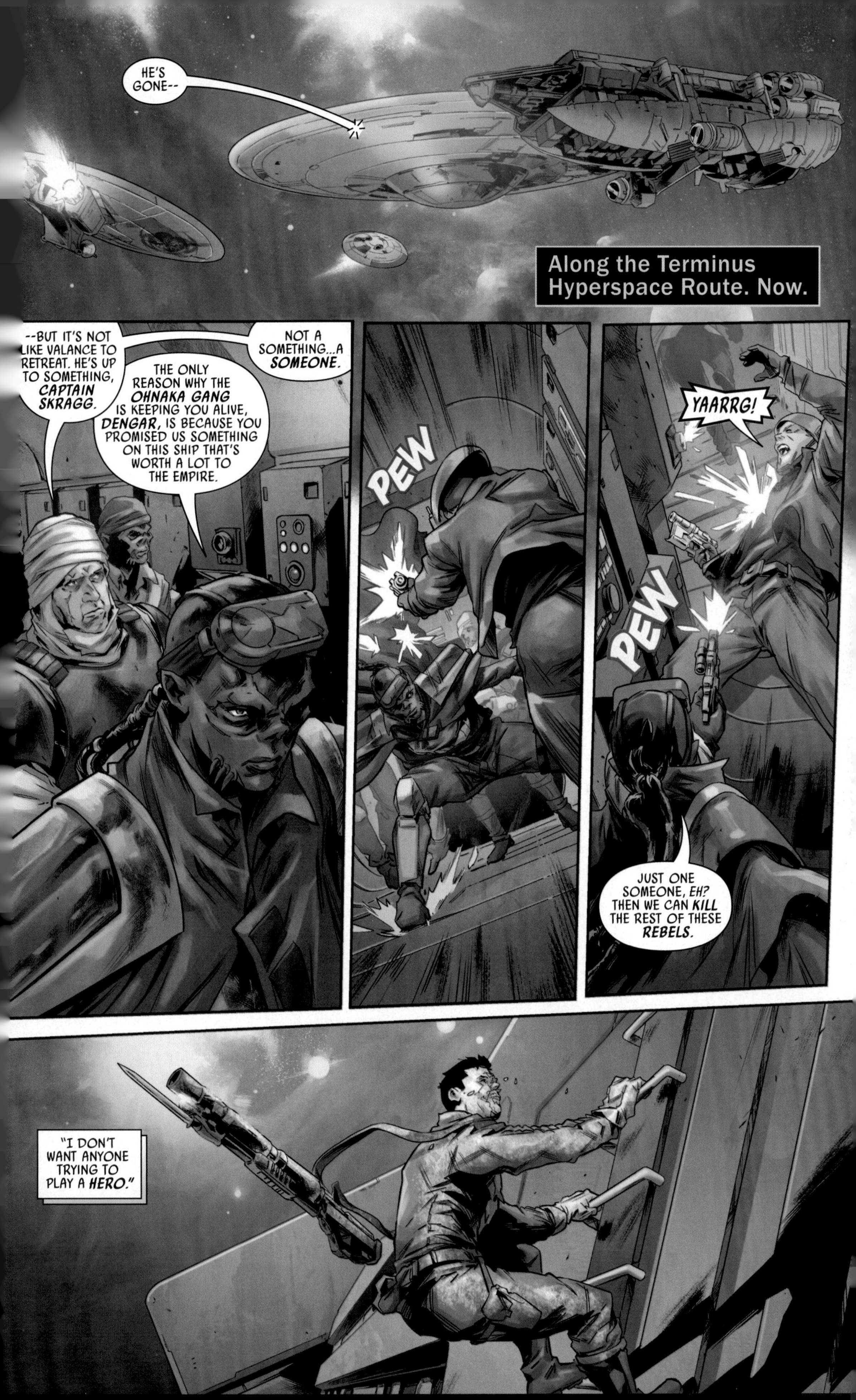
HE'S GONE--
Along the Terminus Hyperspace Route. Now.
--BUT IT'S NOT LIKE VALANCE TO RETREAT. HE'S UP TO SOMETHING, CAPTAIN SKRAGG.
THE ONLY REASON WHY THE OHNAKA GANG IS KEEPING YOU ALIVE, DENGAR, IS BECAUSE YOU PROMISED US SOMETHING ON THIS SHIP THAT'S WORTH A LOT TO THE EMPIRE.
NOT A SOMETHING...A SOMEONE.
PEW
YAARRG!
PEW
JUST ONE SOMEONE, EH? THEN WE CAN KILL THE REST OF THESE REBELS.
"I DON'T WANT ANYONE TRYING TO PLAY A HERO."

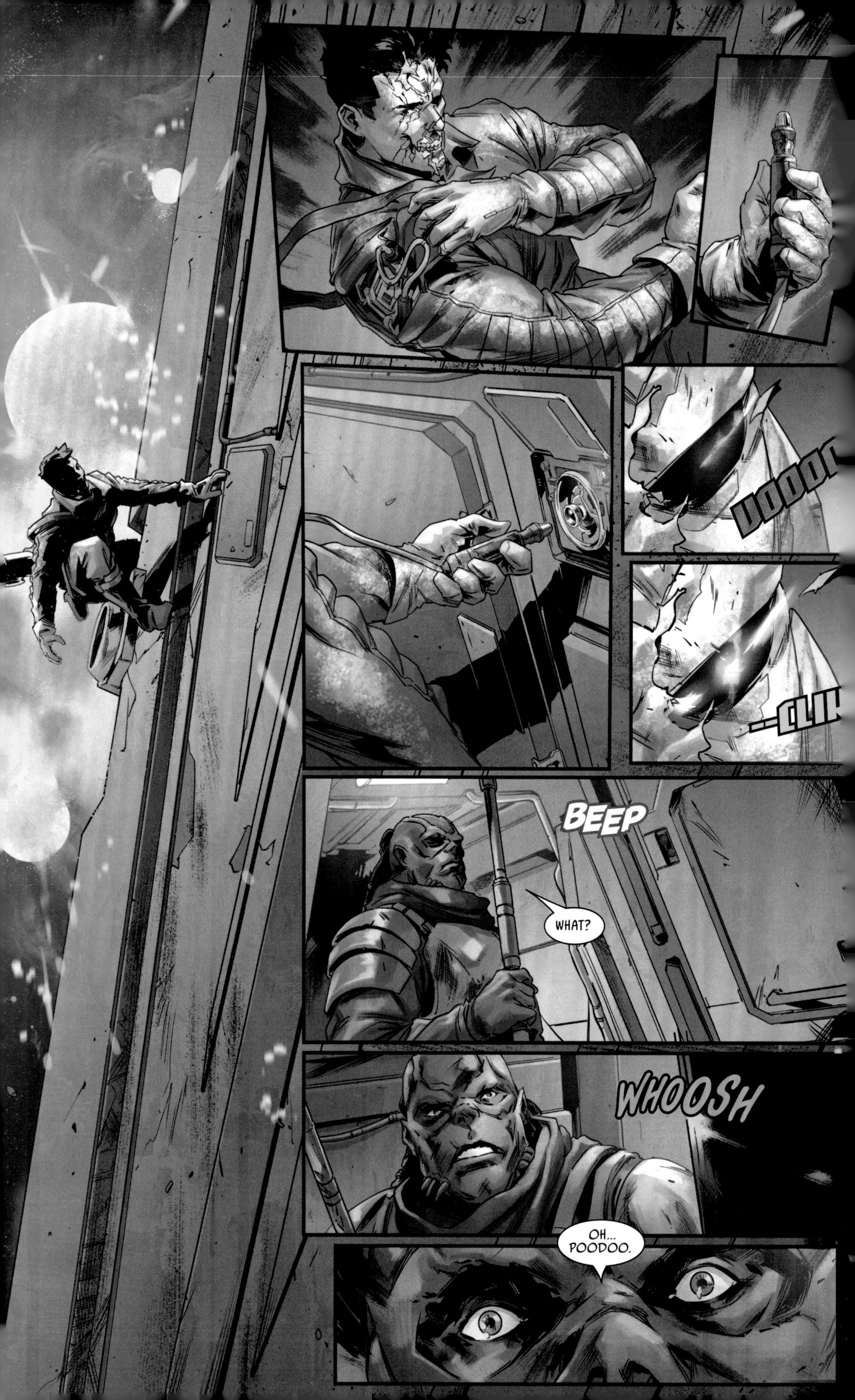
BEEP
WHAT?
WHOOSH
OH... POODOO.

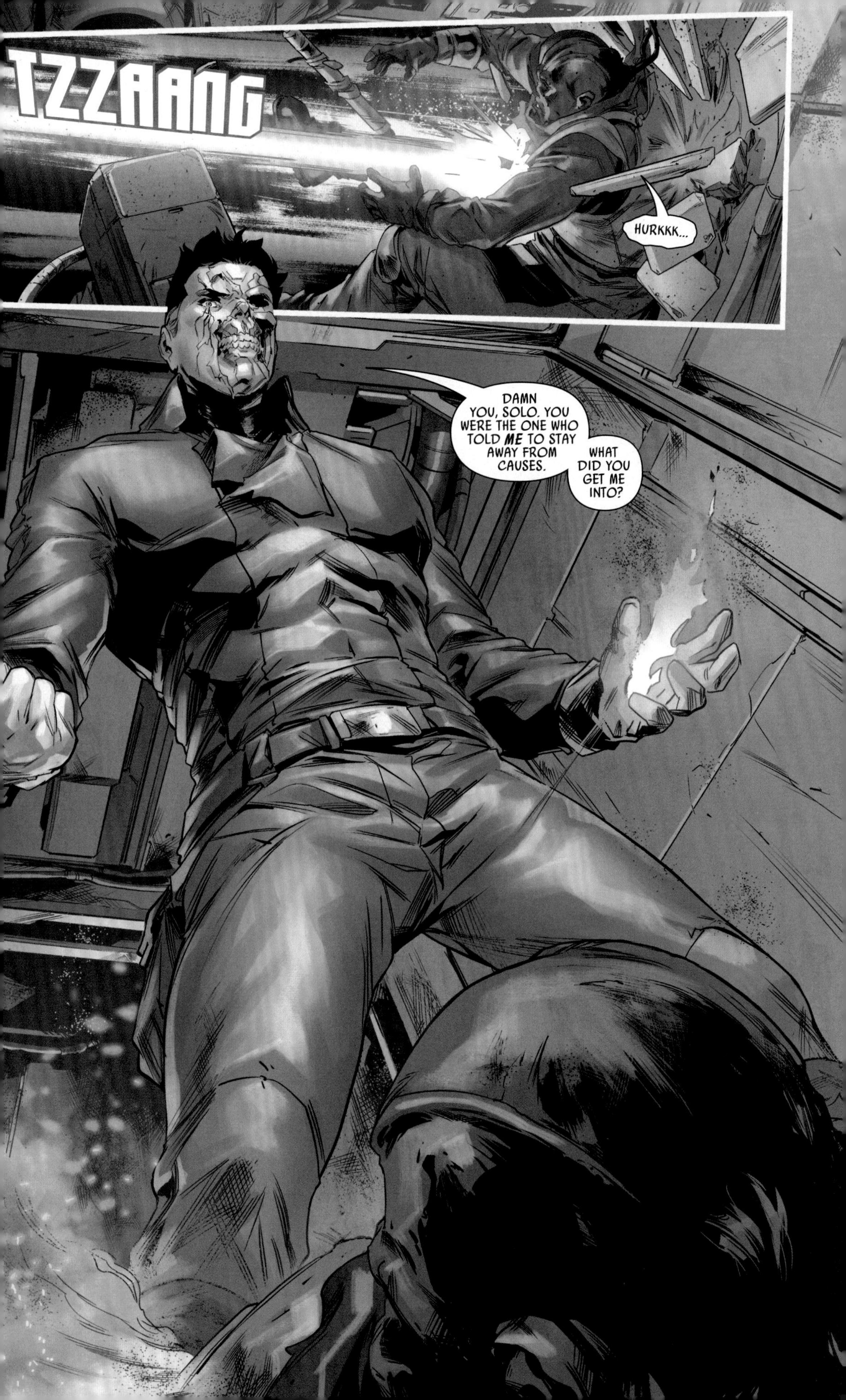
TZZAANG
HURKKK...
DAMN YOU, SOLO. YOU WERE THE ONE WHO TOLD ME TO STAY AWAY FROM CAUSES.
WHAT DID YOU GET ME INTO?

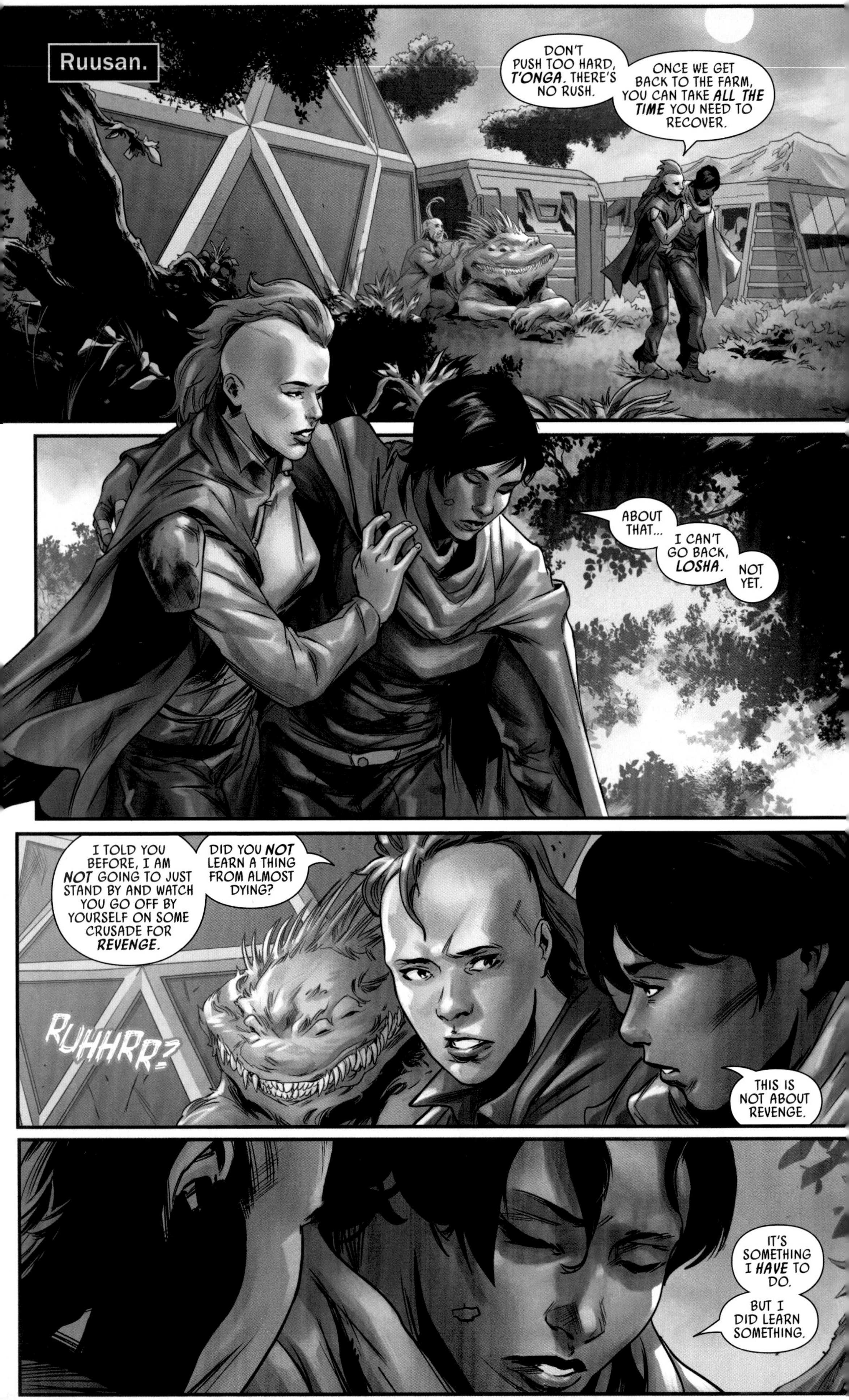
Ruusan.
DON'T PUSH TOO HARD, T'ONGA. THERE'S NO RUSH.
ONCE WE GET BACK TO THE FARM, YOU CAN TAKE ALL THE TIME YOU NEED TO RECOVER.
ABOUT THAT... I CAN'T GO BACK, LOSHA.
NOT YET.
I TOLD YOU BEFORE, I AM NOT GOING TO JUST STAND BY AND WATCH YOU GO OFF BY YOURSELF ON SOME CRUSADE FOR REVENGE.
DID YOU NOT LEARN A THING FROM ALMOST DYING?
RUHHRR?
THIS IS NOT ABOUT REVENGE.
IT'S SOMETHING I HAVE TO DO.
BUT I DID LEARN SOMETHING.

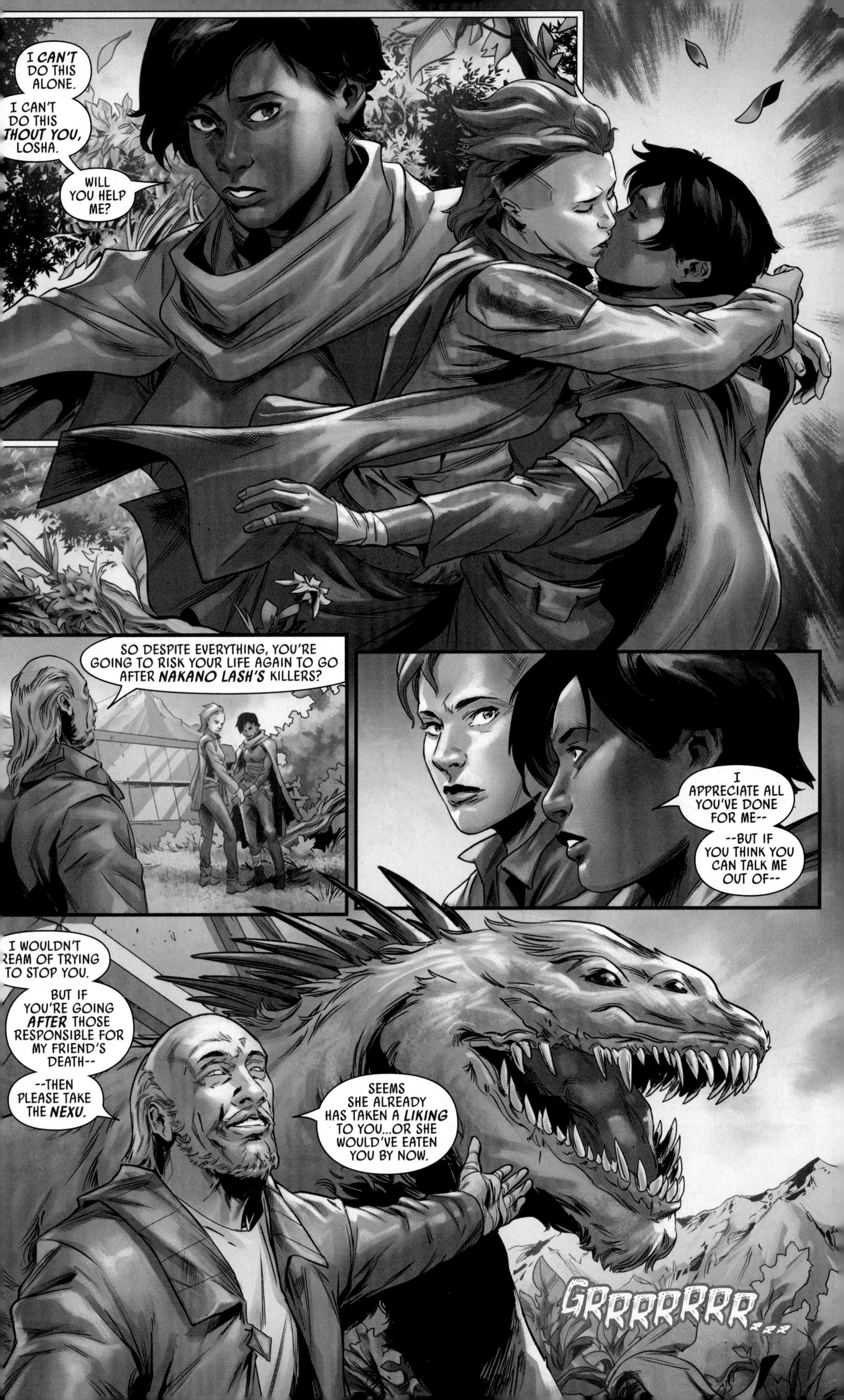
I CAN'T DO THIS ALONE.
I CAN'T DO THIS THOUT YOU, LOSHA.
WILL YOU HELP ME?
SO DESPITE EVERYTHING, YOU'RE GOING TO RISK YOUR LIFE AGAIN TO GO AFTER NAKANO LASH'S KILLERS?
I APPRECIATE ALL YOU'VE DONE FOR ME--
--BUT IF YOU THINK YOU CAN TALK ME OUT OF--
I WOULDN'T REAM OF TRYING TO STOP YOU.
BUT IF YOU'RE GOING AFTER THOSE RESPONSIBLE FOR MY FRIEND'S DEATH--
--THEN PLEASE TAKE THE NEXU.
SEEMS SHE ALREADY HAS TAKEN A LIKING TO YOU...OR SHE WOULD'VE EATEN YOU BY NOW.
GRRRRRRR...

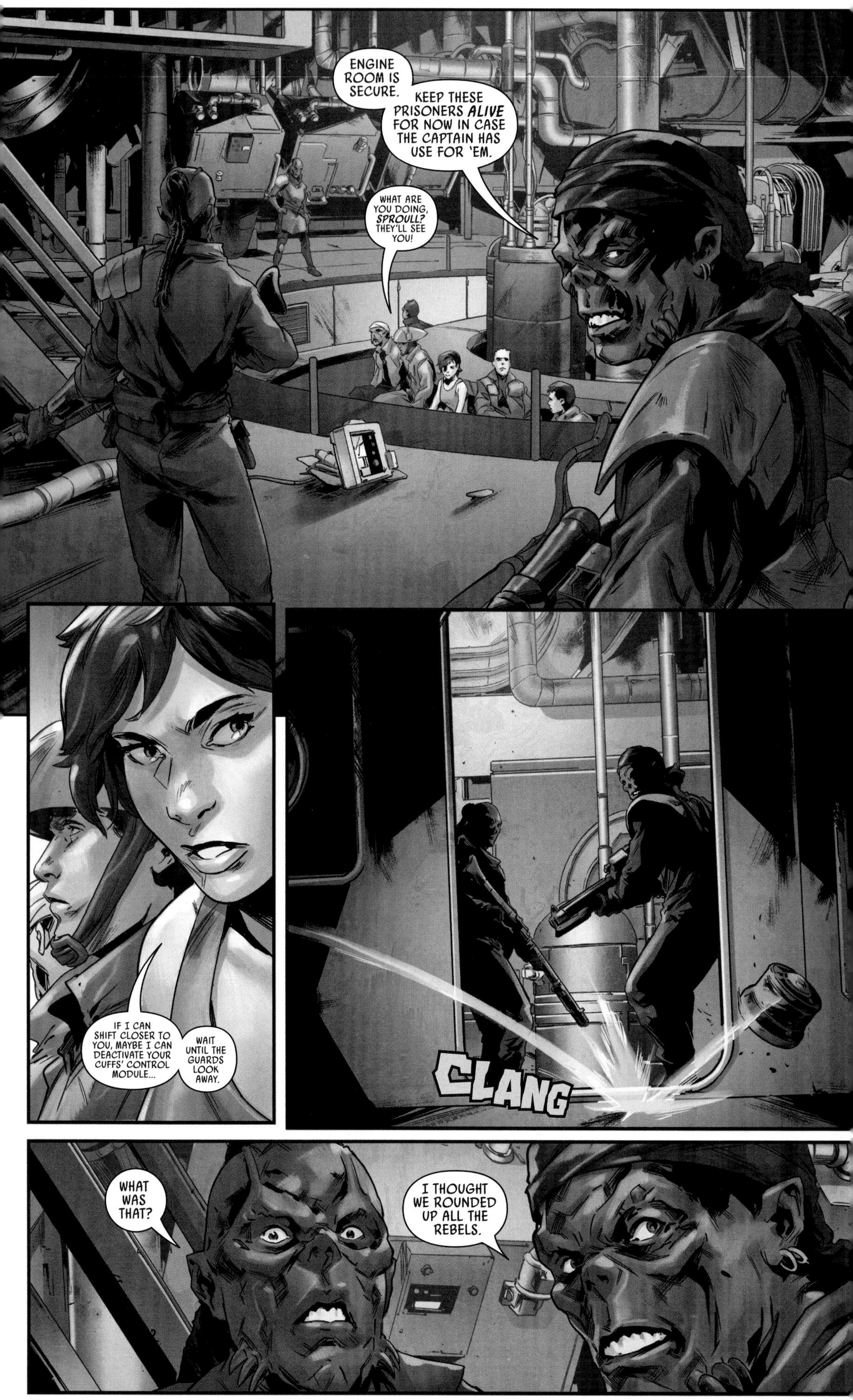
ENGINE ROOM IS SECURE.
KEEP THESE PRISONERS ALIVE FOR NOW IN CASE THE CAPTAIN HAS USE FOR 'EM.
WHAT ARE YOU DOING, SPROULL? THEY'LL SEE YOU!
IF I CAN SHIFT CLOSER TO YOU, MAYBE I CAN DEACTIVATE YOUR CUFFS' CONTROL MODULE...
WAIT UNTIL THE GUARDS LOOK AWAY.
CLANG
WHAT WAS THAT?
I THOUGHT WE ROUNDED UP ALL THE REBELS.

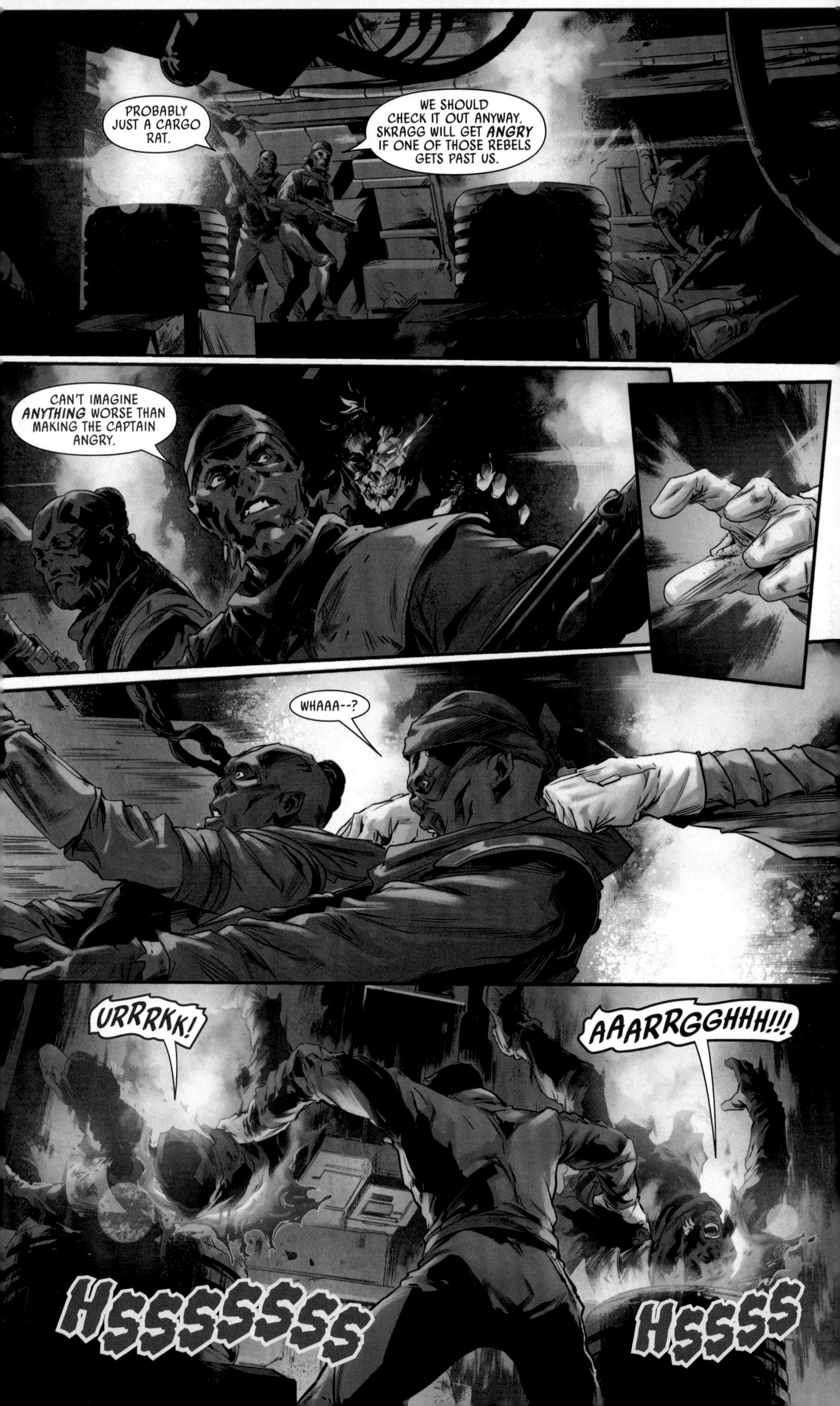
PROBABLY JUST A CARGO RAT.
WE SHOULD CHECK IT OUT ANYWAY. SKRAGG WILL GET ANGRY IF ONE OF THOSE REBELS GETS PAST US.
CAN'T IMAGINE ANYTHING WORSE THAN MAKING THE CAPTAIN ANGRY.
WHAAA--?
URRRKK!
AAARRGGHHH!!!
HSSSSSSS
HSSSS

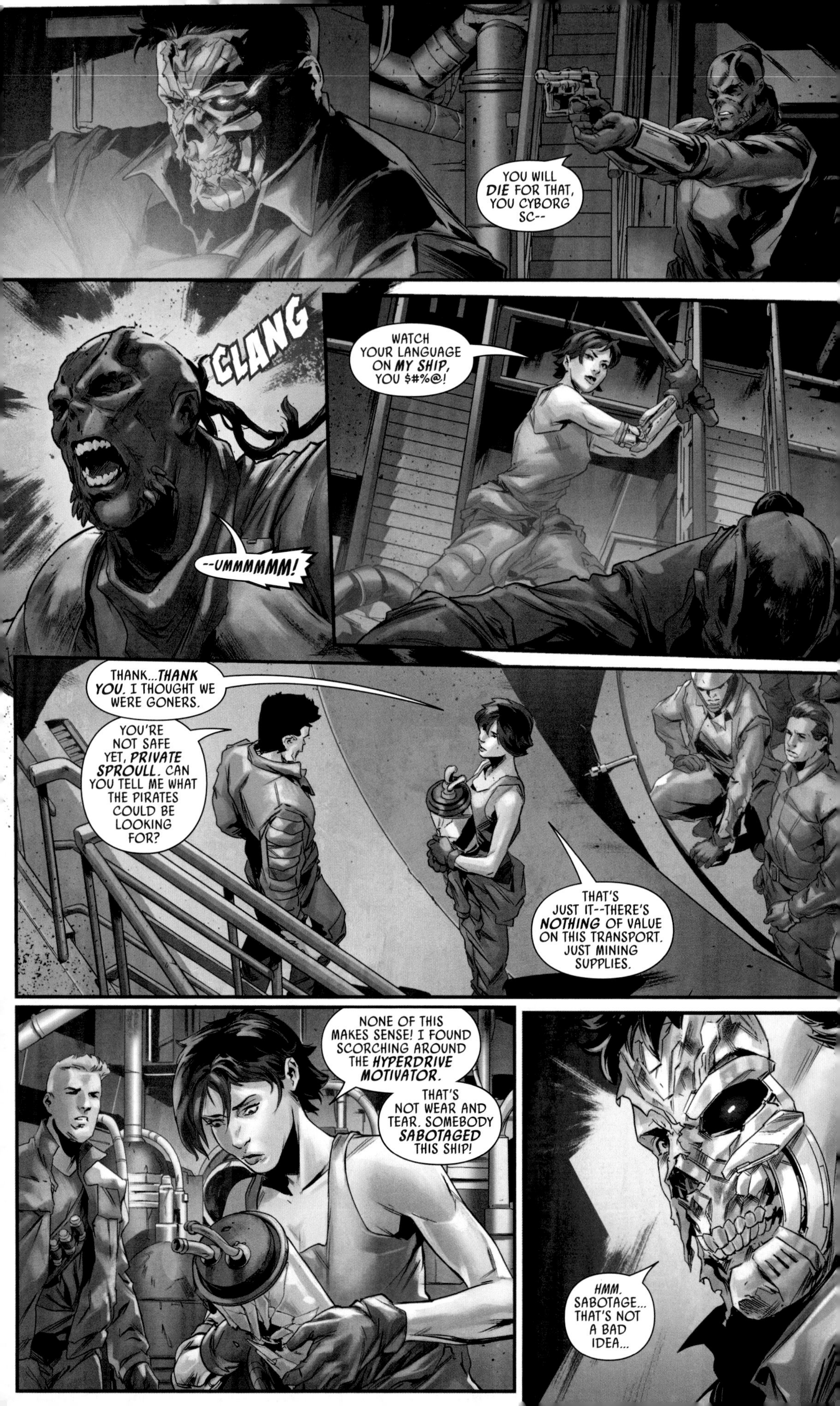
YOU WILL DIE FOR THAT, YOU CYBORG SC--
CLANG
WATCH YOUR LANGUAGE ON MY SHIP, YOU $#%@!
--UMMMMMM!
THANK... THANK YOU. I THOUGHT WE WERE GONERS.
YOU'RE NOT SAFE YET, PRIVATE SPROULL. CAN YOU TELL ME WHAT THE PIRATES COULD BE LOOKING FOR?
THAT'S JUST IT--THERE'S NOTHING OF VALUE ON THIS TRANSPORT. JUST MINING SUPPLIES.
NONE OF THIS MAKES SENSE! I FOUND SCORCHING AROUND THE HYPERDRIVE MOTIVATOR.
THAT'S NOT WEAR AND TEAR. SOMEBODY SABOTAGED THIS SHIP!
HMM. SABOTAGE... THAT'S NOT A BAD IDEA...

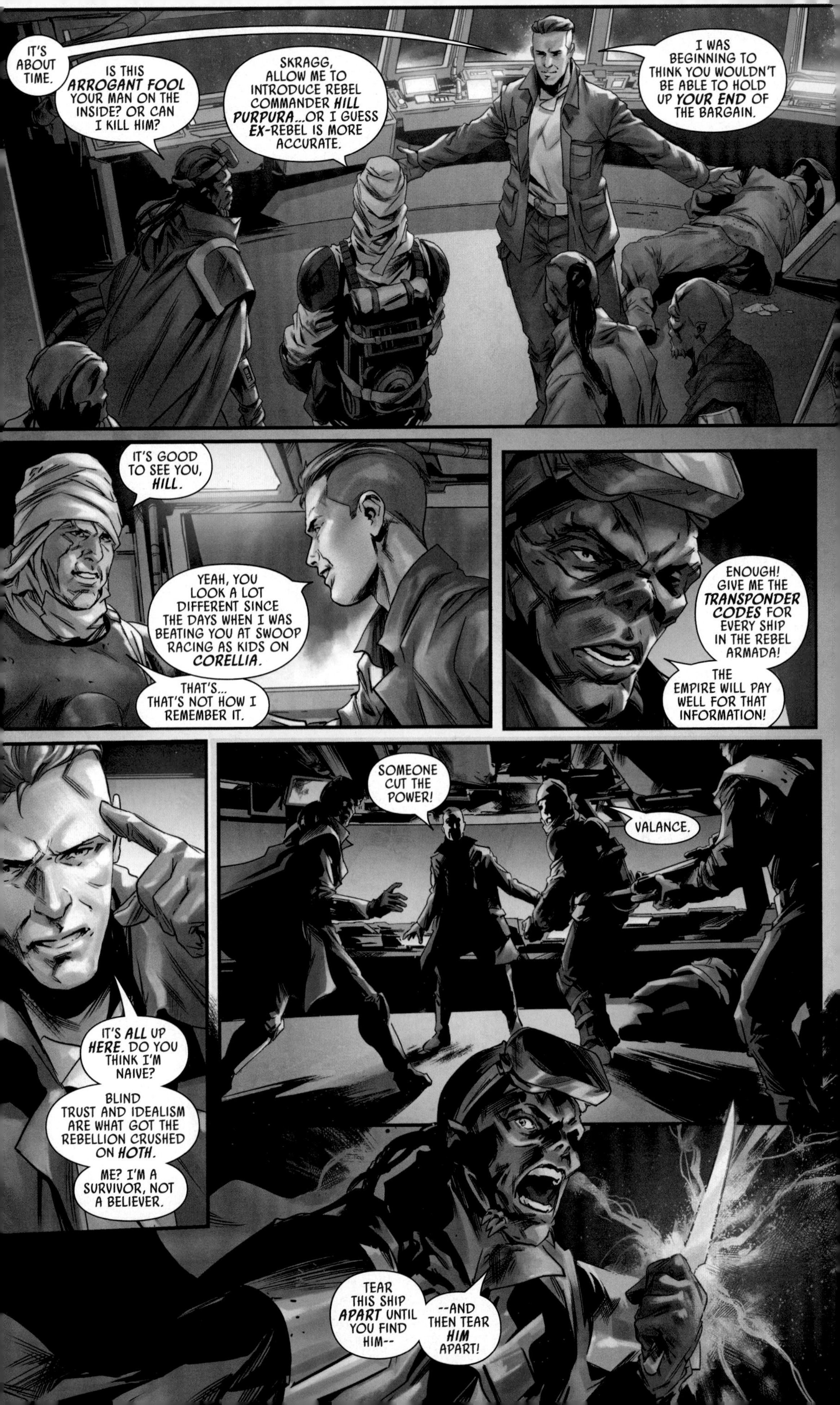
IT'S ABOUT TIME.
IS THIS ARROGANT FOOL YOUR MAN ON THE INSIDE? OR CAN I KILL HIM?
SKRAGG, ALLOW ME TO INTRODUCE REBEL COMMANDER HILL PURPURA...OR I GUESS EX-REBEL IS MORE ACCURATE.
I WAS BEGINNING TO THINK YOU WOULDN'T BE ABLE TO HOLD UP YOUR END OF THE BARGAIN.
IT'S GOOD TO SEE YOU, HILL.
YEAH, YOU LOOK A LOT DIFFERENT SINCE THE DAYS WHEN I WAS BEATING YOU AT SWOOP RACING AS KIDS ON CORELLIA.
THAT'S... THAT'S NOT HOW I REMEMBER IT.
ENOUGH! GIVE ME THE TRANSPONDER CODES FOR EVERY SHIP IN THE REBEL ARMADA!
THE EMPIRE WILL PAY WELL FOR THAT INFORMATION!
IT'S ALL UP HERE. DO YOU THINK I'M NAIVE?
BLIND TRUST AND IDEALISM ARE WHAT GOT THE REBELLION CRUSHED ON HOTH.
ME? I'M A SURVIVOR, NOT A BELIEVER.
SOMEONE CUT THE POWER!
VALANCE.
TEAR THIS SHIP APART UNTIL YOU FIND HIM--
--AND THEN TEAR HIM APART!

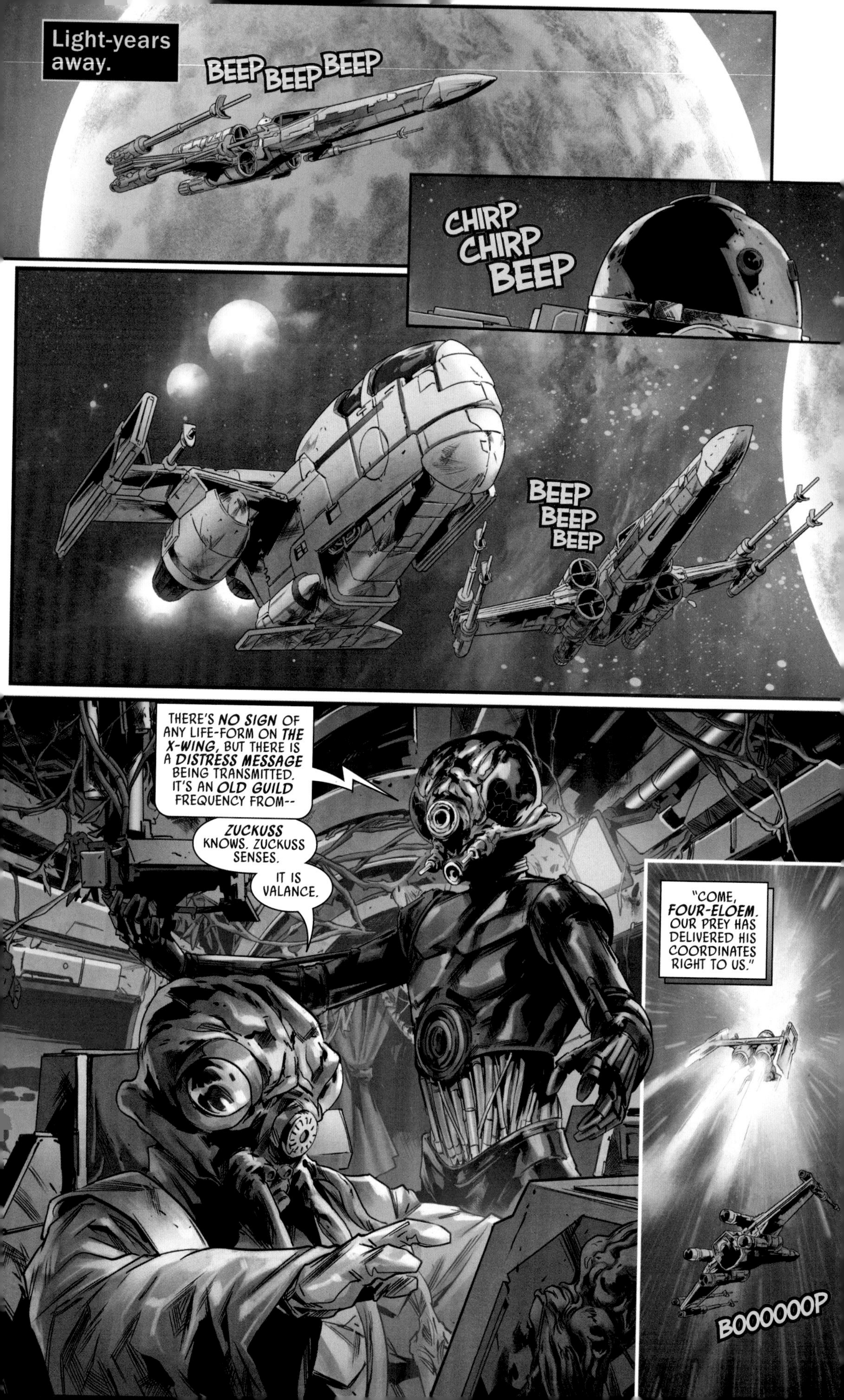
Light-years away.
BEEP BEEP BEEP
CHIRP CHIRP BEEP
BEEP BEEP BEEP
THERE'S NO SIGN OF ANY LIFE-FORM ON THE X-WING, BUT THERE IS A DISTRESS MESSAGE BEING TRANSMITTED. IT'S AN OLD GUILD FREQUENCY FROM--
ZUCKUSS KNOWS. ZUCKUSS SENSES.
IT IS VALANCE.
"COME, FOUR-ELOEM. OUR PREY HAS DELIVERED HIS COORDINATES RIGHT TO US."
BOOOOOOP

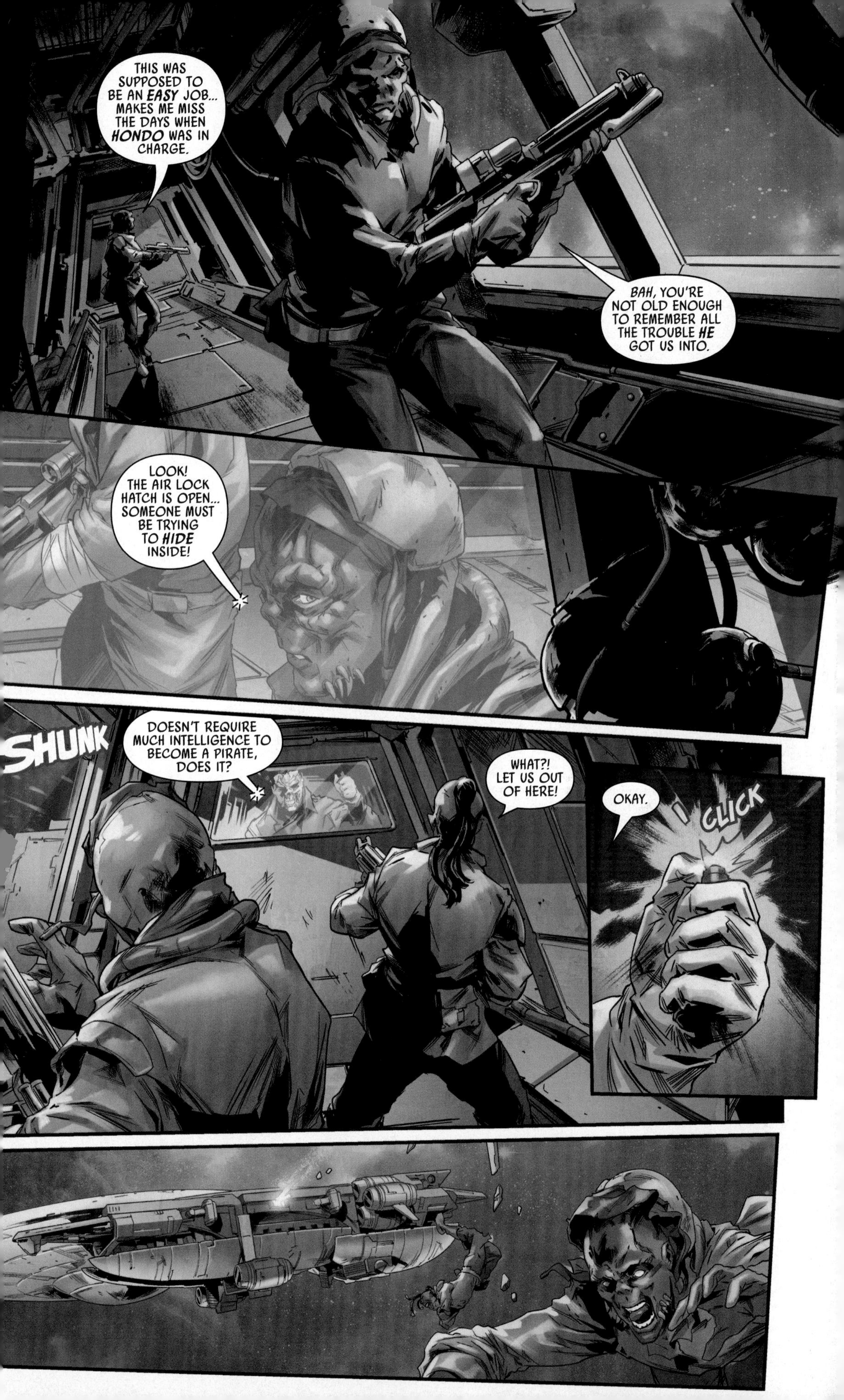

THIS WAS SUPPOSED TO BE AN EASY JOB... MAKES ME MISS THE DAYS WHEN HONDO WAS IN CHARGE.
BAH, YOU'RE NOT OLD ENOUGH TO REMEMBER ALL THE TROUBLE HE GOT US INTO.
LOOK! THE AIR LOCK HATCH IS OPEN... SOMEONE MUST BE TRYING TO HIDE INSIDE!
SHUNK
DOESN'T REQUIRE MUCH INTELLIGENCE TO BECOME A PIRATE, DOES IT?
WHAT?! LET US OUT OF HERE!
OKAY.
CLICK

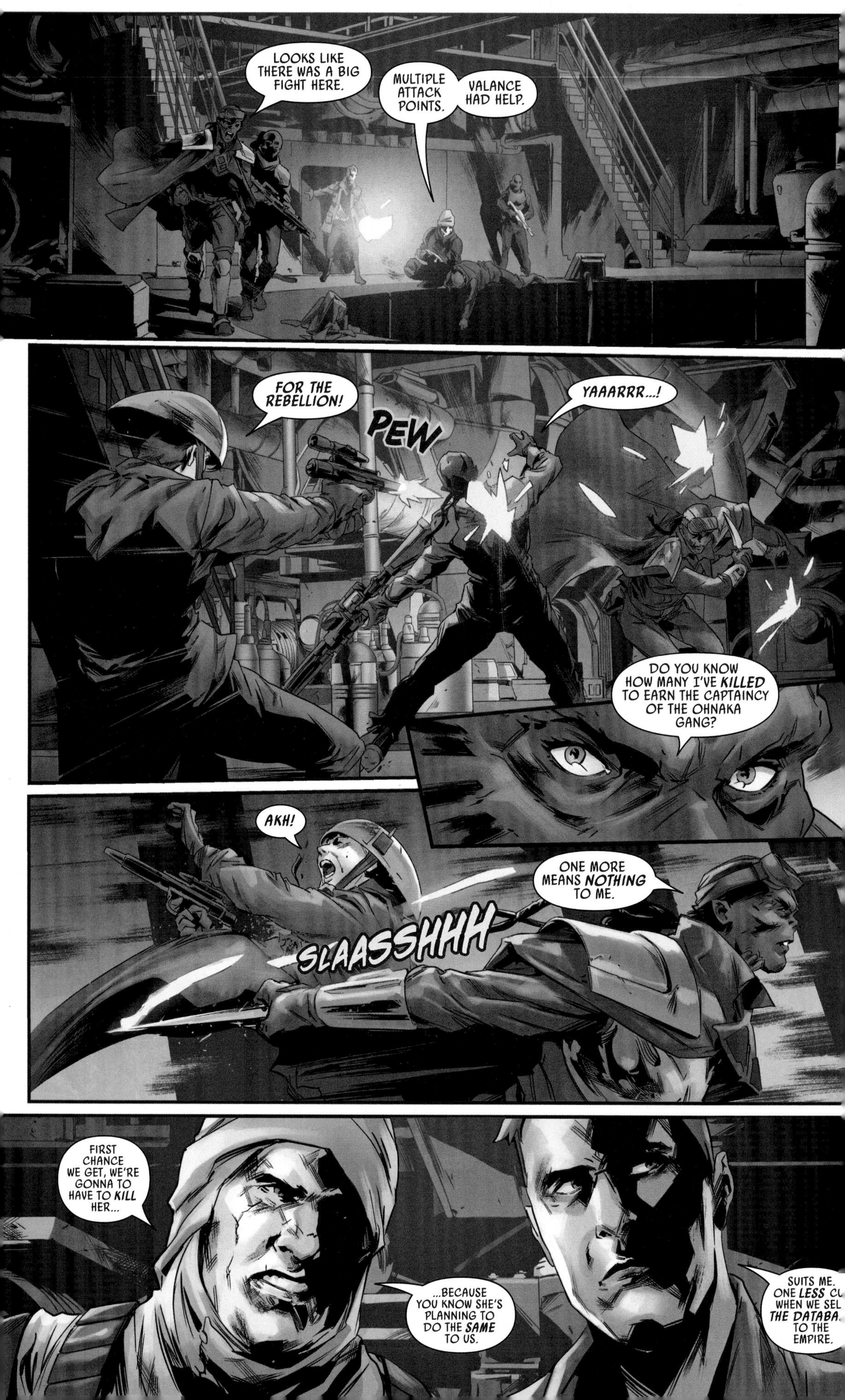
LOOKS LIKE THERE WAS A BIG FIGHT HERE.
MULTIPLE ATTACK POINTS.
VALANCE HAD HELP.
FOR THE REBELLION!
PEW
YAAARRR...!
DO YOU KNOW HOW MANY I'VE KILLED TO EARN THE CAPTAINCY OF THE OHNAKA GANG?
AKH!
ONE MORE MEANS NOTHING TO ME.
SLAASSHHH
FIRST CHANCE WE GET, WE'RE GONNA TO HAVE TO KILL HER...
...BECAUSE YOU KNOW SHE'S PLANNING TO DO THE SAME TO US.
SUITS ME. ONE LESS
WHEN WE SE
TO THE EMPIRE.

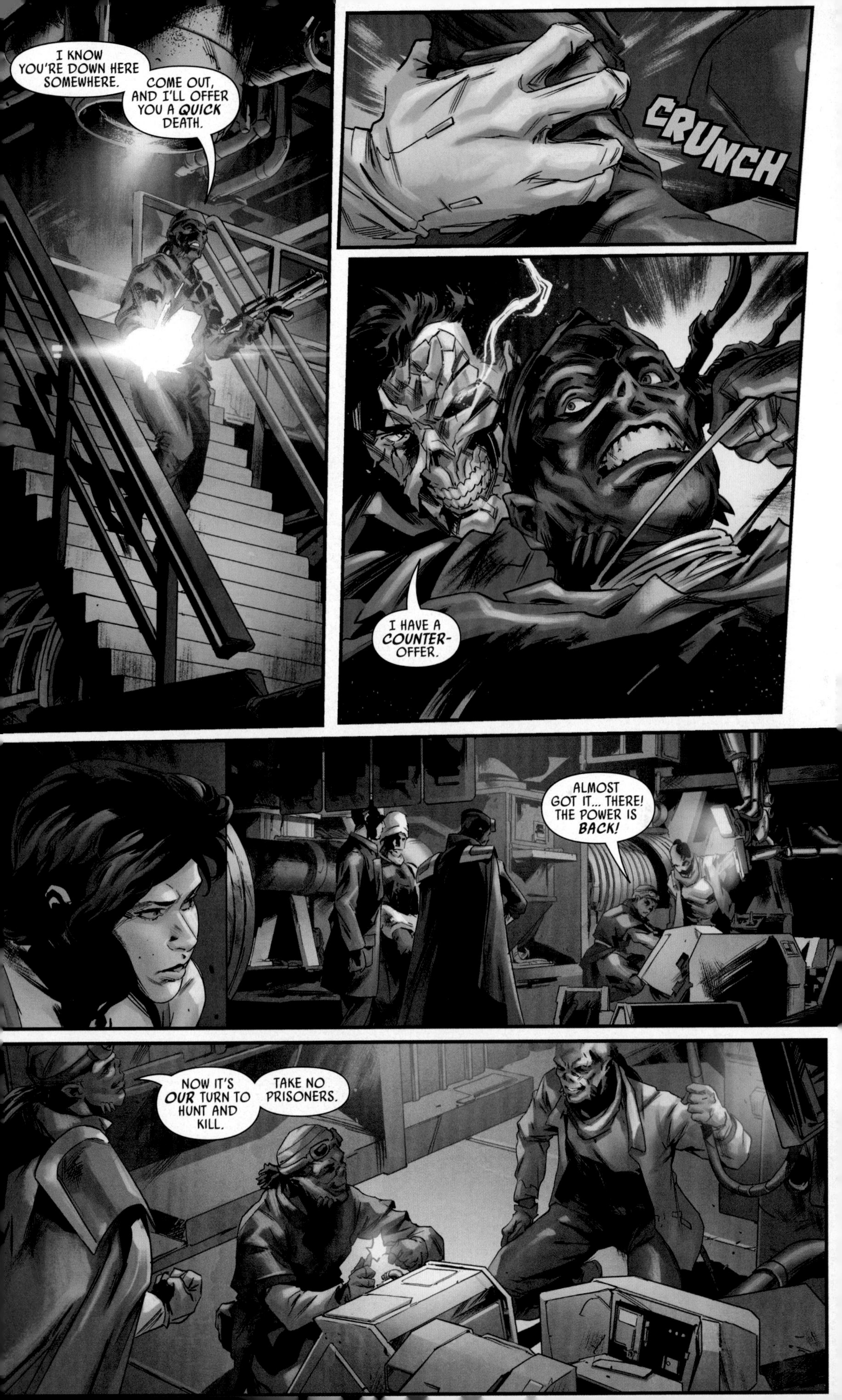
I KNOW YOU'RE DOWN HERE SOMEWHERE.
COME OUT, AND I'LL OFFER YOU A QUICK DEATH.
CRUNCH
I HAVE A COUNTER-OFFER.
ALMOST GOT IT... THERE! THE POWER IS BACK!
NOW IT'S OUR TURN TO HUNT AND KILL.
TAKE NO PRISONERS.

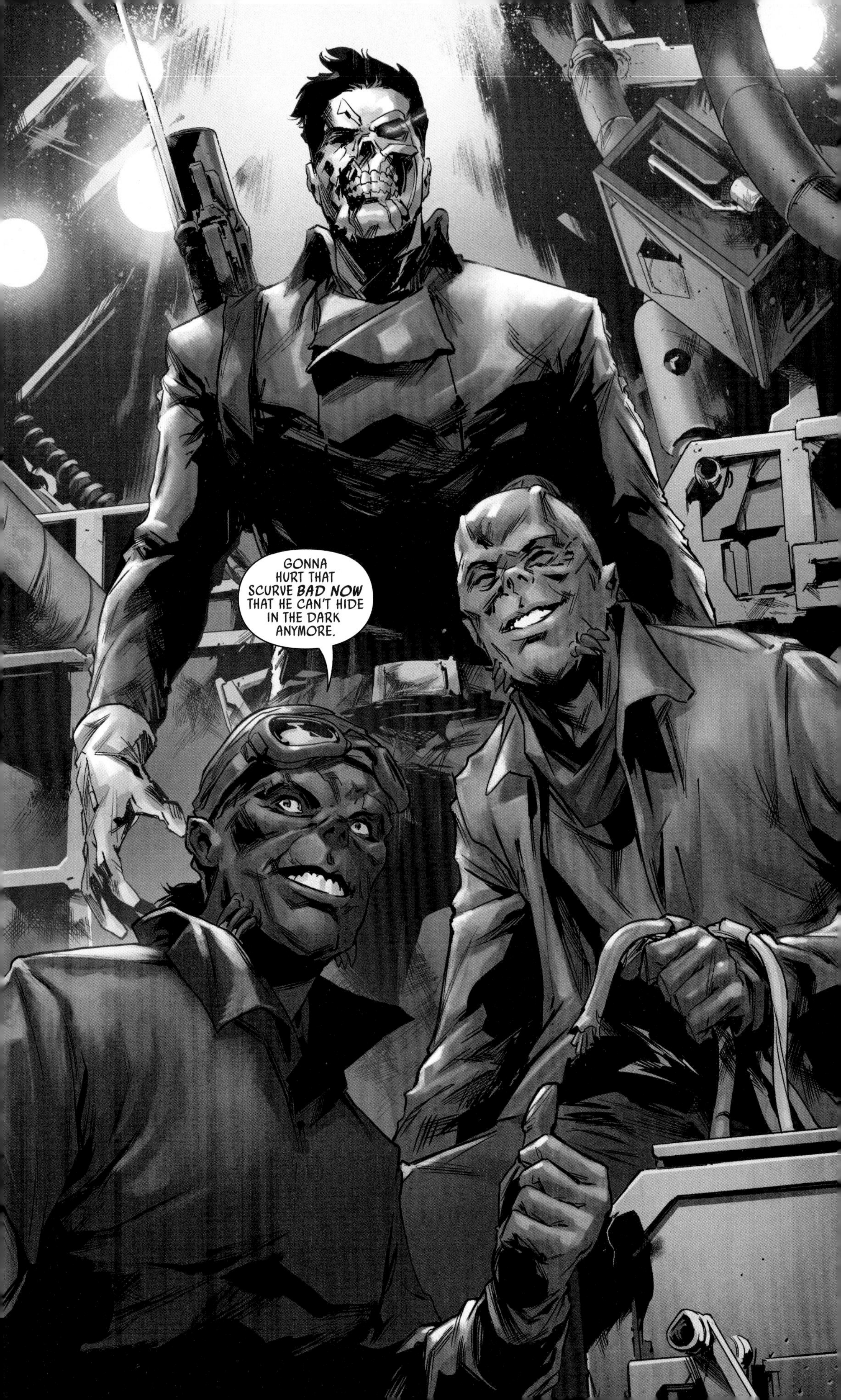
GONNA HURT THAT SCURVE BAD NOW THAT HE CAN'T HIDE IN THE DARK ANYMORE.

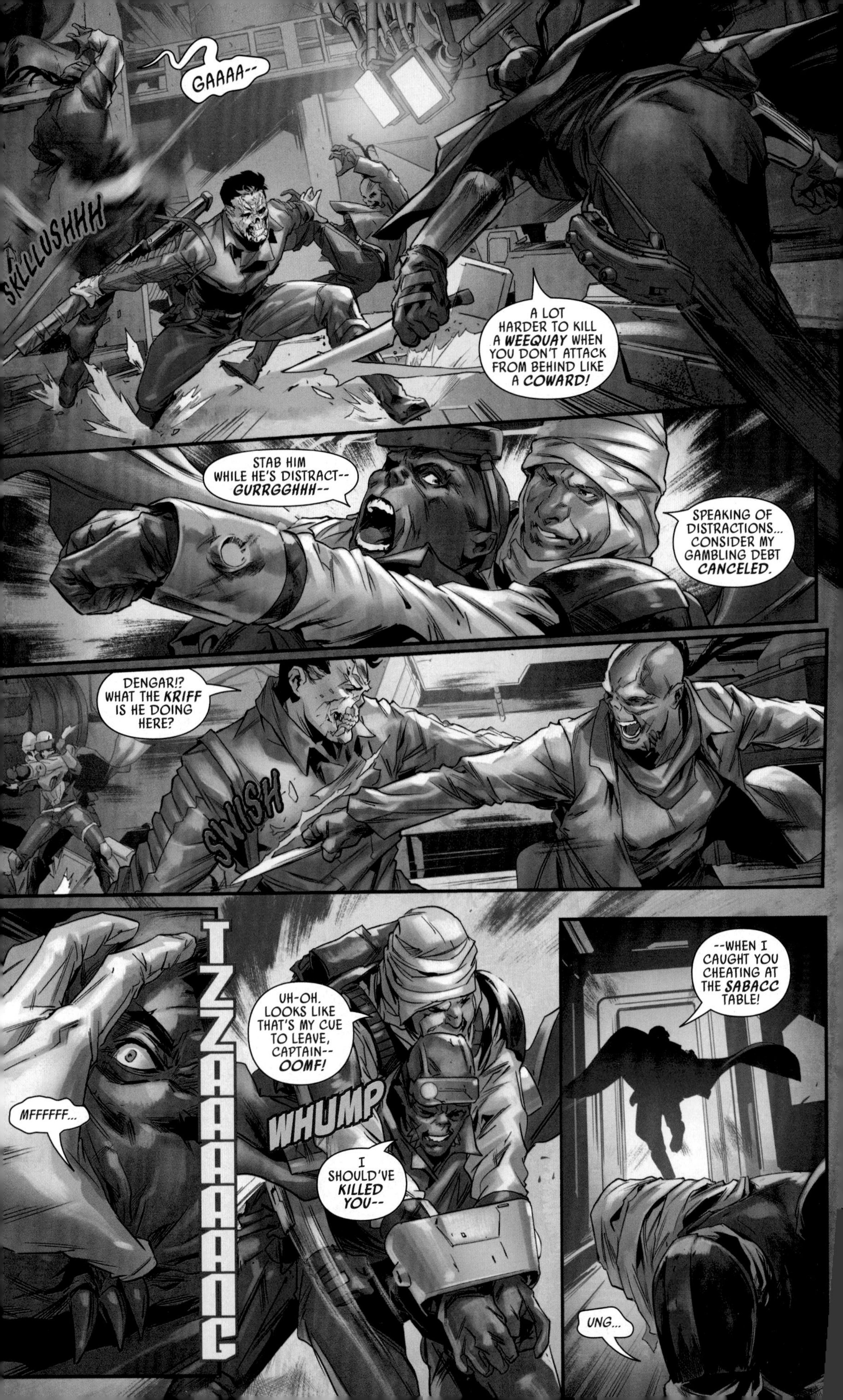
GAAAA--
SKLLLUSHHH
A LOT HARDER TO KILL A WEEQUAY WHEN YOU DON'T ATTACK FROM BEHIND LIKE A COWARD!
STAB HIM WHILE HE'S DISTRACT-- GURRGGHHH--
SPEAKING OF DISTRACTIONS... CONSIDER MY GAMBLING DEBT CANCELED.
DENGAR!? WHAT THE KRIFF IS HE DOING HERE?
SWISH
TZZAAAAAANG
MFFFFFF...
UH-OH. LOOKS LIKE THAT'S MY CUE TO LEAVE, CAPTAIN-- OOMF!
WHUMP
I SHOULD'VE KILLED YOU--
--WHEN I CAUGHT YOU CHEATING AT THE SABACC TABLE!
UNG...

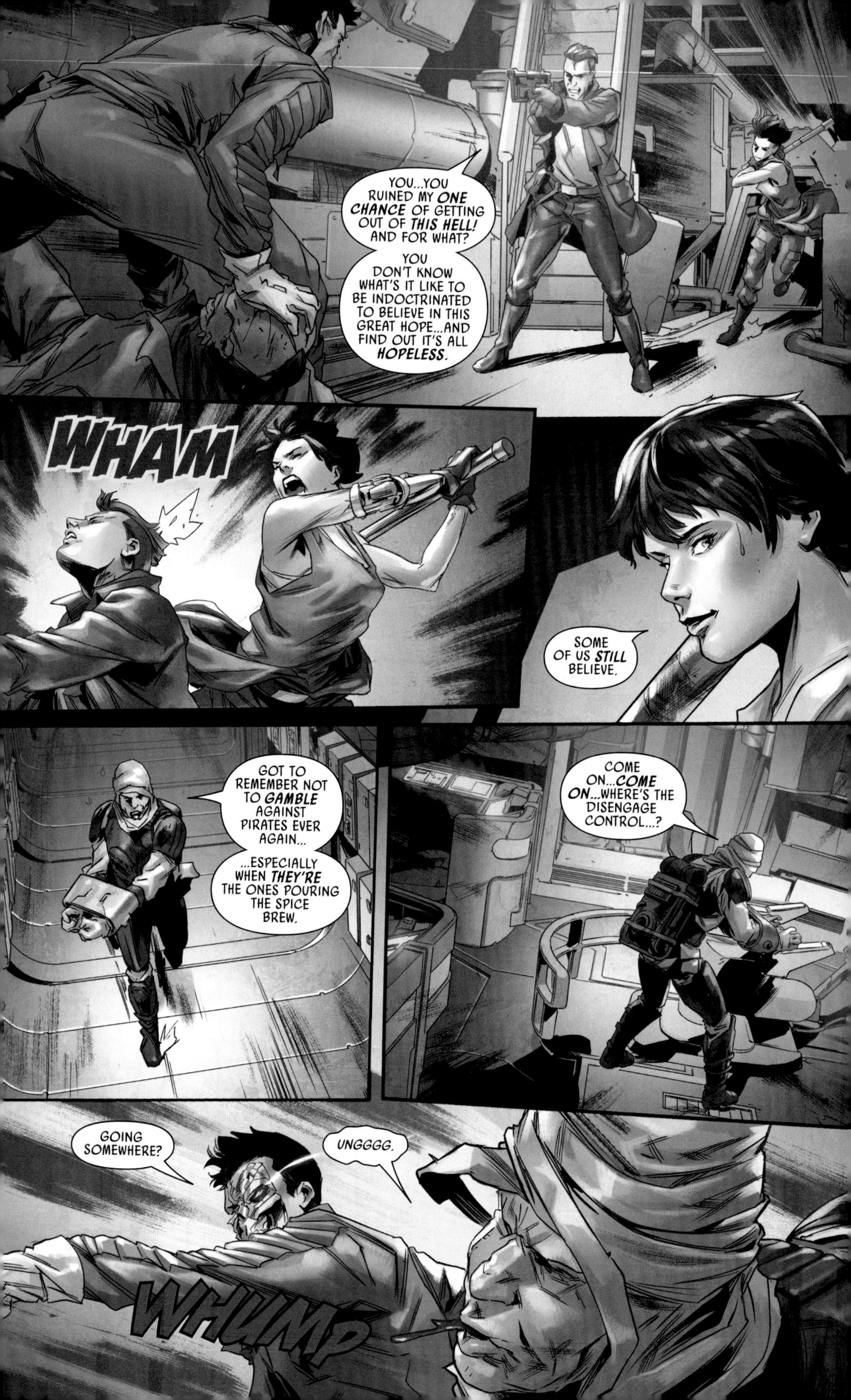
YOU...YOU RUINED MY ONE CHANCE OF GETTING OUT OF THIS HELL! AND FOR WHAT?
YOU DON'T KNOW WHAT'S IT LIKE TO BE INDOCTRINATED TO BELIEVE IN THIS GREAT HOPE...AND FIND OUT IT'S ALL HOPELESS.
WHAM
SOME OF US STILL BELIEVE.
GOT TO REMEMBER NOT TO GAMBLE AGAINST PIRATES EVER AGAIN...
...ESPECIALLY WHEN THEY'RE THE ONES POURING THE SPICE BREW.
COME ON...COME ON...WHERE'S THE DISENGAGE CONTROL...?
GOING SOMEWHERE?
UNGGGG.
WHUMP

SEE YOU 'LL HOLD 'RUDGES.

WELL, YOU UNGRATEFUL NERF HERDER, I *SAVED* YOUR LIFE BACK THERE!

OOF!

WHAM

I GUESS I *DO* HOLD GRUDGES--

--LIKE WHEN A HUNTER ON MY CREW SOLD ME OUT TO *DARTH VADER.*

IF I WEREN'T CUFFED...

JUST MY LUCK. FIRST I LOSE OUT ON THE *HAN SOLO* BOUNTY TO THAT DAMN *BOBA FETT*--WHO'S PROBABLY ALREADY GOT THE CARBONITE TO *JABBA* BY NOW...

...THEN I RUN INTO THE *ONE* PIRATE I OWED MONEY...

...THEN *YOU--*

WHAT... WHAT DID YOU SAY?!?

YOU MEAN THE PART ABOUT THE PIRATE?

CRACK

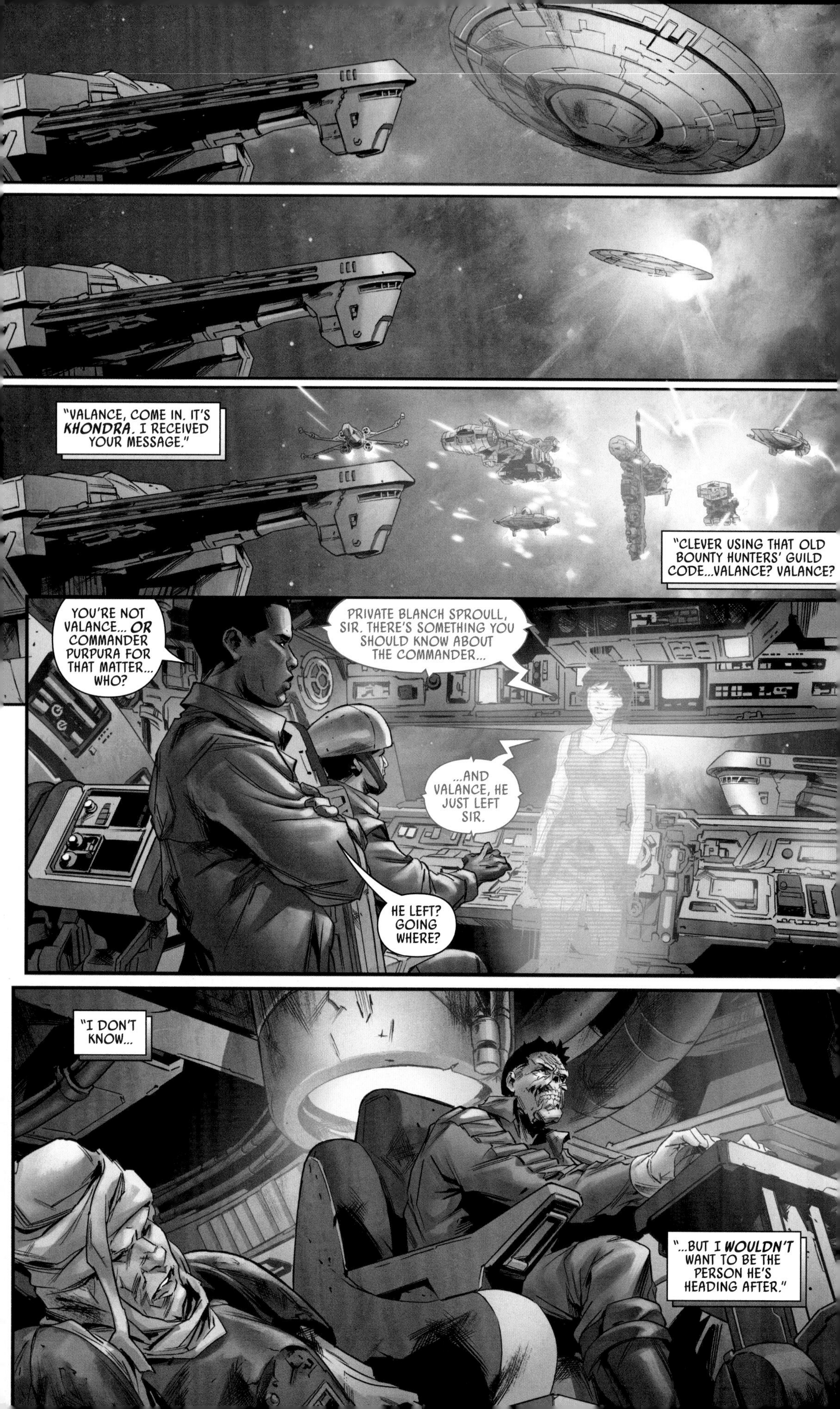
"VALANCE, COME IN. IT'S KHONDRA. I RECEIVED YOUR MESSAGE."
"CLEVER USING THAT OLD BOUNTY HUNTERS' GUILD CODE...VALANCE? VALANCE?
YOU'RE NOT VALANCE... OR COMMANDER PURPURA FOR THAT MATTER... WHO?
PRIVATE BLANCH SPROULL, SIR. THERE'S SOMETHING YOU SHOULD KNOW ABOUT THE COMMANDER...
...AND VALANCE, HE JUST LEFT SIR.
HE LEFT? GOING WHERE?
"I DON'T KNOW...
"...BUT I WOULDN'T WANT TO BE THE PERSON HE'S HEADING AFTER."

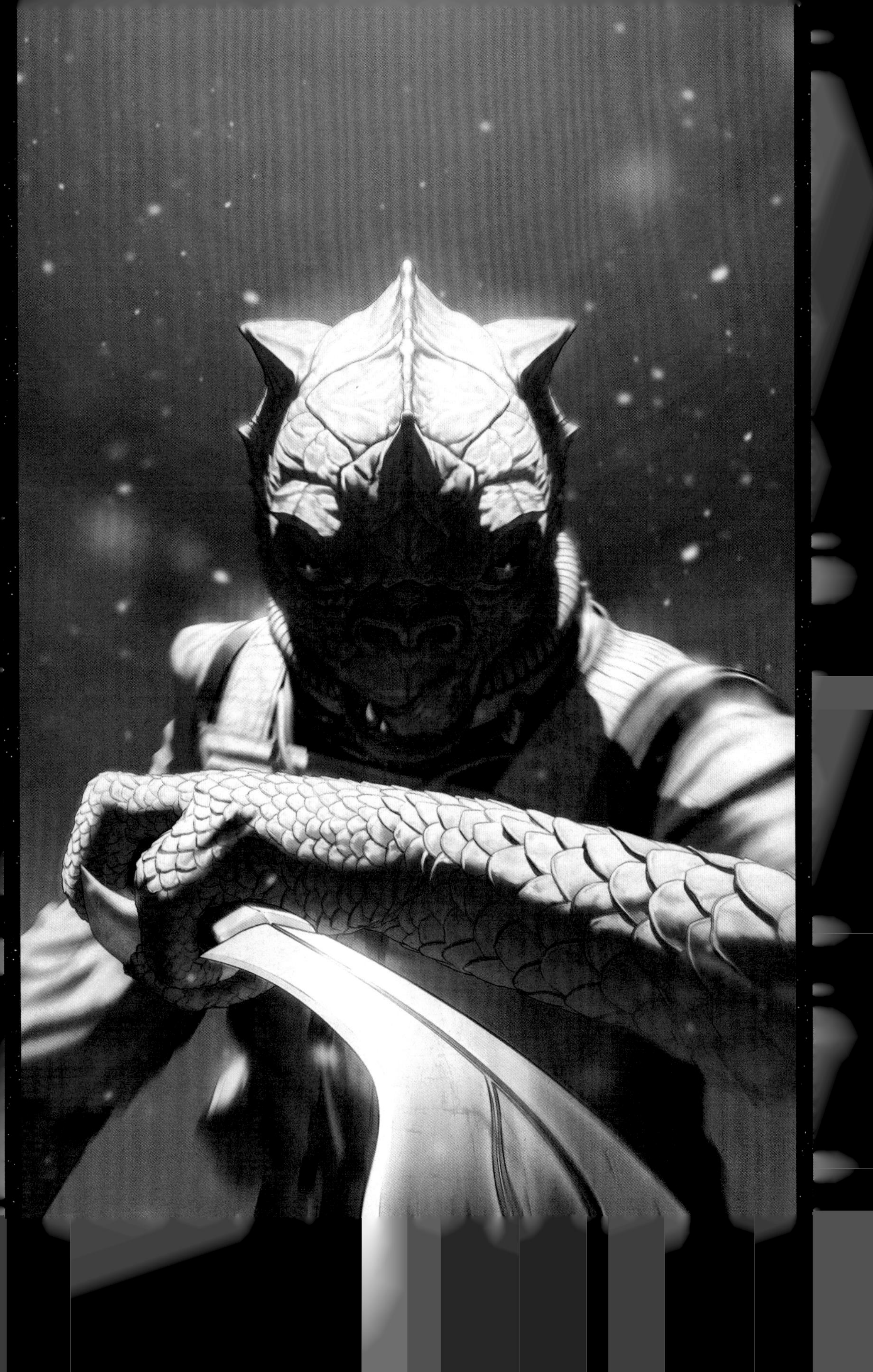

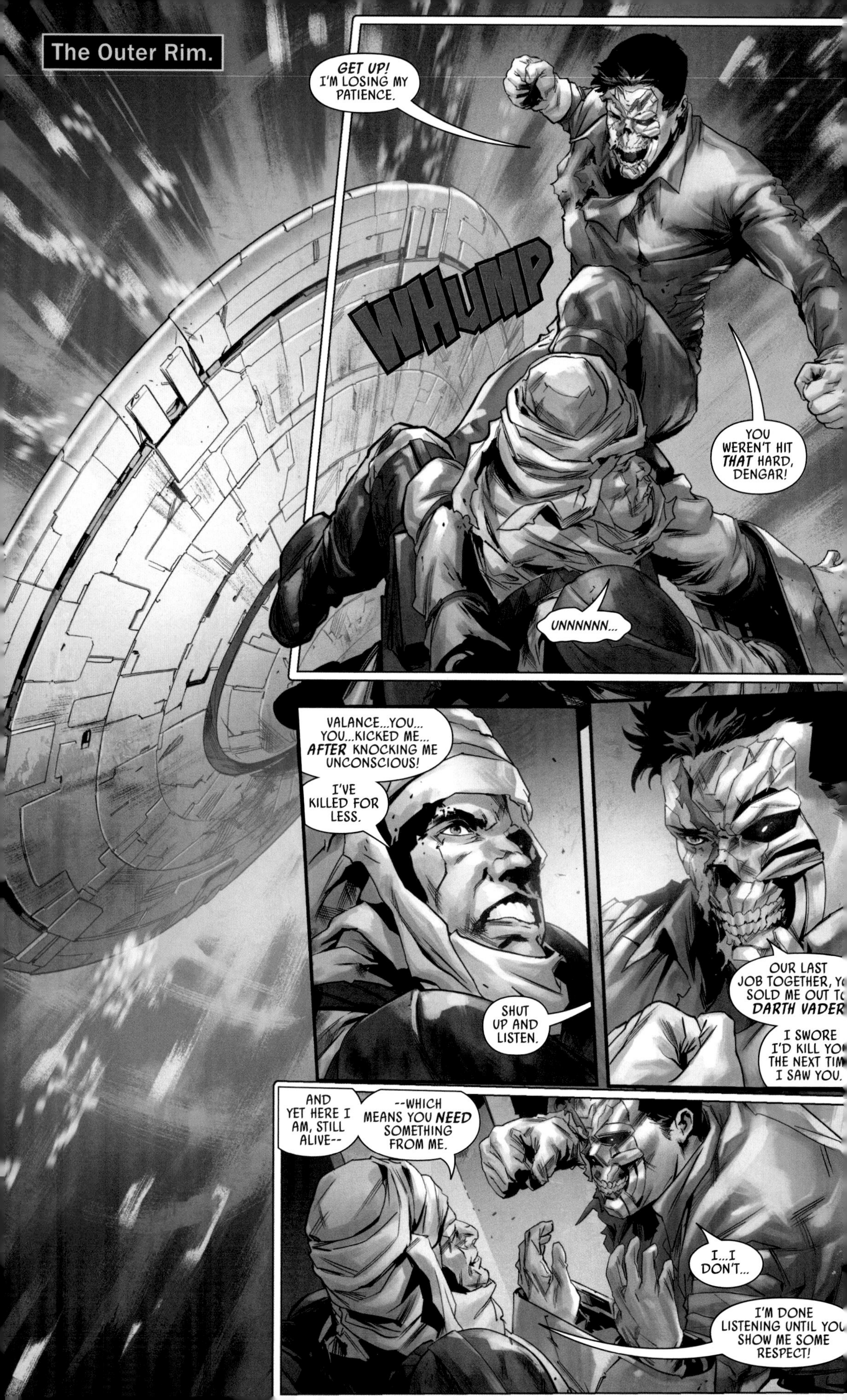
The Outer Rim.
GET UP! I'M LOSING MY PATIENCE.
WHUMP
YOU WEREN'T HIT THAT HARD, DENGAR!
UNNNNNN...
VALANCE...YOU... YOU...KICKED ME... AFTER KNOCKING ME UNCONSCIOUS!
I'VE KILLED FOR LESS.
OUR LAST JOB TOGETHER, YO SOLD ME OUT TO DARTH VADER
I SWORE I'D KILL YO THE NEXT TIM I SAW YOU.
SHUT UP AND LISTEN.
AND YET HERE I AM, STILL ALIVE--
--WHICH MEANS YOU NEED SOMETHING FROM ME.
I...I DON'T...
I'M DONE LISTENING UNTIL YOU SHOW ME SOME RESPECT!

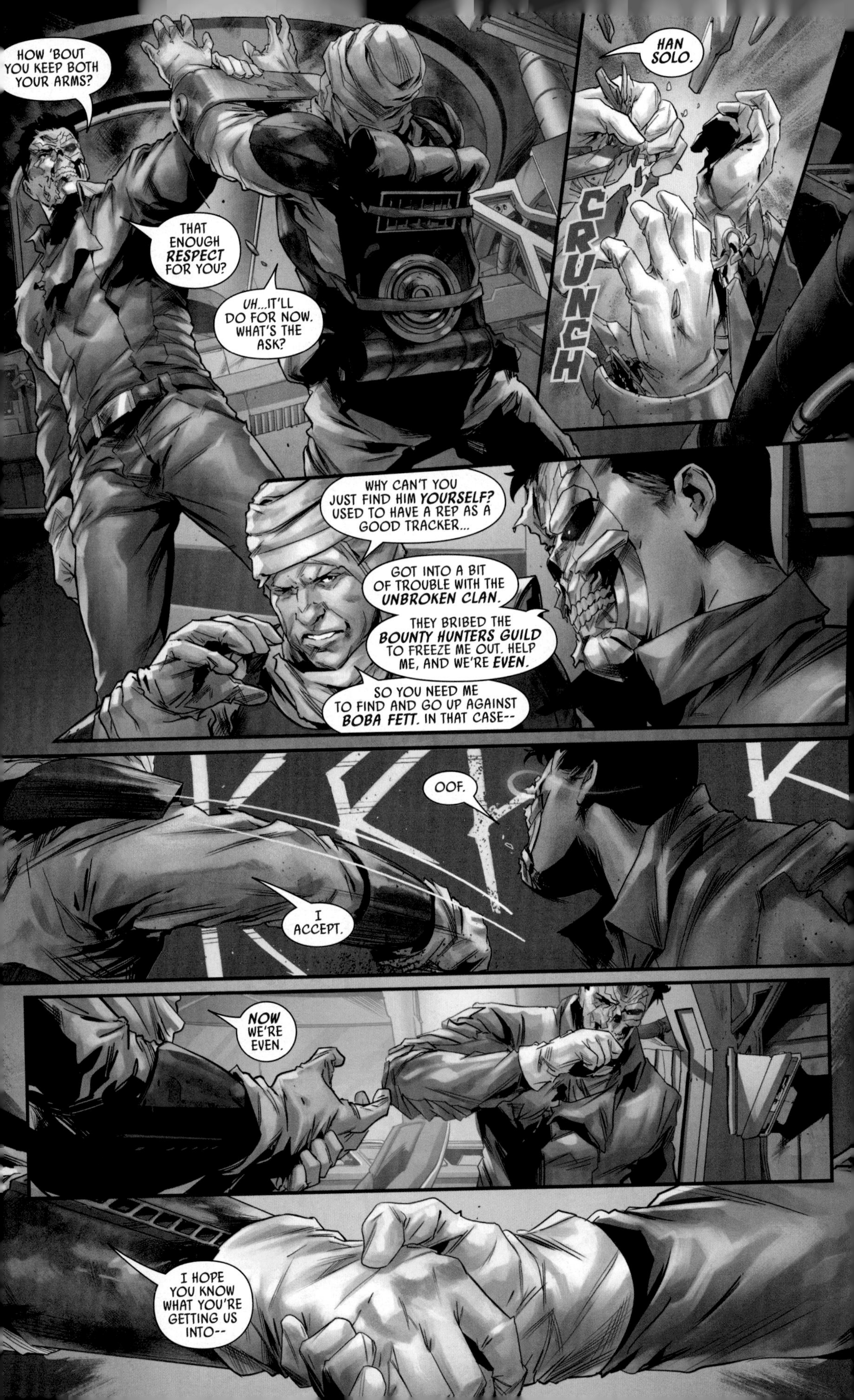
HOW 'BOUT YOU KEEP BOTH YOUR ARMS?
HAN SOLO.
CRUNCH
THAT ENOUGH RESPECT FOR YOU?
UH...IT'LL DO FOR NOW. WHAT'S THE ASK?
WHY CAN'T YOU JUST FIND HIM YOURSELF? USED TO HAVE A REP AS A GOOD TRACKER...
GOT INTO A BIT OF TROUBLE WITH THE UNBROKEN CLAN.
THEY BRIBED THE BOUNTY HUNTERS GUILD TO FREEZE ME OUT. HELP ME, AND WE'RE EVEN.
SO YOU NEED ME TO FIND AND GO UP AGAINST BOBA FETT. IN THAT CASE--
OOF.
I ACCEPT.
NOW WE'RE EVEN.
I HOPE YOU KNOW WHAT YOU'RE GETTING US INTO--

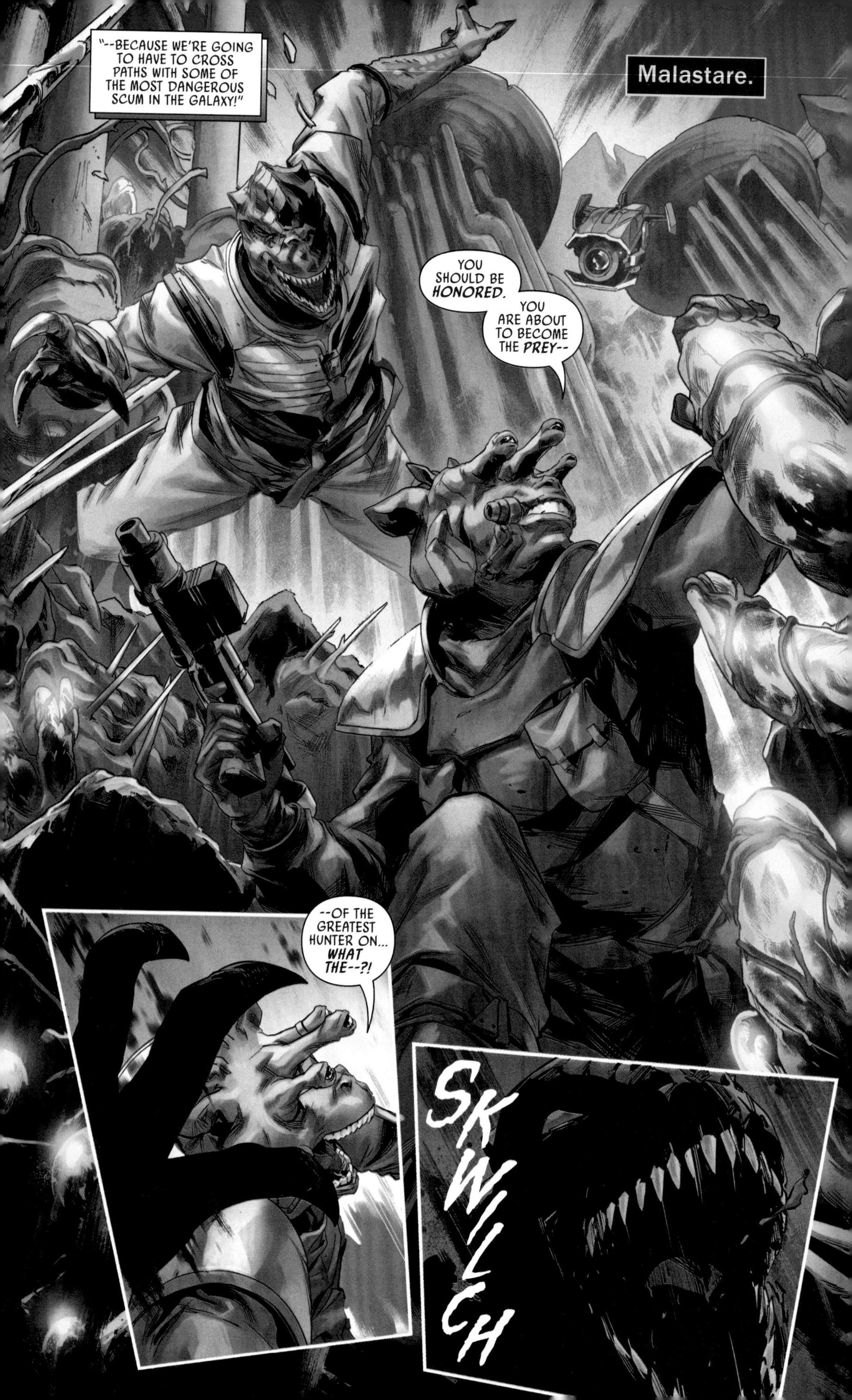
"--BECAUSE WE'RE GOING TO HAVE TO CROSS PATHS WITH SOME OF THE MOST DANGEROUS SCUM IN THE GALAXY!"
Malastare.
YOU SHOULD BE *HONORED.*
YOU ARE ABOUT TO BECOME THE *PREY*--
--OF THE GREATEST HUNTER ON... *WHAT THE*--?!
SKWILCH

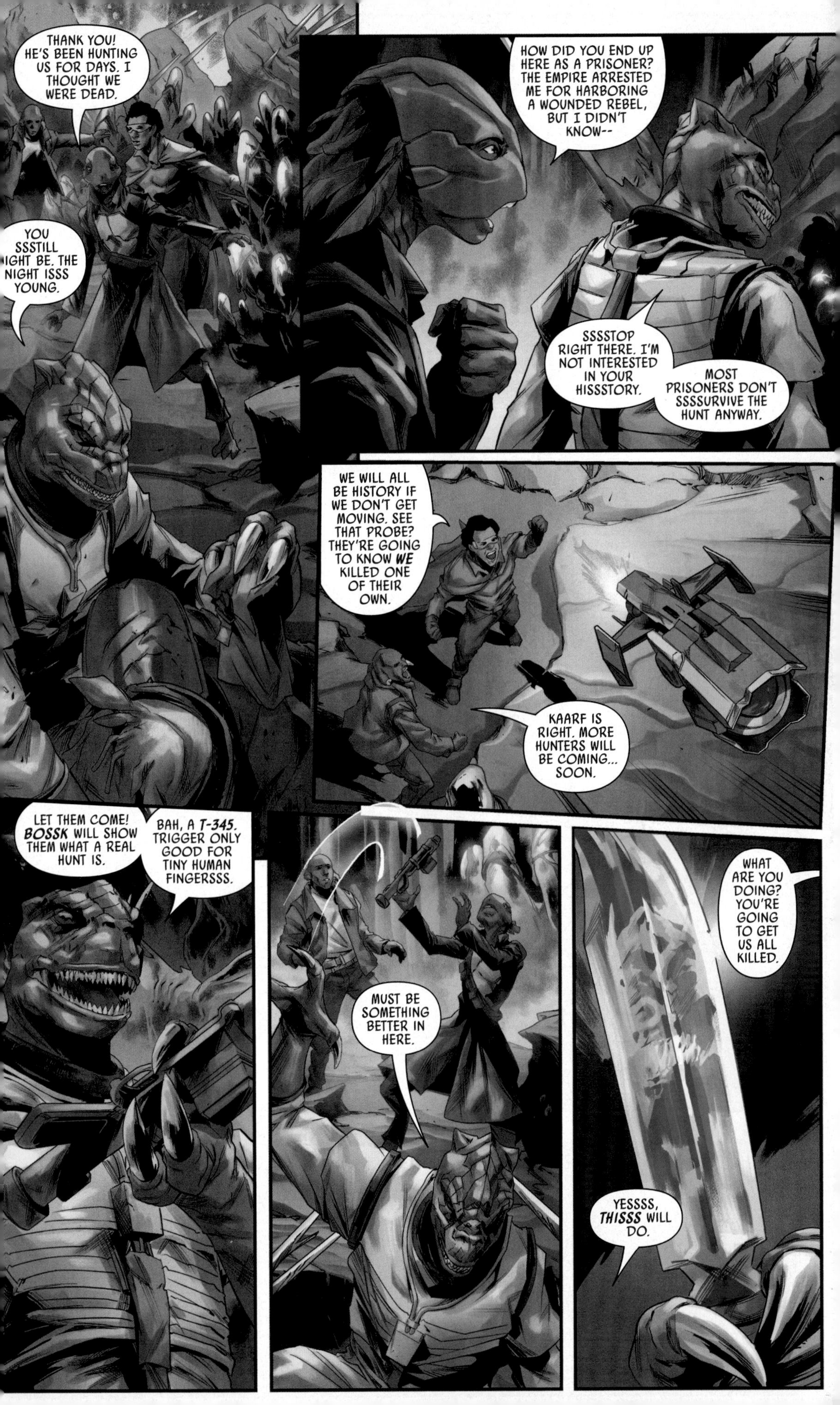
THANK YOU! HE'S BEEN HUNTING US FOR DAYS. I THOUGHT WE WERE DEAD.
YOU SSSTILL IGHT BE. THE NIGHT ISSS YOUNG.
HOW DID YOU END UP HERE AS A PRISONER? THE EMPIRE ARRESTED ME FOR HARBORING A WOUNDED REBEL, BUT I DIDN'T KNOW--
SSSSTOP RIGHT THERE. I'M NOT INTERESTED IN YOUR HISSSTORY.
MOST PRISONERS DON'T SSSSURVIVE THE HUNT ANYWAY.
WE WILL ALL BE HISTORY IF WE DON'T GET MOVING. SEE THAT PROBE? THEY'RE GOING TO KNOW WE KILLED ONE OF THEIR OWN.
KAARF IS RIGHT. MORE HUNTERS WILL BE COMING... SOON.
LET THEM COME! BOSSK WILL SHOW THEM WHAT A REAL HUNT IS.
BAH, A T-345. TRIGGER ONLY GOOD FOR TINY HUMAN FINGERSSS.
MUST BE SOMETHING BETTER IN HERE.
WHAT ARE YOU DOING? YOU'RE GOING TO GET US ALL KILLED.
YESSSS, THISSS WILL DO.

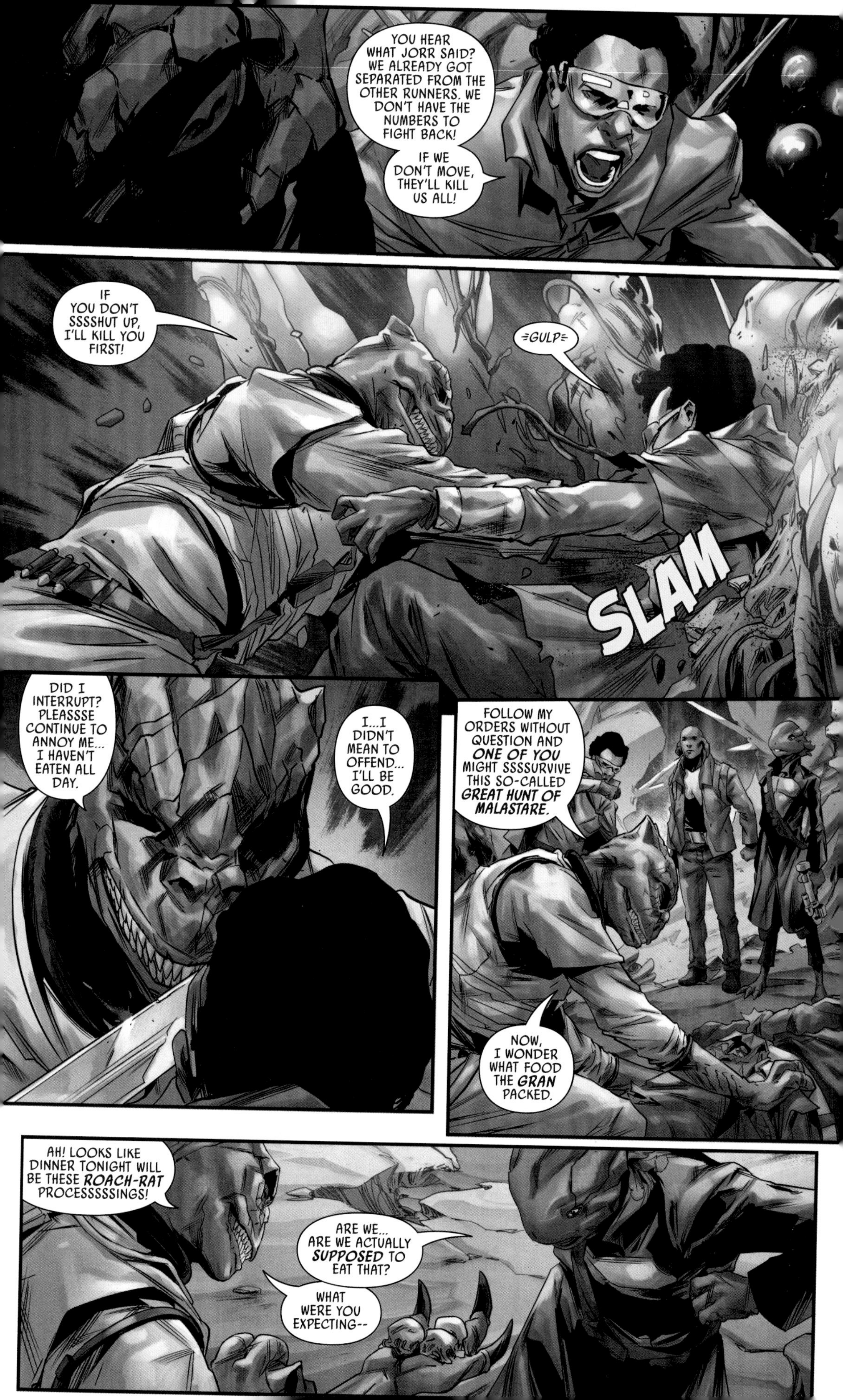

YOU HEAR WHAT JORR SAID? WE ALREADY GOT SEPARATED FROM THE OTHER RUNNERS. WE DON'T HAVE THE NUMBERS TO FIGHT BACK!
IF WE DON'T MOVE, THEY'LL KILL US ALL!
IF YOU DON'T SSSSHUT UP, I'LL KILL YOU FIRST!
=GULP=
SLAM
DID I INTERRUPT? PLEASSSE CONTINUE TO ANNOY ME... I HAVEN'T EATEN ALL DAY.
I...I DIDN'T MEAN TO OFFEND... I'LL BE GOOD.
FOLLOW MY ORDERS WITHOUT QUESTION AND ONE OF YOU MIGHT SSSSURVIVE THIS SO-CALLED GREAT HUNT OF MALASTARE.
NOW, I WONDER WHAT FOOD THE GRAN PACKED.
AH! LOOKS LIKE DINNER TONIGHT WILL BE THESE ROACH-RAT PROCESSSSSINGS!
ARE WE... ARE WE ACTUALLY SUPPOSED TO EAT THAT?
WHAT WERE YOU EXPECTING--

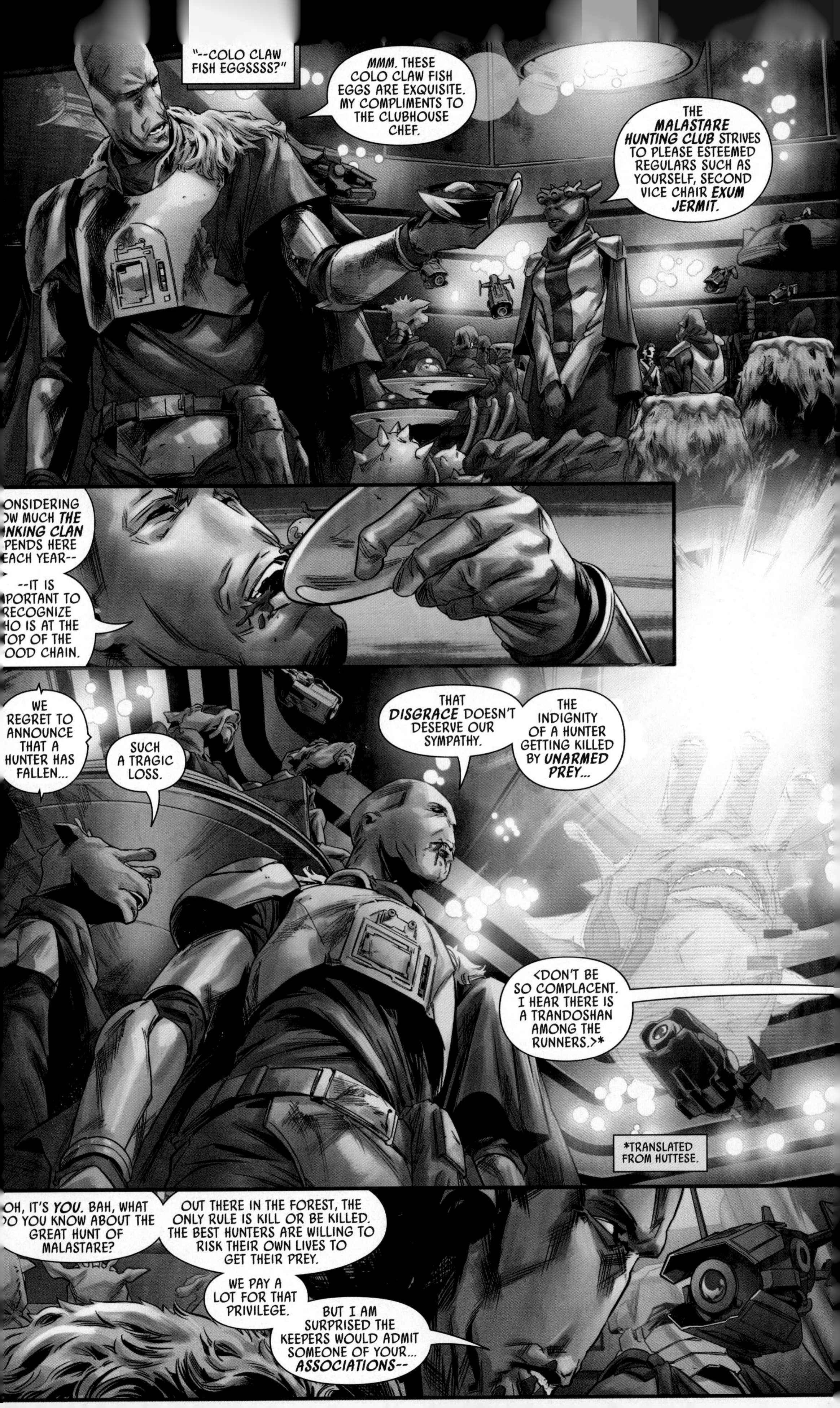
"--COLO CLAW FISH EGGSSSS?"
MMM. THESE COLO CLAW FISH EGGS ARE EXQUISITE. MY COMPLIMENTS TO THE CLUBHOUSE CHEF.
THE MALASTARE HUNTING CLUB STRIVES TO PLEASE ESTEEMED REGULARS SUCH AS YOURSELF, SECOND VICE CHAIR EXUM JERMIT.
ONSIDERING OW MUCH THE INKING CLAN PENDS HERE EACH YEAR--
--IT IS PORTANT TO RECOGNIZE HO IS AT THE TOP OF THE OOD CHAIN.
WE REGRET TO ANNOUNCE THAT A HUNTER HAS FALLEN...
SUCH A TRAGIC LOSS.
THAT DISGRACE DOESN'T DESERVE OUR SYMPATHY.
THE INDIGNITY OF A HUNTER GETTING KILLED BY UNARMED PREY...
<DON'T BE SO COMPLACENT. I HEAR THERE IS A TRANDOSHAN AMONG THE RUNNERS.>*
*TRANSLATED FROM HUTTESE.
OH, IT'S YOU. BAH, WHAT DO YOU KNOW ABOUT THE GREAT HUNT OF MALASTARE?
OUT THERE IN THE FOREST, THE ONLY RULE IS KILL OR BE KILLED. THE BEST HUNTERS ARE WILLING TO RISK THEIR OWN LIVES TO GET THEIR PREY.
WE PAY A LOT FOR THAT PRIVILEGE.
BUT I AM SURPRISED THE KEEPERS WOULD ADMIT SOMEONE OF YOUR... ASSOCIATIONS--

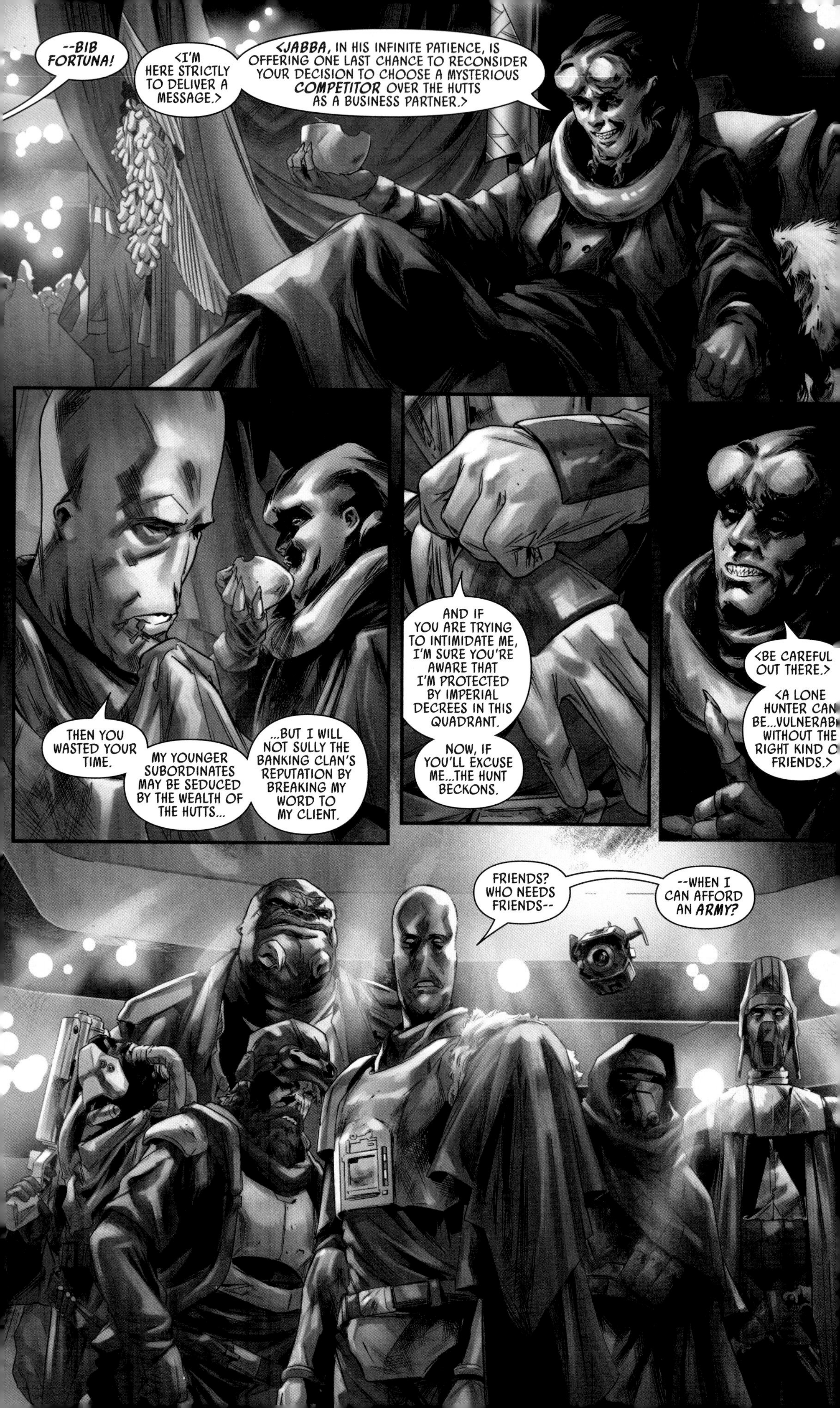
--BIB FORTUNA!
<I'M HERE STRICTLY TO DELIVER A MESSAGE.>
<JABBA, IN HIS INFINITE PATIENCE, IS OFFERING ONE LAST CHANCE TO RECONSIDER YOUR DECISION TO CHOOSE A MYSTERIOUS COMPETITOR OVER THE HUTTS AS A BUSINESS PARTNER.>
THEN YOU WASTED YOUR TIME.
MY YOUNGER SUBORDINATES MAY BE SEDUCED BY THE WEALTH OF THE HUTTS...
...BUT I WILL NOT SULLY THE BANKING CLAN'S REPUTATION BY BREAKING MY WORD TO MY CLIENT.
AND IF YOU ARE TRYING TO INTIMIDATE ME, I'M SURE YOU'RE AWARE THAT I'M PROTECTED BY IMPERIAL DECREES IN THIS QUADRANT.
NOW, IF YOU'LL EXCUSE ME...THE HUNT BECKONS.
<BE CAREFUL OUT THERE.>
FRIENDS? WHO NEEDS FRIENDS--
--WHEN I CAN AFFORD AN ARMY?

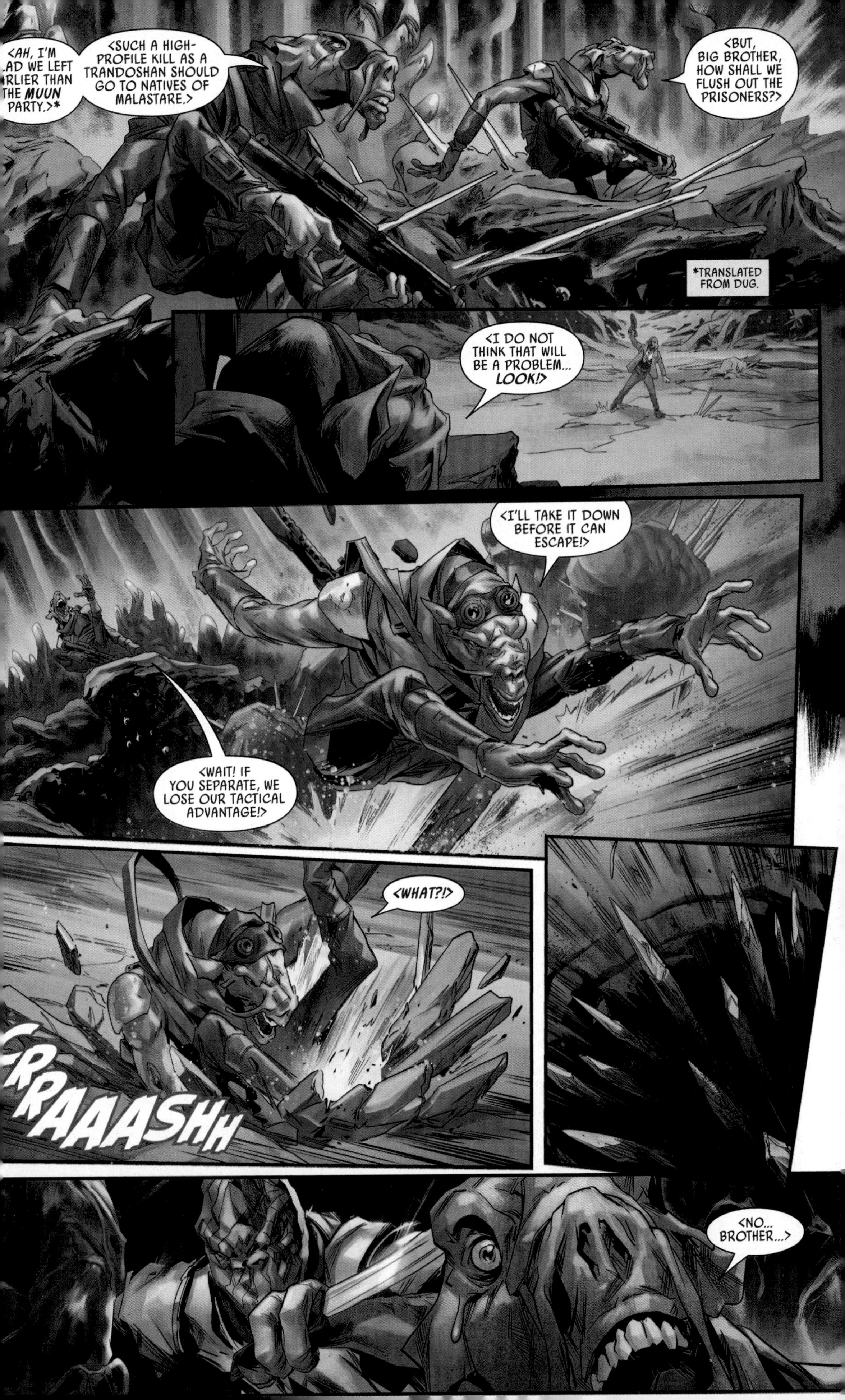

<AH, I'M LAD WE LEFT RLIER THAN THE MUUN PARTY.>*
<SUCH A HIGH-PROFILE KILL AS A TRANDOSHAN SHOULD GO TO NATIVES OF MALASTARE.>
<BUT, BIG BROTHER, HOW SHALL WE FLUSH OUT THE PRISONERS?>
*TRANSLATED FROM DUG.
<I DO NOT THINK THAT WILL BE A PROBLEM... LOOK!>
<I'LL TAKE IT DOWN BEFORE IT CAN ESCAPE!>
<WAIT! IF YOU SEPARATE, WE LOSE OUR TACTICAL ADVANTAGE!>
<WHAT?!>
RRAAAASHH
<NO... BROTHER...>

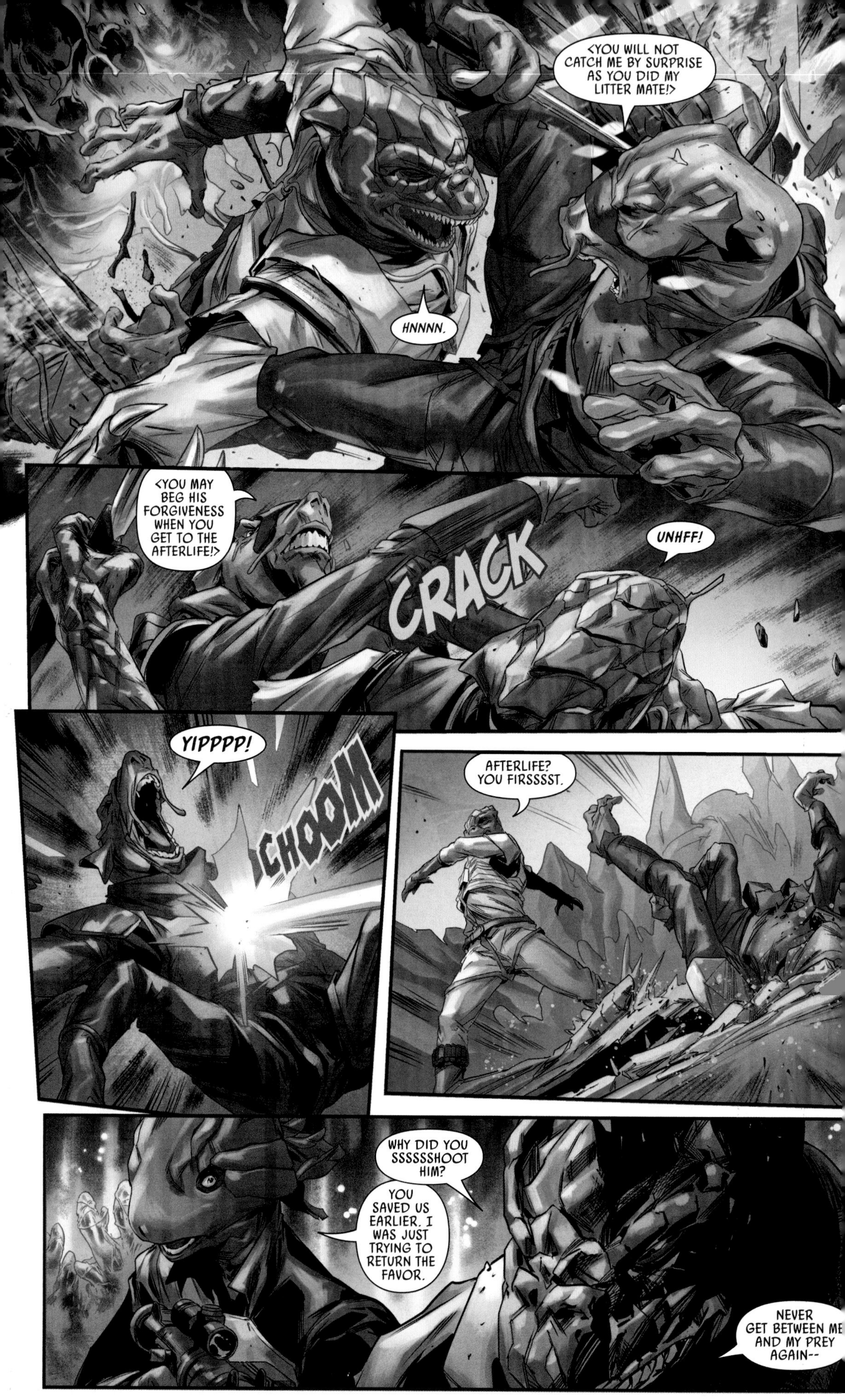
<YOU WILL NOT CATCH ME BY SURPRISE AS YOU DID MY LITTER MATE!>
HNNNN.
<YOU MAY BEG HIS FORGIVENESS WHEN YOU GET TO THE AFTERLIFE!>
CRACK
UNHFF!
YIPPPP!
CHOOM
AFTERLIFE? YOU FIRSSSST.
WHY DID YOU SSSSSSHOOT HIM?
YOU SAVED US EARLIER. I WAS JUST TRYING TO RETURN THE FAVOR.
NEVER GET BETWEEN ME AND MY PREY AGAIN--

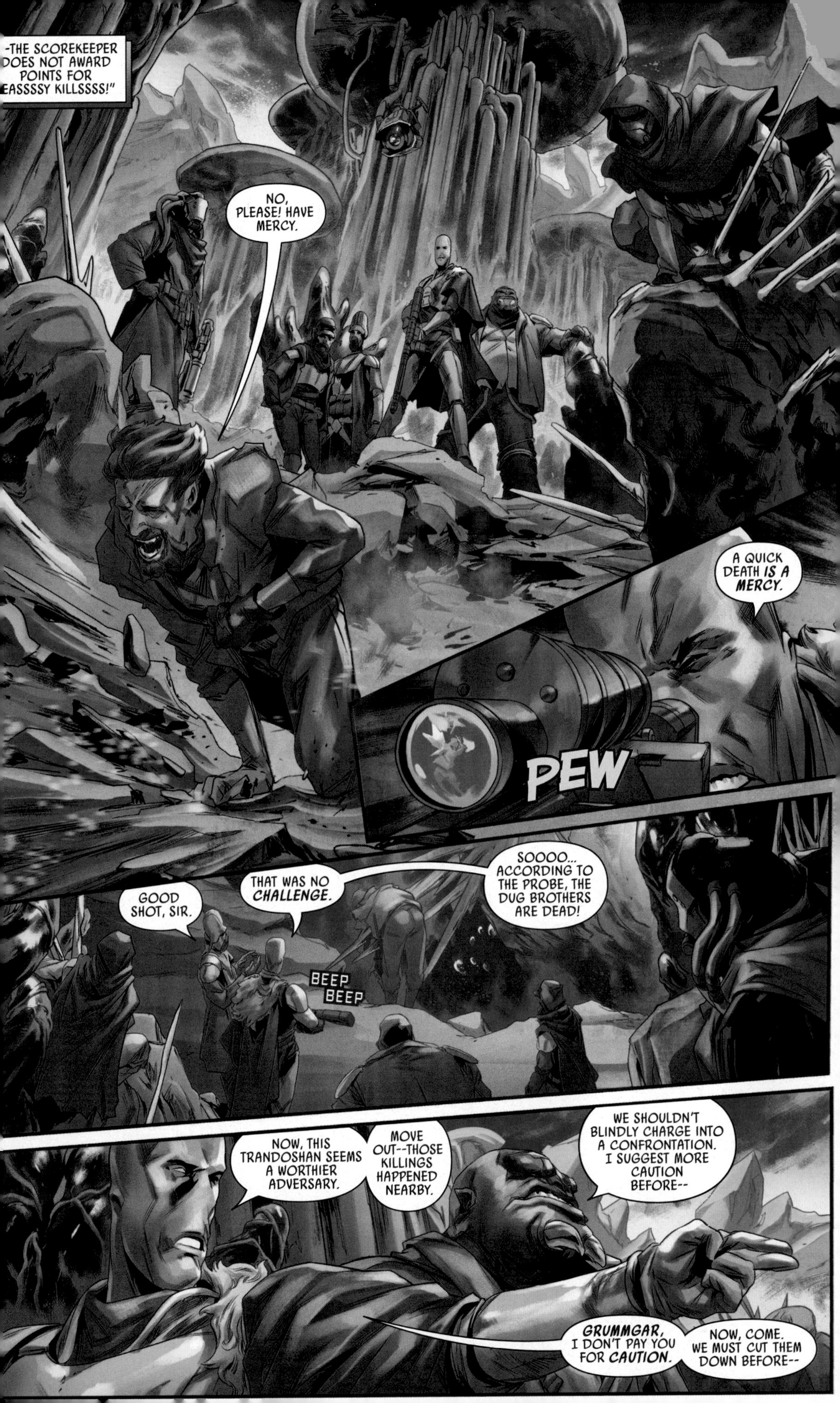
-THE SCOREKEEPER DOES NOT AWARD POINTS FOR EASSSSY KILLSSSS!"
NO, PLEASE! HAVE MERCY.
A QUICK DEATH IS A MERCY.
PEW
GOOD SHOT, SIR.
THAT WAS NO CHALLENGE.
SOOOO... ACCORDING TO THE PROBE, THE DUG BROTHERS ARE DEAD!
BEEP BEEP
NOW, THIS TRANDOSHAN SEEMS A WORTHIER ADVERSARY.
MOVE OUT--THOSE KILLINGS HAPPENED NEARBY.
WE SHOULDN'T BLINDLY CHARGE INTO A CONFRONTATION. I SUGGEST MORE CAUTION BEFORE--
GRUMMGAR, I DON'T PAY YOU FOR CAUTION.
NOW, COME. WE MUST CUT THEM DOWN BEFORE--

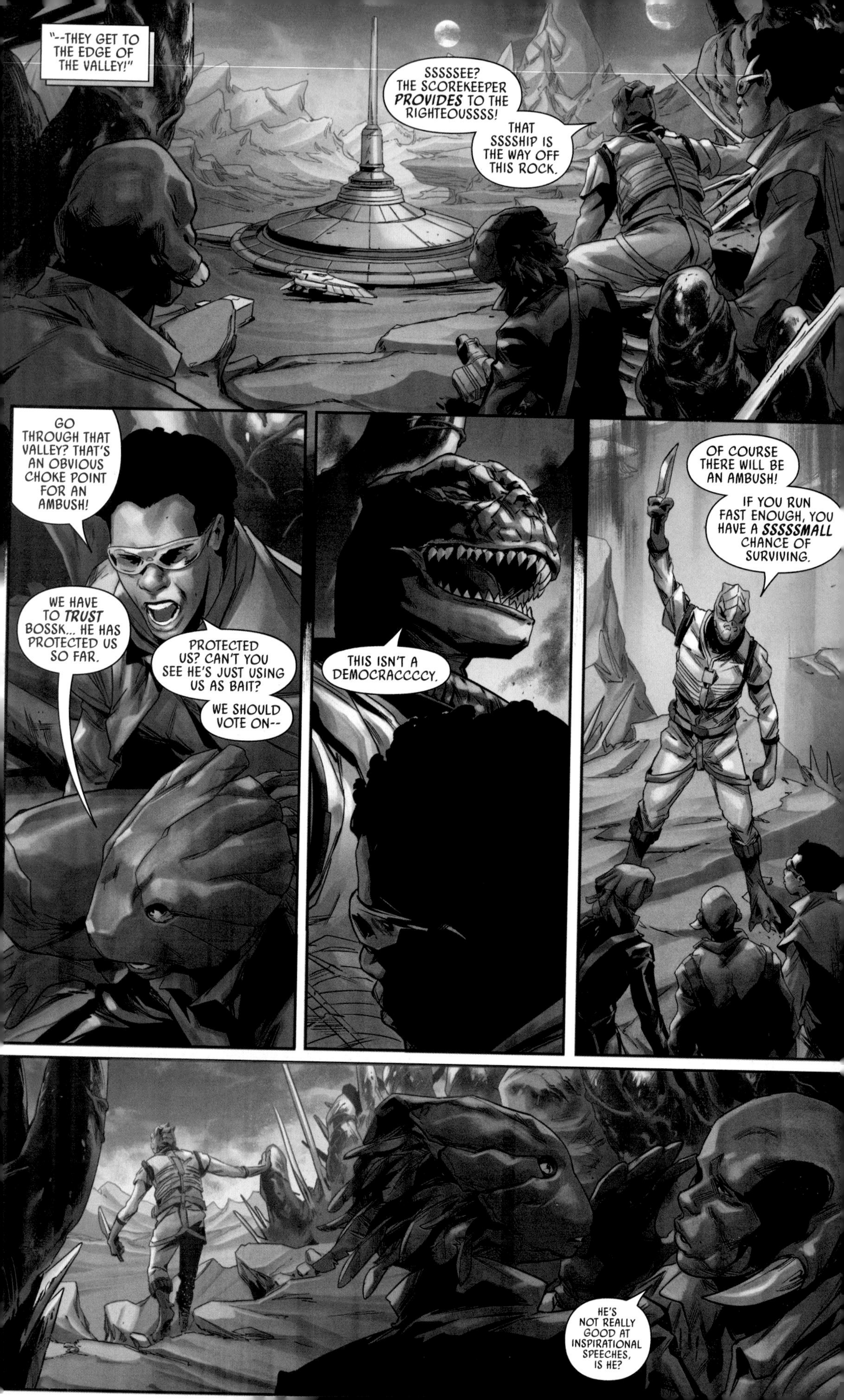
"--THEY GET TO THE EDGE OF THE VALLEY!"
SSSSSEE? THE SCOREKEEPER PROVIDES TO THE RIGHTEOUSSSS!
THAT SSSSHIP IS THE WAY OFF THIS ROCK.
GO THROUGH THAT VALLEY? THAT'S AN OBVIOUS CHOKE POINT FOR AN AMBUSH!
WE HAVE TO TRUST BOSSK... HE HAS PROTECTED US SO FAR.
PROTECTED US? CAN'T YOU SEE HE'S JUST USING US AS BAIT?
WE SHOULD VOTE ON--
THIS ISN'T A DEMOCRACCCCY.
OF COURSE THERE WILL BE AN AMBUSH!
IF YOU RUN FAST ENOUGH, YOU HAVE A SSSSSMALL CHANCE OF SURVIVING.
HE'S NOT REALLY GOOD AT INSPIRATIONAL SPEECHES, IS HE?

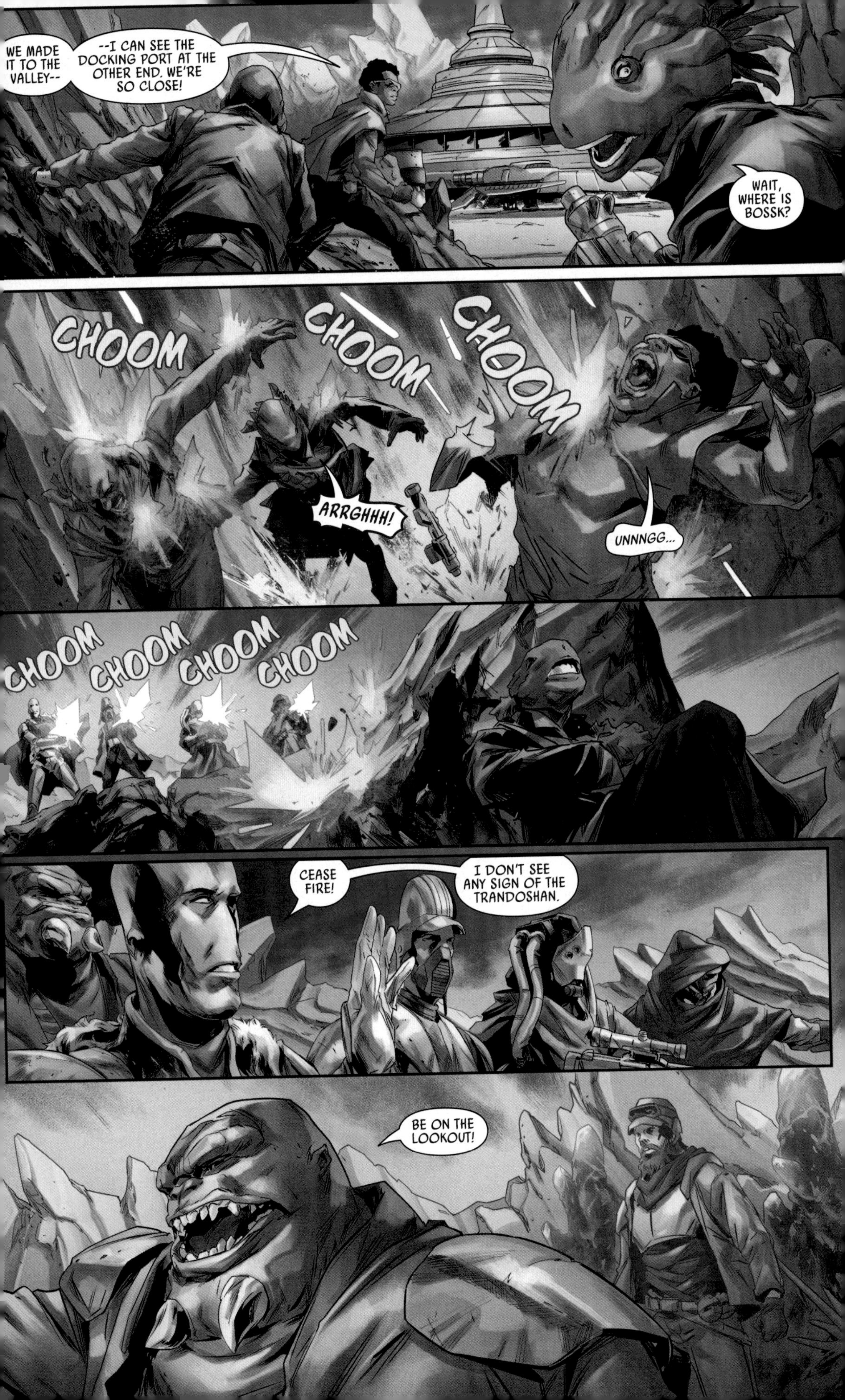

WE MADE IT TO THE VALLEY--
--I CAN SEE THE DOCKING PORT AT THE OTHER END. WE'RE SO CLOSE!
WAIT, WHERE IS BOSSK?
CHOOM
CHOOM
CHOOM
ARRGHHH!
UNNNGG...
CHOOM
CHOOM
CHOOM
CHOOM
CEASE FIRE!
I DON'T SEE ANY SIGN OF THE TRANDOSHAN.
BE ON THE LOOKOUT!

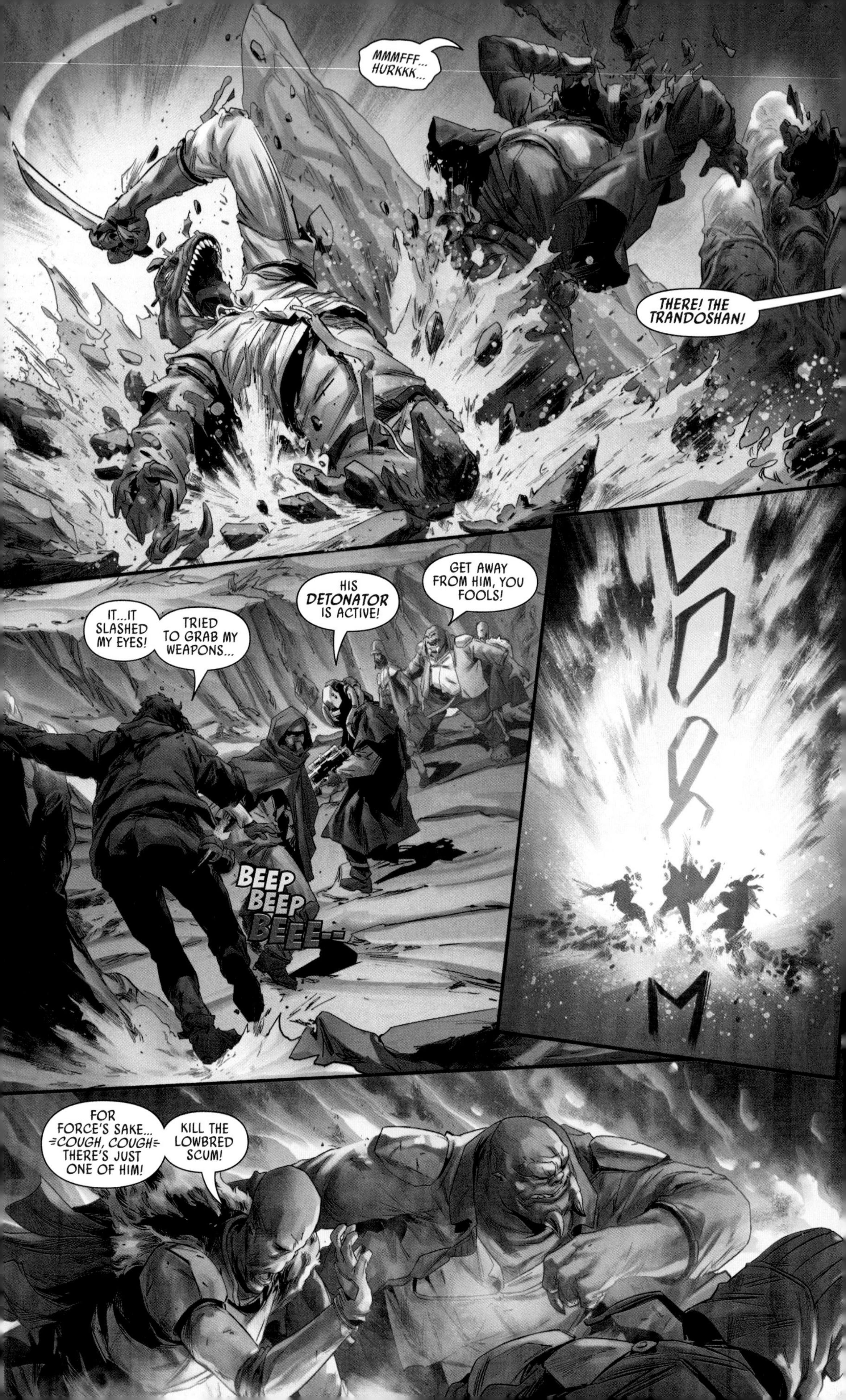
MMMFFF... HURKKK...
THERE! THE TRANDOSHAN!
IT...IT SLASHED MY EYES!
TRIED TO GRAB MY WEAPONS...
HIS DETONATOR IS ACTIVE!
GET AWAY FROM HIM, YOU FOOLS!
BEEP BEEP BEEE--
BOOM
FOR FORCE'S SAKE... =COUGH, COUGH= THERE'S JUST ONE OF HIM!
KILL THE LOWBRED SCUM!

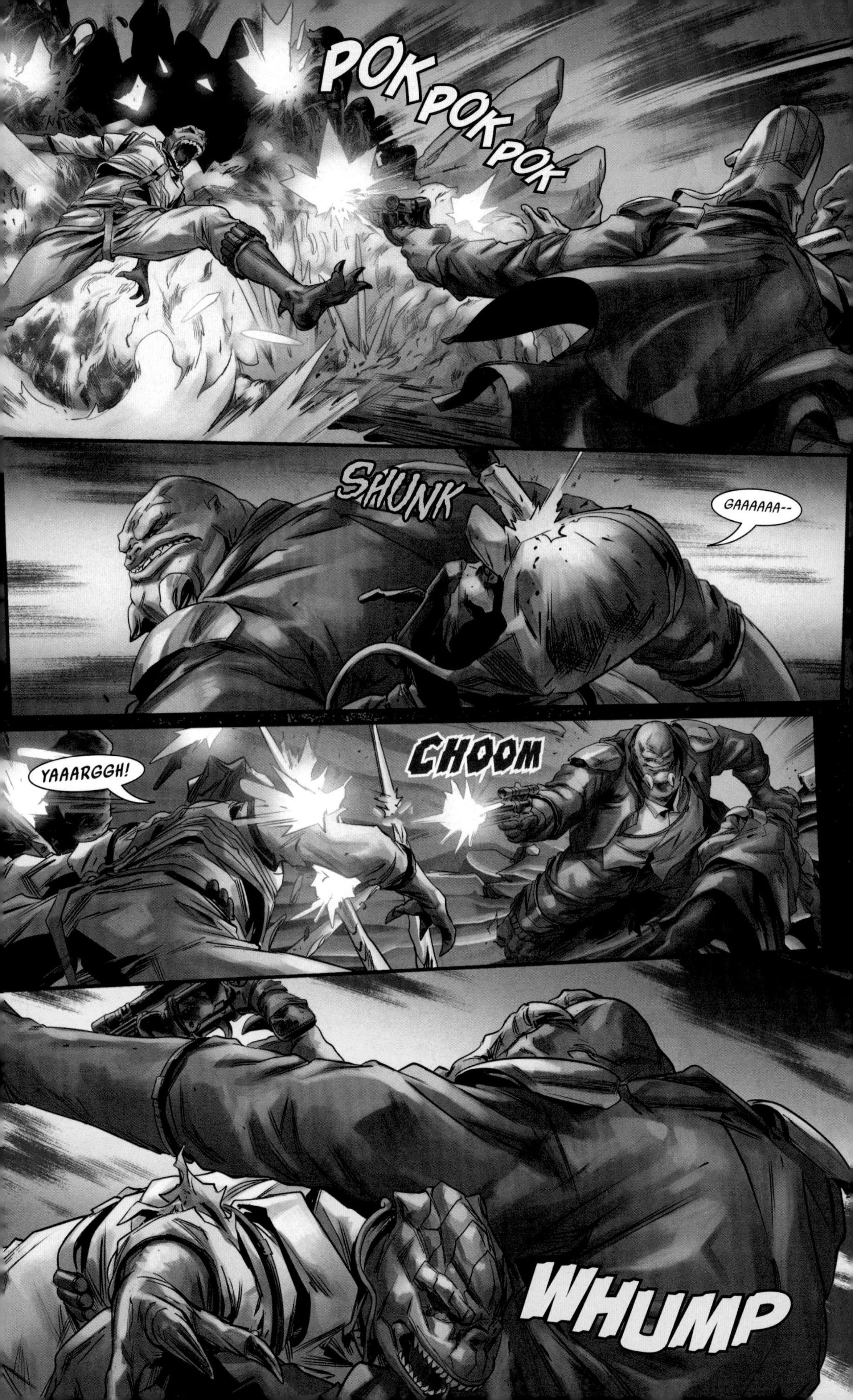
POK
POK
POK
POK
SHUNK
GAAAAAA--
YAAARGGH!
CHOOM
WHUMP

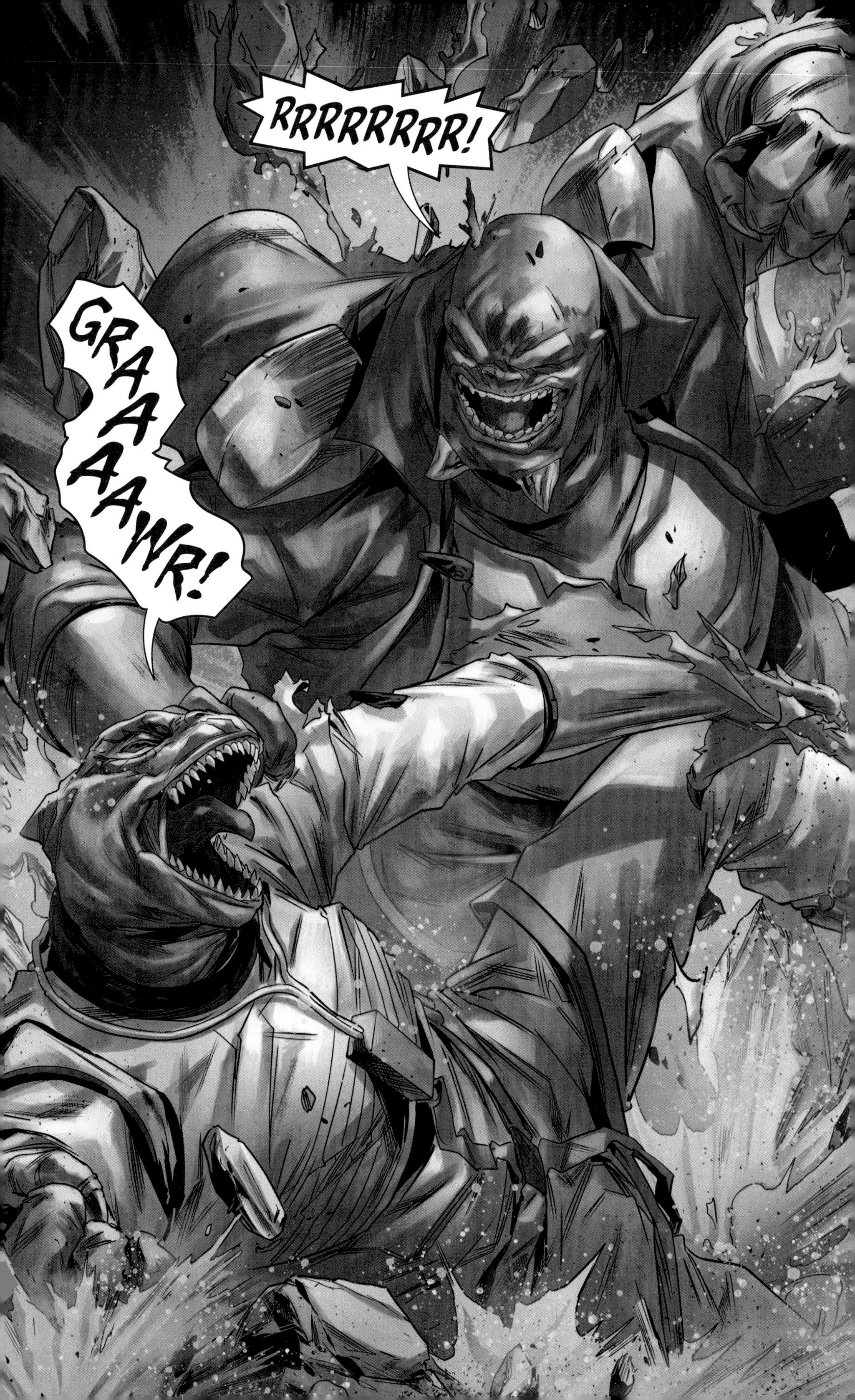
RRRRRRRRR!
GRAAAAAWR!

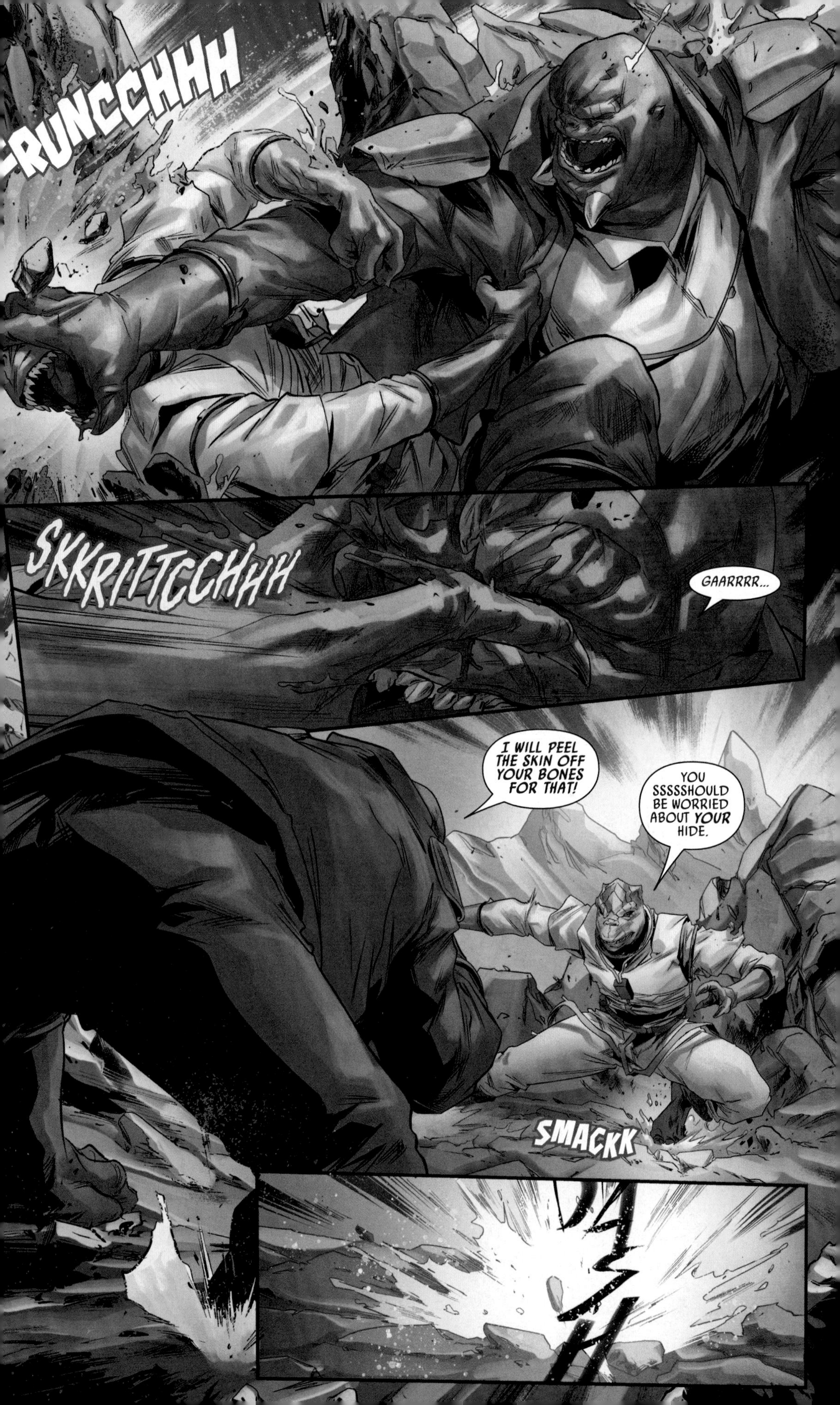

-RUNCCHHH
SKKRITTCCHHH
GAARRRR...
I WILL PEEL THE SKIN OFF YOUR BONES FOR THAT!
YOU SSSSSHOULD BE WORRIED ABOUT YOUR HIDE.
SMACKK

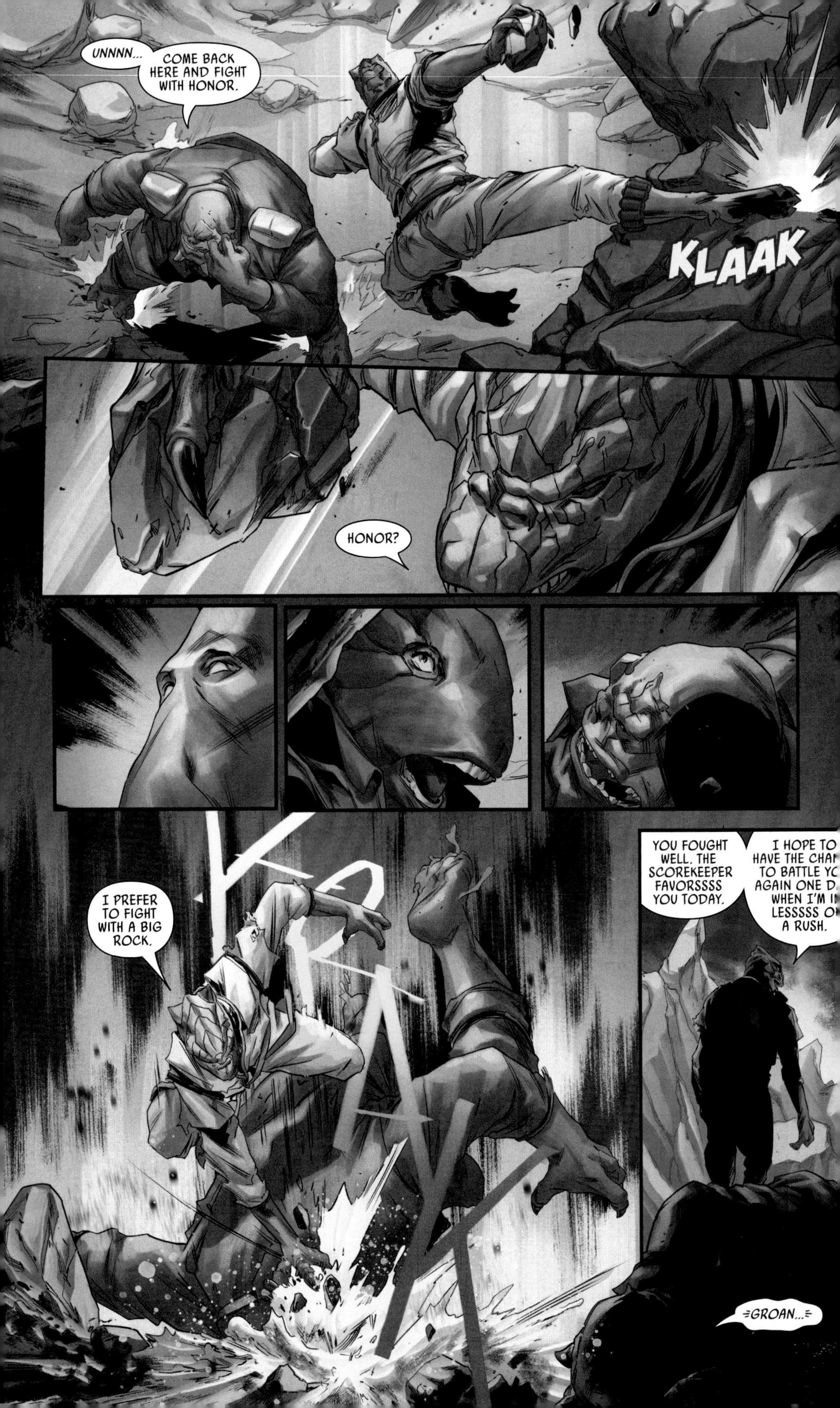
UNNNN...
COME BACK HERE AND FIGHT WITH HONOR.
KLAAK
HONOR?
I PREFER TO FIGHT WITH A BIG ROCK.
YOU FOUGHT WELL. THE SCOREKEEPER FAVORSSSS YOU TODAY.
≡GROAN...≡

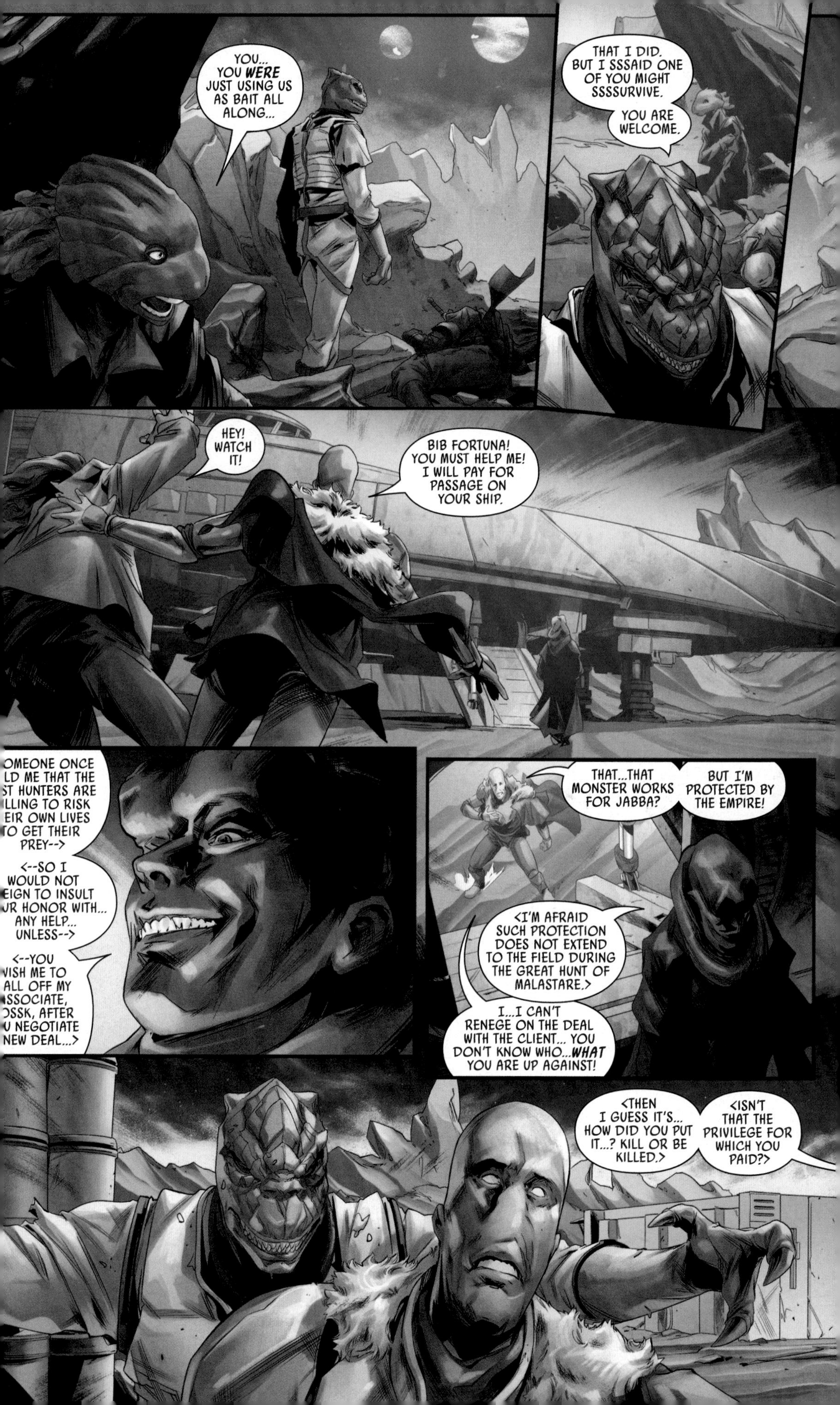
YOU... YOU WERE JUST USING US AS BAIT ALL ALONG...
THAT I DID. BUT I SSSAID ONE OF YOU MIGHT SSSSURVIVE.
YOU ARE WELCOME.
HEY! WATCH IT!
BIB FORTUNA! YOU MUST HELP ME! I WILL PAY FOR PASSAGE ON YOUR SHIP.
OMEONE ONCE LD ME THAT THE ST HUNTERS ARE LLING TO RISK EIR OWN LIVES TO GET THEIR PREY-->
<--SO I WOULD NOT EIGN TO INSULT UR HONOR WITH... ANY HELP... UNLESS-->
<--YOU VISH ME TO ALL OFF MY SSOCIATE, OSSK, AFTER U NEGOTIATE NEW DEAL...>
THAT...THAT MONSTER WORKS FOR JABBA?
BUT I'M PROTECTED BY THE EMPIRE!
<I'M AFRAID SUCH PROTECTION DOES NOT EXTEND TO THE FIELD DURING THE GREAT HUNT OF MALASTARE.>
I...I CAN'T RENEGE ON THE DEAL WITH THE CLIENT... YOU DON'T KNOW WHO...WHAT YOU ARE UP AGAINST!
<THEN I GUESS IT'S... HOW DID YOU PUT IT...? KILL OR BE KILLED.>
<ISN'T THAT THE PRIVILEGE FOR WHICH YOU PAID?>

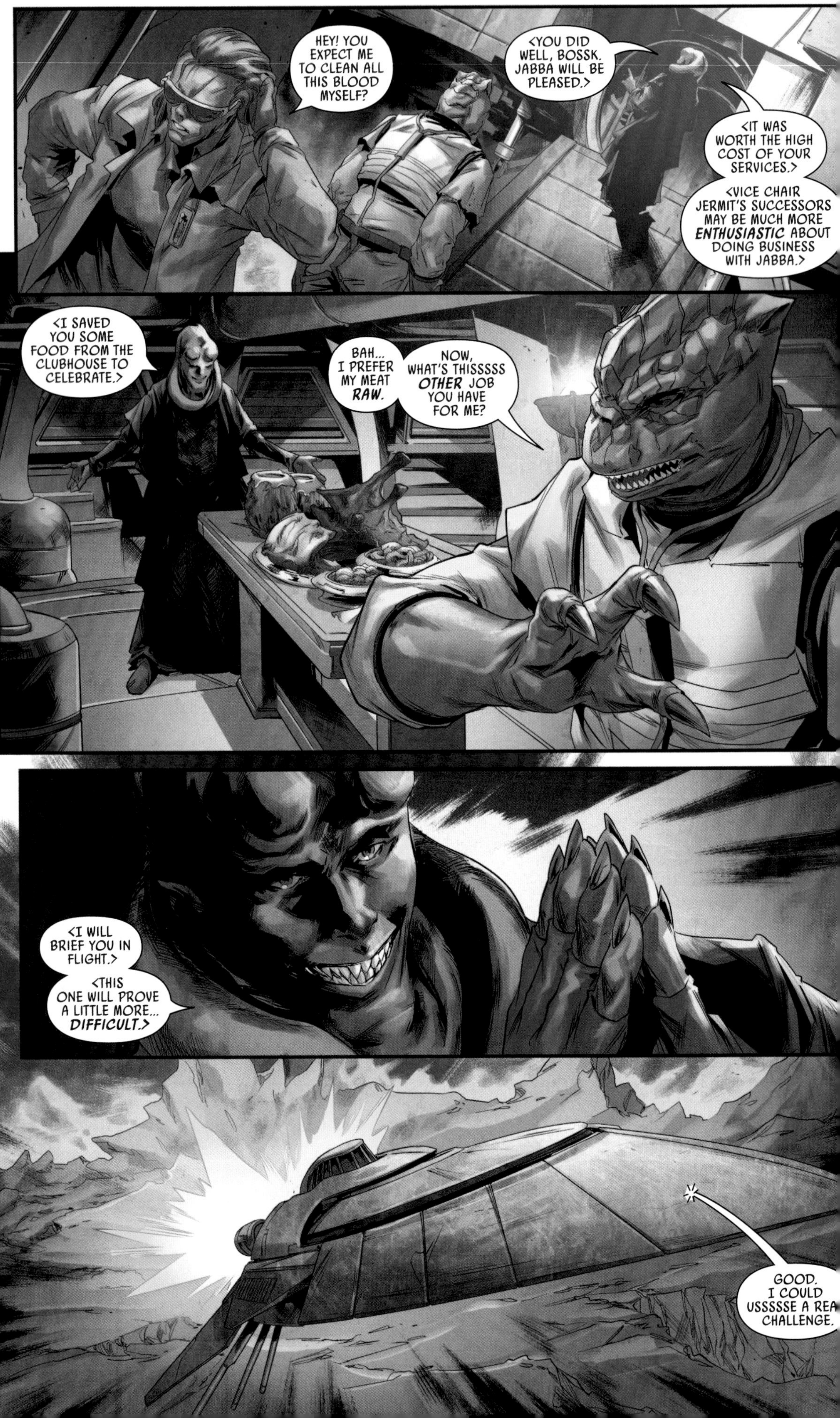
HEY! YOU EXPECT ME TO CLEAN ALL THIS BLOOD MYSELF?
<YOU DID WELL, BOSSK. JABBA WILL BE PLEASED.>
<IT WAS WORTH THE HIGH COST OF YOUR SERVICES.>
<VICE CHAIR JERMIT'S SUCCESSORS MAY BE MUCH MORE ENTHUSIASTIC ABOUT DOING BUSINESS WITH JABBA.>
<I SAVED YOU SOME FOOD FROM THE CLUBHOUSE TO CELEBRATE.>
BAH... I PREFER MY MEAT RAW.
NOW, WHAT'S THISSSSS OTHER JOB YOU HAVE FOR ME?
<I WILL BRIEF YOU IN FLIGHT.>
<THIS ONE WILL PROVE A LITTLE MORE... DIFFICULT.>
GOOD. I COULD USSSSSE A REA CHALLENGE.

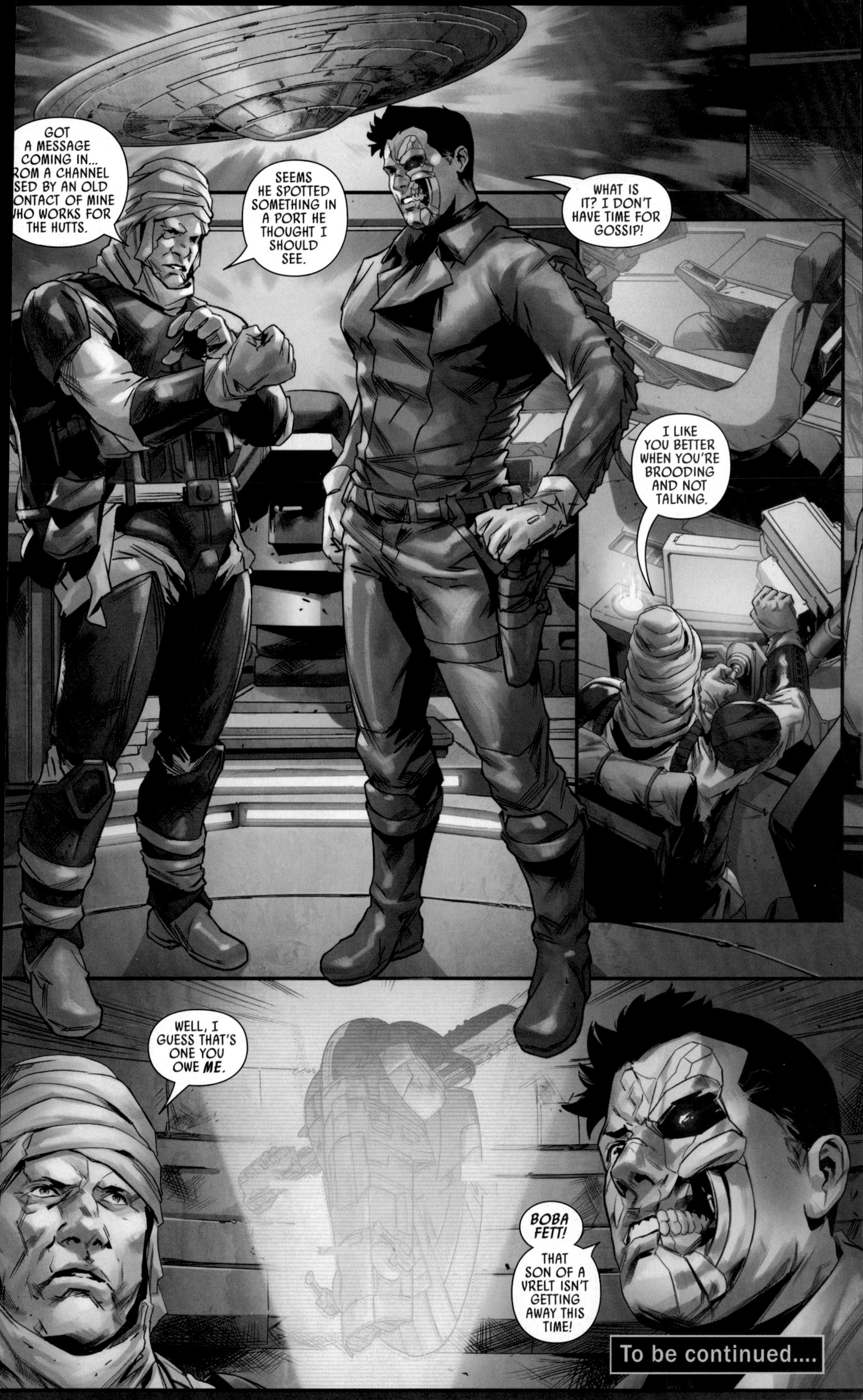
GOT A MESSAGE COMING IN... FROM A CHANNEL USED BY AN OLD CONTACT OF MINE WHO WORKS FOR THE HUTTS.
SEEMS HE SPOTTED SOMETHING IN A PORT HE THOUGHT I SHOULD SEE.
WHAT IS IT? I DON'T HAVE TIME FOR GOSSIP!
I LIKE YOU BETTER WHEN YOU'RE BROODING AND NOT TALKING.
WELL, I GUESS THAT'S ONE YOU OWE *ME*.
BOBA FETT!
THAT SON OF A VRELT ISN'T GETTING AWAY THIS TIME!
To be continued....

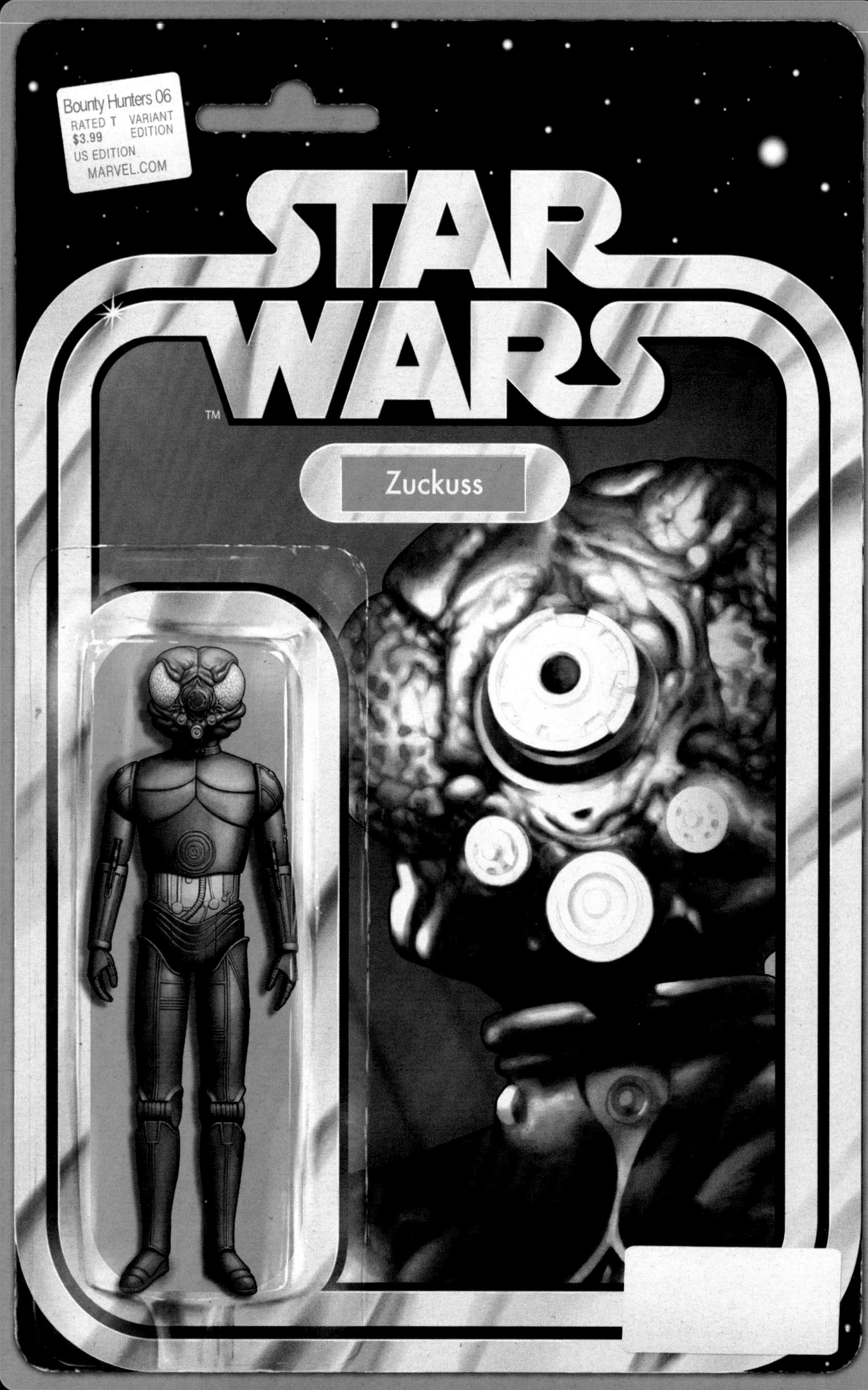
Bounty Hunters 06
RATED T
VARIANT EDITION
$3.99
US EDITION
MARVEL.COM
STAR WARS
TM
Zuckuss

#6 Action Figure Variant by
JOHN TYLER CHRISTOPHER

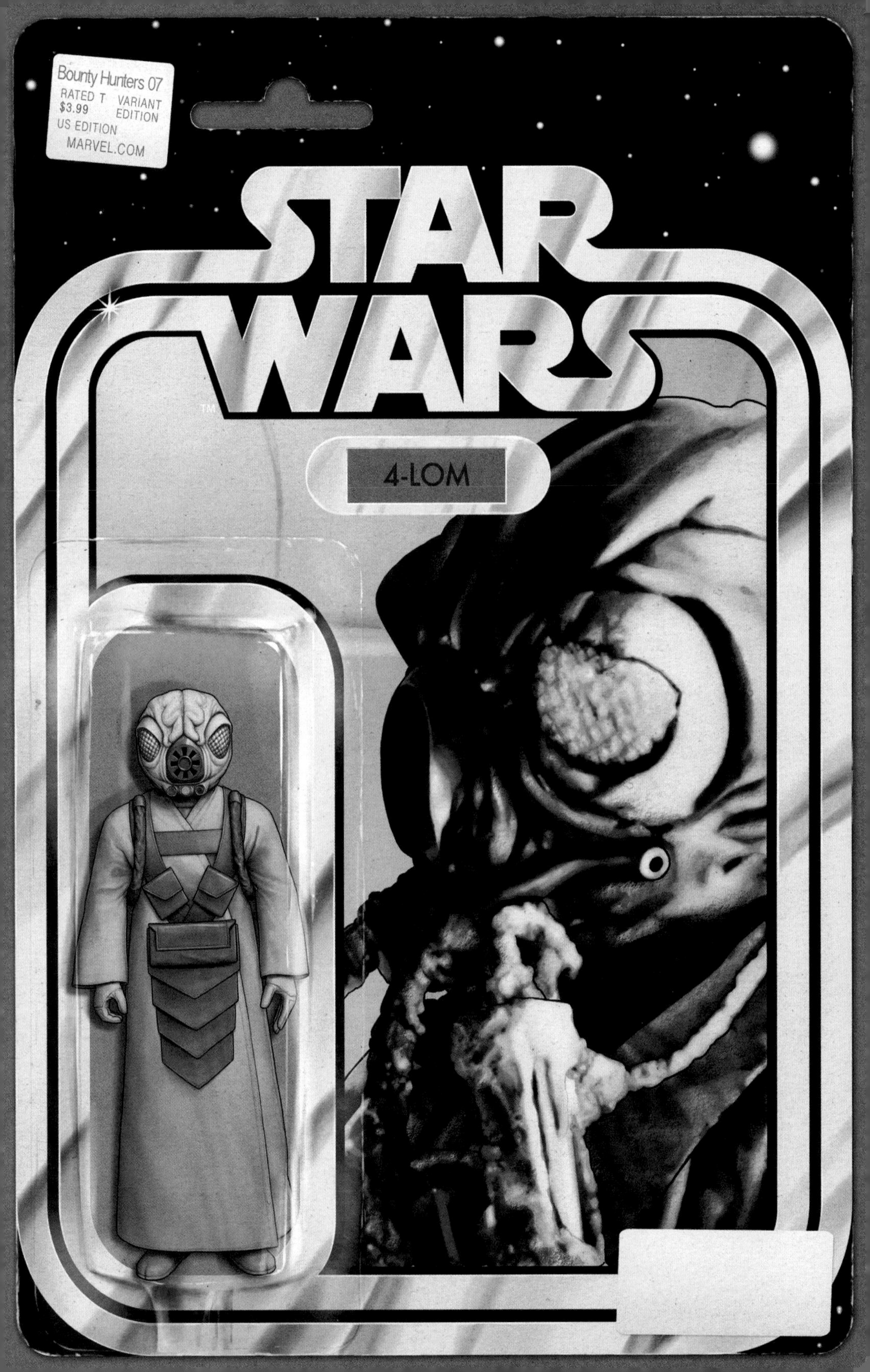
Bounty Hunters 07
RATED T
VARIANT EDITION
$3.99
US EDITION
MARVEL.COM
STAR WARS
TM
4-LOM

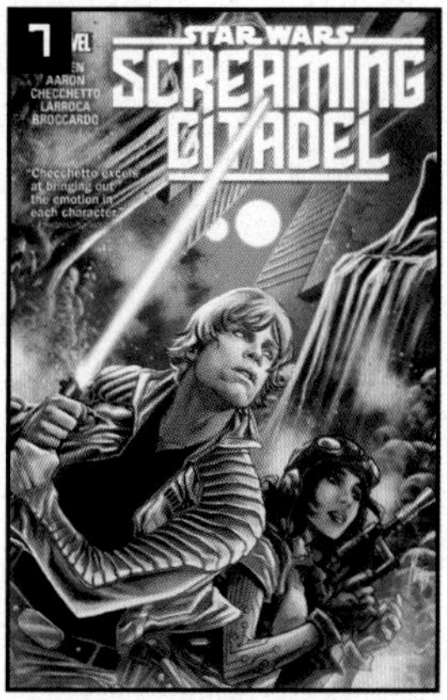
7
STAR WARS
SCREAMING CITADEL
AARON
CHECCHETTO
LARROCA
BROCCARDO

Star Wars:
The Screaming Citadel
ISBN 978-1-302-90678-8

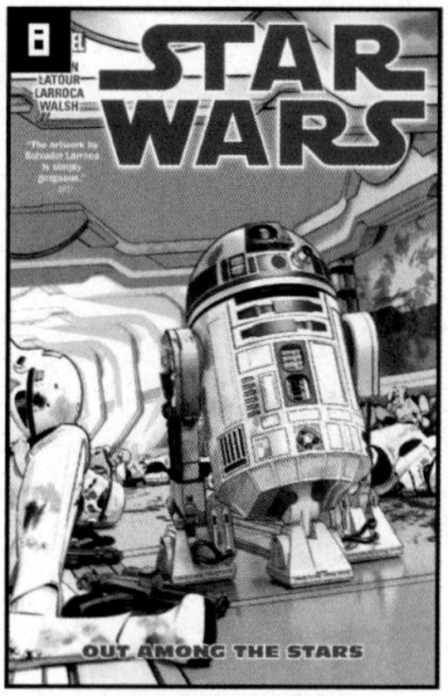
8
LATOUR
LARROCA
WALSH
STAR WARS
OUT AMONG THE STARS

Star Wars Vol. 6:
Out Among the Stars
ISBN 978-1-302-90553-8

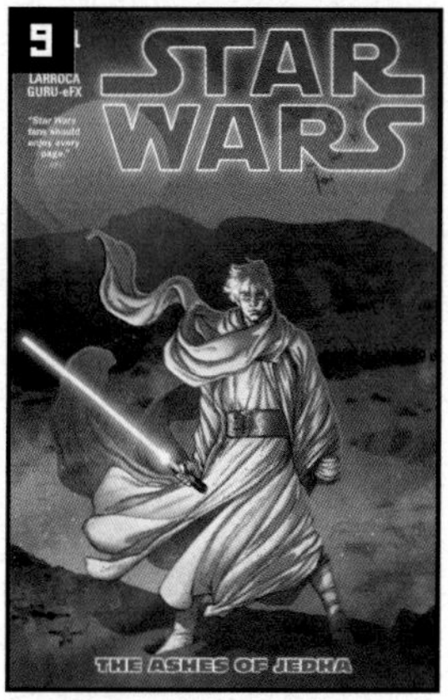
9
LARROCA
GURU-eFX
STAR WARS
THE ASHES OF JEDHA

Star Wars Vol. 7:
The Ashes of Jedha
ISBN 978-1-302-91052-5

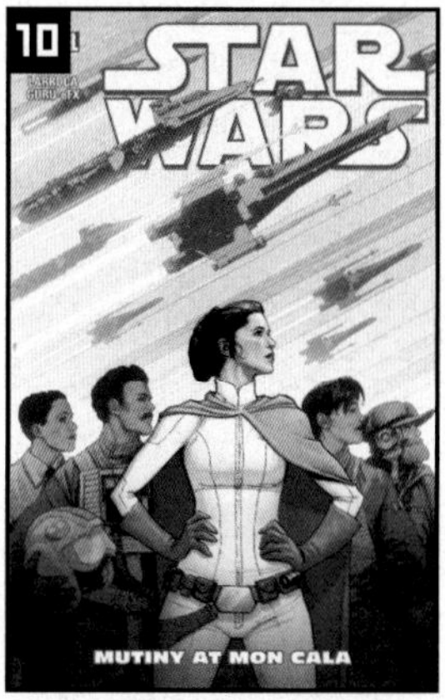
10
STAR WARS
MUTINY AT MON CALA

Star Wars Vol. 8:
Mutiny at Mon Cala
ISBN 978-1-302-91053-2

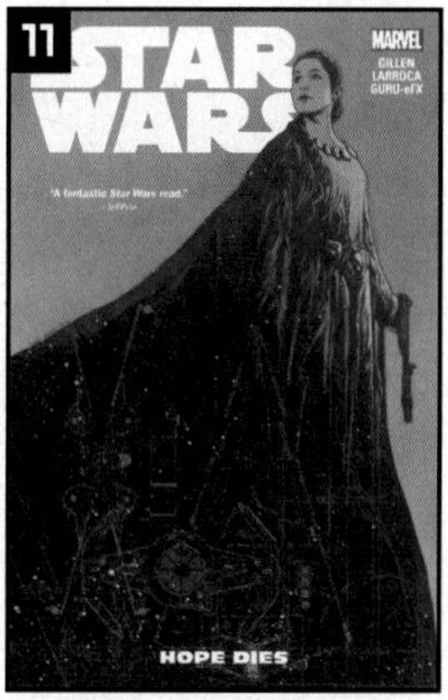
11
STAR WARS
MARVEL
GILLEN
LARROCA
GURU-eFX
HOPE DIES

Star Wars Vol. 9:
Hope Dies
ISBN 978-1-302-91054-9

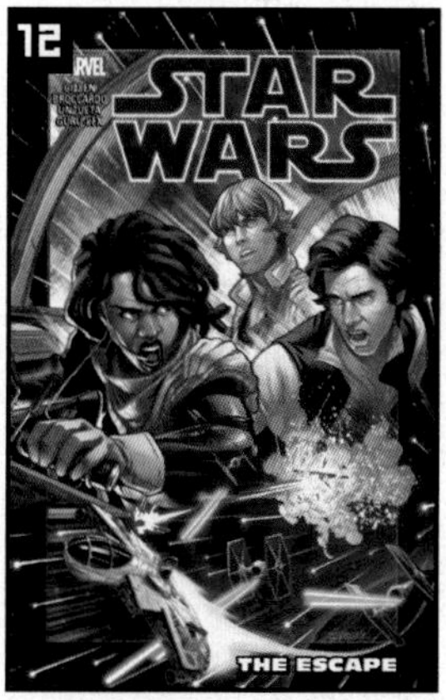
12
STAR WARS
THE ESCAPE

Star Wars Vol. 10:
The Escape
ISBN 978-1-302-91449-3

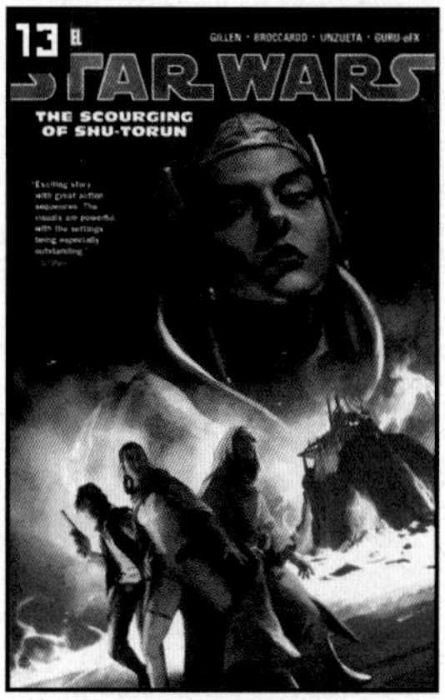
13
GILLEN · BROCCARDO · UNZUETA · GURU-eFX
STAR WARS
THE SCOURGING OF SHU-TORUN

Star Wars Vol. 11:
The Scourging of Shu-Torun
ISBN 978-1-302-91450-9

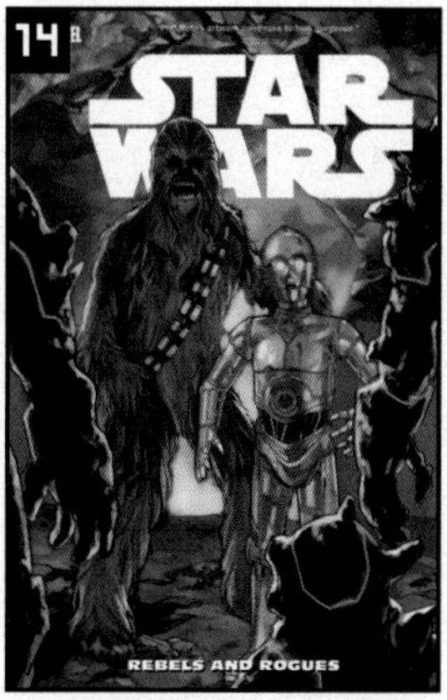
14
STAR WARS
REBELS AND ROGUES

Star Wars Vol. 12:
Rebels and Rogues
ISBN 978-1-302-91451-6

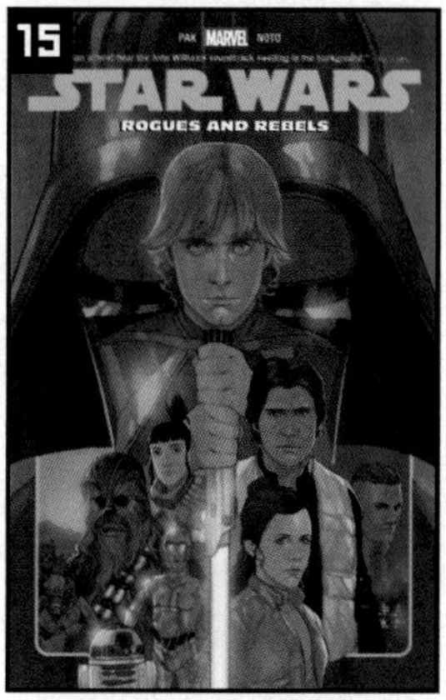
15
PAK
MARVEL
NOTO
STAR WARS
ROGUES AND REBELS

Star Wars Vol. 13:
Rogues and Rebels
ISBN 978-1-302-91450-9

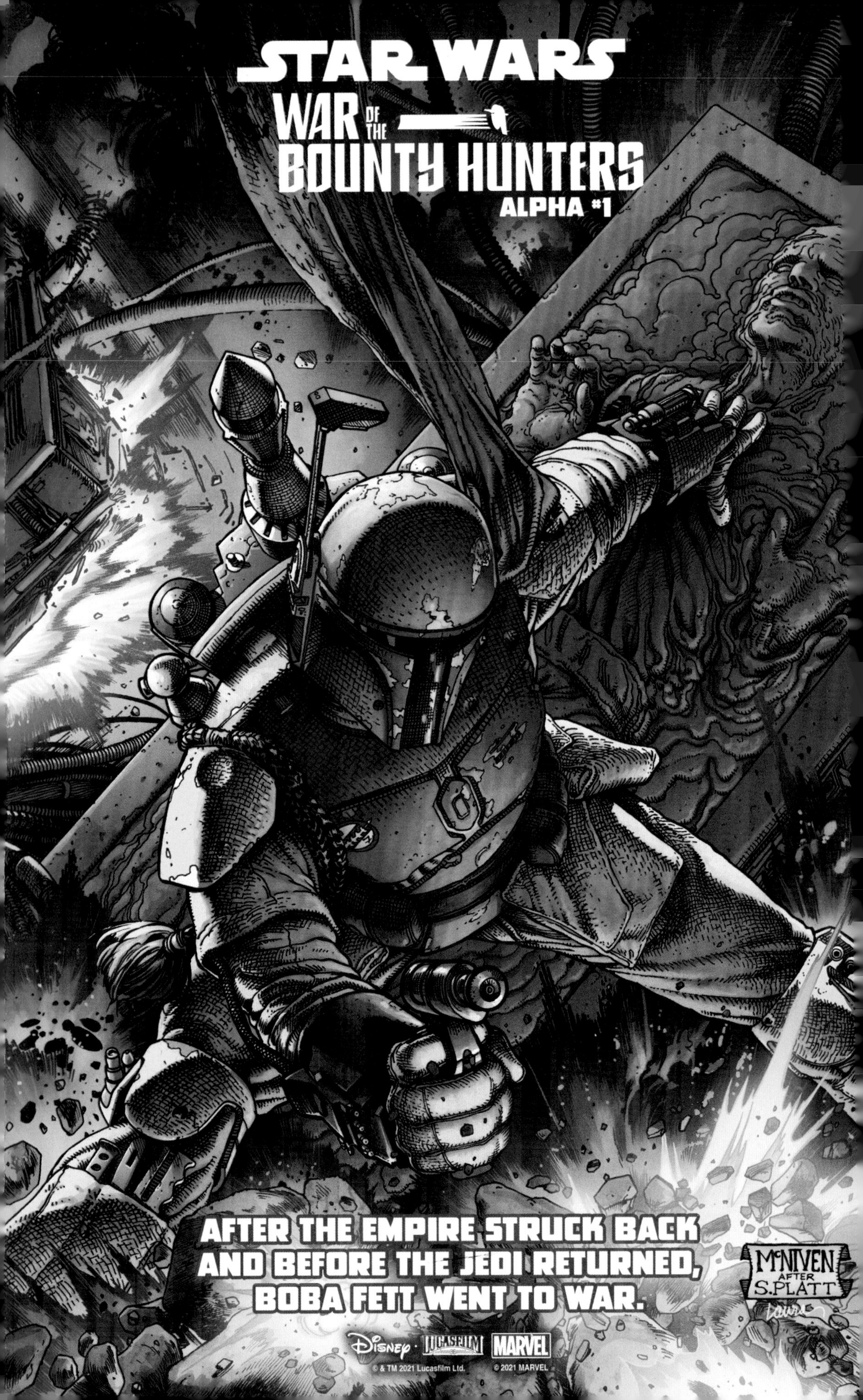

STAR WARS
WAR OF THE BOUNTY HUNTERS
ALPHA #1
AFTER THE EMPIRE STRUCK BACK
AND BEFORE THE JEDI RETURNED,
BOBA FETT WENT TO WAR.
McNIVEN AFTER S.PLATT
Disney · LUCASFILM MARVEL
© & TM 2021 Lucasfilm Ltd.
© 2021 MARVEL